REFLECTIVE HISTORY SERIES

Barbara Finkelstein and William J. Reese, Series Editors

American Educational History Revisited

A CRITIQUE OF PROGRESS

Milton Gaither

TEACHERS
COLLEGE
PRESS

Teachers College, Columbia University
New York and London

Published by Teachers College Press, 1234 Amsterdam Avenue, New York, NY 10027

Copyright © 2003 by Teachers College, Columbia University

Library of Congress Cataloging-in-Publication Data

Gaither, Milton.
    American educational history revisited : a critique of progress / Milton Gaither.
      p.   cm. — (Reflective history series)
    Includes bibliographical references (p.) and index.
    ISBN 0-8077-4290-2 (cloth : alk. paper)
    1. Education—United States—History. I. Title. II. Series.

  LA205 .G35 2003
  370'.973—dc21   2002074033

ISBN 0-8077-4290-2 (cloth)

Printed on acid-free paper
Manufactured in the United States of America

10 09 08 07 06 05 04 03   8 7 6 5 4 3 2 1

To Elizabeth, *mater virtutum*

Contents

Acknowledgments

The notes in this work have a tale to tell. Taken as a whole, they reveal that very little of this book is original with me. At best I have rearranged and organized the ideas and works of other people in a new pattern. But this pattern itself is not my own, as my very phrasings and vocabulary betray. To properly acknowledge all the sources that have led to the interpretation promulgated here would be a tedious affair. Let it suffice to mention a few names that have been particularly helpful in a more tangible way. Any errors of fact or interpretation that follow are entirely my own responsibility.

The original idea for this project was scribbled by Ed McClellan on the bottom of a seminar paper. His editor's instincts and encyclopedic knowledge have improved my work at every stage, and his generous friendship and mentoring have sustained me throughout.

Several colleagues have offered insightful criticism and encouragement over the years as this study was taking shape. These include Alan Jacobs, William Reese, Jürgen Herbst, Andrea Walton, Donald Warren, Kate Cruikshank, David Setran, Sevan Terzian, David Martin, Laurie Moses Hines, Stuart McAninch, and Stephen Arch.

Edie MacMullen first introduced me to the riches of educational history and historiography through her legendary pedagogical skills. Sheila Moss taught me whatever I know about prose style.

Thanks go out to the members of the History of Education Society. Our numbers are relatively small, but the quality of intellectual exchange and cordiality are rare delights in the academic world today. I cannot list them all, but many colleagues have inspired me with their own work and with their professional camaraderie. Thanks in particular to Roberta Wollons and the Barnard Committee for helping this study become publishable.

Brian Ellerbeck of Teachers College Press has throughout been an encouraging and dedicated editor. Thanks to the staff at Teachers College Press, especially my excellent editor, Siddhartha Deb, and to the editors of this series, Bill Reese and Barbara Finkelstein. Thanks to the dedicated library staff at

Indiana University, Bloomington, who filled countless requests with professional competence and ceaseless courtesy. Thanks also to Mary Ellen Charbonnier and the rest of the staff at Messiah College faculty services for their help in printing and reprinting the manuscript.

Paul and Cathy Gutjahr merit special thanks for their friendship and for the use of coveted library space to do the writing. Paul will recognize many of his own insights in these pages. Thanks to Red Leader for much-needed funding.

Finally, I would like to thank my wife and intellectual companion, Elizabeth. Her name should probably be on the title page along with mine, so pervasive is her influence on this text. After our many years together it is difficult to tell just where her thoughts end and mine begin. Three of our collaborations have willingly shared their father while he was completing this project, and I thank Rachel, Aidan, and Susanna for their patience and love throughout.

The Myth of the New History of Education and the Progress Principle

The educator-historian . . . stands . . . in a no-man's land between the practical educators, whose chief interest centers in operating a vast, machine-like enterprise, and the historians who concentrate all their efforts on history as a field of academic specialization. To the practical mind of the former, the labor of the educator-historians may well seem unlikely to be of any direct use; while to specialists in history their work seems often to fall far short in respect to technical standards. . . . The educator-historian himself assumes a problematic guise. If he and his kind last long enough, they too may become a problem for historical investigation!

—Thomas Woody

The year 1960 was critical for educational historians. It was, in one sense, a fallow time, when the profession's publication organ of ten years, the *History of Education Journal*, ceased publication, only for the *History of Education Quarterly* to emerge in its stead in 1961. The *Journal*, established by professors of education as "an avenue for the publication of the views and research reports of those interested in the teaching of the historical and comparative foundations of education," had for a decade been devoted to questions concerning the relationship between educational history and teacher preparation as practiced in professional schools of education. Its replacement struck a different tone from its very first article, a piece by Raymond E. Callahan on the educational scientist Leonard Ayres, which concluded with a sarcastic flourish directed at two of the giants of educational historiography, signaling a new spirit:

In appraising the contributions of Leonard Ayres in regard to the problems of retardation and elimination it is difficult to agree with Ellwood Cubberley that his *Laggards in Our Schools* was "A valuable study of retardation and elimination of pupils." But it is impossible to agree with Edgar W. Knight that his work constituted a "careful study of the subject."[1]

The first issue of the *History of Education Quarterly* also included an obituary notice for veteran educational historian Thomas Woody. His death in 1960 may be taken to symbolize the end of one era and the beginning of another, for Woody more than perhaps any of his contemporaries possessed unalloyed the intellectual qualities and historical sensibilities that post-1960 educational history would stringently reject. His greatest works stand at the apex of a tradition of historical writing whose roots descend deep into the colonial period and whose fruit had been ripening for centuries thereafter. History, for Woody, was a series of successive and progressive revolutions in consciousness, as humanity fought its way up from "local primitive enclaves" to "the highest civilizations" through a gradual accumulation of intelligence. Historians could reconstruct the dynamics of this advance by examining each era's educational institutions. For Thomas Woody, the history of education was nothing less than the history of Western civilization, a sublime tale of the triumph of the human spirit over the obstacles of environment, prejudice, tradition, and ignorance as it has wended its way toward "the Golden Age, a better civilization than any yet known" that may lie just ahead.[2]

But Woody was not yet cold in the ground when the silence of the year was interrupted by a call that would shake the field of educational history to its "foundations." In 1960 Bernard Bailyn's *Education in the Forming of American Society* was published, and the response from educators and historians alike electrified the field. Bailyn's book stunned the old-guard educators who had birthed and nurtured the *History of Education Journal* and its parent society, the History of Education Section of the National Society of College Teachers of Education. In eleven short pages Bailyn rejected the entire tradition that gave their lives meaning and their writings significance. Educational historiography suffers, said Bailyn,

> from an excess of writing along certain lines and an almost undue clarity of direction. . . . Since at least the end of the nineteenth century the lines of interpretation and the framework of ideas have been unmistakable. And yet, for all of this, the role of education in American history is obscure. We have almost no historical leverage on the problems of American education. The facts, or at least a great quantity of them, are there, but they lie inert; they form no significant pattern.[3]

Bailyn went on to explain how educational historiography as practiced in professional schools was woefully inadequate to the task at hand. The field was suffused with an apologetic sensibility deriving from the felt need by professional educators to justify their own position to the rest of the academy and to inspire their students with the greatness of their calling. The historical tale they concocted therefore derived "directly from their professional interests": they wrote almost exclusively about schools, and did so in terms that made past eras significant only to the extent that they foreshadowed present educational conditions. The past, for schoolmen from Thomas Davidson to Ellwood Cubberley and R. G. Boone, "was simply the present writ small." Thus their accounts were filled with anachronistic misreadings because of an inability to understand the past on its own terms and the tendency to "read present issues and definitions back into the past." The schoolmen's historiography assumed what Bailyn termed "a condescension toward the past," an attitude whereby "the past could be differentiated from the present mainly by its primitivism, the rudimentary character of the institutions and ideas whose ultimate development the writers were privileged to know so well."[4]

Reviews of the book make it clear that Bailyn's message was one that many historians were eager to receive. "It will be a book of major importance if it succeeds in removing the blinders that have long kept historians of education from seeing their subject as a whole," wrote one reviewer. Another concurred:

> A consummation devoutly to be wished is that it will shift writing on the history of education away from the professional educators and administrators into the hands of historians of American life and culture where it obviously belongs.

Frederick D. Kershner could "only endorse . . . wholeheartedly" Bailyn's "polite but scathing denunciation of the Cubberley school of educationist history." And Frederick B. Tolles exulted in the "withering and irrefutable criticism of most of the work that has been done in the field hitherto."[5]

Although there were a few objections to aspects of Bailyn's characterization, his account has swept the field to such an extent that it has for some time been the default understanding among practicing educational historians of their discipline's history. Surely no work has done more to bring about this consensus than Lawrence Cremin's *Wonderful World of Ellwood Patterson Cubberley*, to date the most complete treatment of educational historiography, and written by the most eminent educational historian of our time. Substantially, it is an extension of Bailyn's thesis via detailed embellishments that trace the evolution of the perspective Bailyn found so distasteful from Henry Barnard's *American Journal of Education* up to Cubberley's *Public Education in the United States*. Bailyn's opening section to *Education in the Forming of American Society* and Cremin's *Wonderful World of Ellwood Patterson Cubberley* have together provided those educational historians who have cared to inquire at all into the history of their discipline with an account that is at once coherent, convincing, and flattering.[6]

One does not have to look far into the literature to find evidence that Bailyn's condemnation, seconded and augmented by Cremin, informs the self-image of current practitioners. Here is Maris Vinovskis, for example, in 1985:

> During most of the twentieth century, analysis of educational history in the United States was a relatively undeveloped and narrowly focused field. In the past fifteen years, however, there has been a dramatic increase in the quantity and quality of work in educational history. Education in the past is now being analyzed from the broad perspective of the transmission of culture, including and expanding on the narrowly focused perspective of the development of public schools used in earlier studies.

Sterling Fishman, writing in 1989, concurred:

> Ever since Bernard Bailyn and Lawrence Cremin cast their pebbles in the pond, the circular wake emanating from their splash has continued to grow. The history of education has been transformed into cultural history, social history, and other entities too numerous to mention. Clearly, none but the most hirsute antiquarian or confirmed middlebrow would research and write a history of schooling any longer.

Jürgen Herbst, similarly, declared triumphantly in 1980:

> It has now been twenty years and more since Bernard Bailyn warned us against seeing the past simply as the present writ small. In the interval the history of education . . . has become an immensely fruitful and rewarding branch of historical scholarship. . . . Certainly it can be said without unduly encouraging our pride and sense of self-importance that we have . . . incorporated educational developments into the mainstream of American historiography. This has been done, I would say, in large measure because we have heeded Bernard Bailyn's admonition.

Lawrence Veysey was convinced that had revisionism never taken place, the history of education "would have remained a somnolent academic field." Thomas Bender considered that "the great value of Bailyn's work was his success in vastly broadening the dimensions of what educational history might include." Paul Mattingly understood that "from the time of Bailyn's book we are now aware that education is a singularly rich area of study." And Peter Dobkin Hall agreed:

> What we have since Bailyn's essay is a really remarkable transformation of our basic viewpoint . . . the field is no longer the special property of a strange cult

of people celebrating the virtues of particular institutions but, rather, it has become the common property of all those who are seriously concerned with American history.[7]

One could go on, but these few examples are sufficient to demonstrate the powerful hold that Bailyn's interpretation of educational historiography has on the discipline's self-understanding. For more than forty years now it has provided educational historians with a usable past that affirms the significance of our own project at our predecessors' expense. Gradually, the few reservations expressed at the outset about Bailyn's account have been forgotten, and since the old historians are no longer read save as primary source references or foils for new interpretations, our self-congratulatory disciplinary history has passed into unchallenged orthodoxy.[8]

The goal of this study is to do for pre-1960 educational historiography what Bernard Bailyn urged be done for early American education generally. Bailyn is known both in his own work and in his many comments on historical method as the great champion of contextualization. Throughout his career he has stressed that the past must be understood in its own context, on its own terms, that the greatest enemy of historical study is the sin of presentism, of what Herbert Butterfield famously called the "Whig interpretation of history." Unfortunately, Bailyn's educational historiography is far less sensitive to context, to the entire cultural world of past educational historians, than is his own superlative historical work. In this one area he did not practice what he preached. In this study I propose to test Bailyn's and Cremin's account of the discipline's history by attending to the works of the past—not judging them according to contemporary historiographical standards, but relating them to the intellectual and cultural history of their own time. When they are evaluated in this light, a strikingly different interpretation of the history of educational history writing in America emerges.[9]

It is entirely correct to see a critical shift in educational historiography in 1960, but it is not the shift that Bailyn and his many followers thought they were describing. It is simply false that pre-1960 historiography revealed "no significant pattern," nor is it true that the early works focused exclusively on schools because of their narrow definition of education. They did not isolate education from what they took to be the broader context within which it operated, nor were they out of touch with the mainstream of historical writing. What they present to us is in fact a deeply contextual historical account perfectly attuned to the intellectual currents fashionable in their time. What happened in 1960 was not that educational history discovered context, but that by then the intellectual context within which educational history was written had changed.[10]

To understand the profound alteration in intellectual sensibility that occurred in the second quarter of the twentieth century is to understand why Bailyn's revolution met with so little resistance despite the fact that his historiographical argument was specious. In this study I will seek to re-create the older context and show how it was overturned. We will see how from colonial times to the middle of the twentieth century an underlying consensus held in American intellectual life concerning the reality of human progress and of the New World's role therein. Although on the surface these centuries were weltered by waves of revisionist campaigns and impassioned debates over particular historical conclusions, underneath the calm of an underlying commitment to progress held everything together. It was only when the horrors wrought by race science and technological warfare rendered this commitment untenable that educational historiography was compelled to change its tone, but the postwar generation of educational historians on the whole failed to recognize this situation. It was Bailyn's achievement to bring educational historiography up to date, to reimagine it so that intellectuals sensitive to the death of the principle of progress could believe in educational history again.

Although thesis driven, this study is as comprehensive as possible. To date, no single study has covered the entire history of American educational historiography. A great deal of what I treat has not been previously explored. Isolated studies do exist on particular elements of the story, but no overarching thesis emerges from them to give us a coherent picture. That said, it must be acknowledged that the study is by no means exhaustive. A truly plenary treatment would find much of value in such sources as nineteenth-century middle-class fiction, newspaper editorials, or anniversary orations honoring individual educational institutions. Perhaps most egregiously, I have not even begun to address evidence (much of it doubtless preserved in languages other than English) that would shed light on the way various minority ethnic communities have understood educational history. Much work, a good deal of it beyond my competence, remains to be done. Nevertheless, it is hoped that the selected themes and sources are those most important for constructing an account of the topic more accurate than any yet attempted.[11]

An anonymous author once observed in an old number of the *Nation*: "The American mind does not dwell on the past, does not easily recall it, forgets as easily as it forgives, and only by a miracle secures for its legislation and its institutions a historical development." This study originated in an attempt by a novice graduate student to provide himself with a sense of his chosen discipline's history. It is now submitted to a wider audience in the conviction that historians, of all people, ought to stand as counterevidence to such a characterization of the "American mind." Herein lies an account with the potential to secure for one discipline a historical development. Whether it deserves to do so will be for the reader to decide.[12]

Ideology and Historical Practice in Early America

> In history a great volume is unrolled for our instruction, drawing the materials of future wisdom from the past errors and infirmities of mankind.
> —Edmund Burke

PURITANS AND PLANTERS

Writing about the history of education in this country is almost as old as history writing itself. While some of the European explorers who scouted out the New World composed annals that could justifiably be termed historical, for the first significant interpretive accounts we must turn to the Puritans. They are important for our story in many ways, not only for their chronological primacy in composing historical narrative concerned with matters educational, but also for the influence that their understanding of history's meaning has had upon all who followed. The Puritans transmitted to the New World the linear historical narrative that had been the hallmark of Semitic and then Christian historical thought for millennia, and they introduced in complex and sometimes conflicting ways the two directions in which the line of history could be drawn. Depending on the fit that the Puritan historian found between contemporary circumstance and biblical witness, the line of history would either tend upward toward the celestial city or downward into deepest darkness.

In many ways the Protestant Reformation was a return to Saint Augustine; but in terms of scriptural interpretation, it was not. The Roman Church had inherited from this great Western father a tendency to allegorize and moralize scriptural passages that was rejected unequivocally by the reformers. True to the Renaissance spirit in which they were reared, they sought a return to the original, historical, and literal meaning of the text. This move is of immense significance for understanding Puritan historiography, for the Puritan conception of history was merely an extension of their literal reading of the scriptures. Separated from the allegorical method, Protestants began reading apocalyptic literature in a literal sense and then finding in current events the fulfillment of prophetic utterance. A particularly striking example of this rebirth of millennialism is to be found in what is perhaps the greatest work of English Protestant history, John Foxe's *Actes and Monuments*, or as it is more often called, the *Book of Martyrs*.[1]

For Foxe, as for his fellow Protestants, the Bible was the source of the deepest historical knowledge. Prophecy and history were two sides of the same coin, for both displayed the will of God and His plan for the world. When the revelator John prophesied a one-thousand-year reign of peace for Christ and his church, to be followed by a period of harsh persecution under the auspices of an unchained Antichrist, Foxe expected to find a corresponding history. The one thousand years, for Foxe, commenced with Constantine's conversion and the cessation of persecution as Christianity triumphed over its pagan rivals, and it came to an end in around 1327, when persecution of the saints was revived, beginning with John Wycliffe. His history took as its framework a literalist interpretation of prophetic biblical literature, which provided the structure on which he built his account of more recent events. This approach of beginning with a literalist interpretation of the Bible and using it as a template for explaining the significance of more recent political history became the standard method of English Protestant historiography. Foxe's book, explains historian William Haller,

> was for its own time and for several succeeding generations a comprehensive history of England based upon a conception of human nature and of the meaning and course of history which few of its readers were in any state of mind to do anything but accept as universally true.

"Generations of Englishmen," says Peter Gay, "saw history through Foxe's eyes." Foxe transmitted to English Puritans a linear, directional conception of history, updated for the Elizabethan context, and he provided an authoritative justification for the necessity of creating and maintaining Puritan institutions if the forces of darkness, the forces of Rome, were to be defeated.[2]

For John Foxe the progress of history was seemingly pointing to the emergence of a Protestant kingdom in an England governed by the Protestant queen Elizabeth, whose dominion would be a light to the rest of the world. But by the time the first English colonists arrived in the New World, the Puritan vision of a reformed England seemed to them phantasmic. The millennial fervor of Foxe's book and the sharp distinction it canonized between Christian Protestants and antichristian Papists was retained, but the locus of hope shifted from old England to New England. What in the sixteenth century had seemed like a broad-based political and religious consensus for reform became by the seventeenth a struggle between various Protestant factions for the soul of England. Margo Todd has suggested that

> it is only after the disintegration of the Renaissance consensus that it becomes possible to speak first of a "Protestant" and then of a "Puritan" social ethic. . . . As long as the mainstream of English Protestantism operated within the reformist assumptions of Christian humanism, Puritans and conformists could cooperate in building the New Jerusalem in England. It was only when Laud and Charles, in their drive for control and conformity, attempted to divert the mainstream into an apparently absolutist channel, that Puritans found themselves in opposition.

And many of these Puritans found opposition so difficult that they looked to the New World for space in which to build their holy city.[3]

It was in the passage across the Atlantic that the motif of colonial history was founded, but it was a passage interpreted according to Puritan textual authorities. One cannot overstress the significance of the Old Testament for the Puritan understanding of history. Two particular elements of this Testament were explicitly appropriated by these latter-day Hebrews as tropes for their own experiences. The first was the call of Abraham out from his home country to go to a land that God would show him, and the second was the passage of the Israelites through the Red Sea as they left behind their condition of slavery and prepared to enter the promised land. To these biblical motifs was added a somewhat solipsistic understanding of history that saw the entire sweep of world events culminating with the Puritan errand into the wilderness. But how did the story unfold? We require one more piece of the Puritan historical imagination before we can proceed to investigate the particulars of their history of education. That piece can be approached by means of what is surely the paradigmatic Puritan story, John Bunyan's *Pilgrim's Progress*.

G. Stanley Hall is still remembered for popularizing the Herbartian recapitulation theory ("ontogeny recapitulates phylogeny") that human fetal growth extends to postnatal child development. In this view the individual relives in his or her life span the entire history of race experience. We can perhaps best understand Puritan history if we invert Hall's formulation. For the Puritans, phylogeny recapitulates ontogeny—the group experience follows and is analogous to the experience of the individual. And the individual's story is the story of Pilgrim, the story of progress in grace as the individual faces the perils and pitfalls of the world's temptations, the flesh's weaknesses, and the devil's wiles. To understand the individual conversion story is to understand the national story as well.[4]

Bunyan's allegory of Pilgrim is itself patterned after the history of Israel. It begins with a decisive departure from the old country and customs, as with the call of Abraham. This is the moment of conversion, which in addition to being a break from the past is also the first step in the journey of the future. Progress is made along the path of life with each step taken, and endurance is the hallmark of progress:

> [W]hat begins as a flight from sin, Egypt, Babylon, Laud, becomes for the saint a pilgrimage to Canaan. As his experience grows during the middle of his story, "progress" shifts from its original sense of "journey" to its modern sense of "improvement," "movement towards."

It is this combined sense of progress as both journey and improvement that must be understood to properly read Puritan historiography. The colonists, having once left their homeland, have embarked on a journey filled with potential pitfalls, but at the same time they have created the possibility of advancement. Their journey is a journey *upward*, a journey *toward* the celestial city. This perspective is abundantly clear in the first history of the Puritan experience written in the New World that contained explicitly educational material, Edward Johnson's *Wonder Working Providence of Sions Savior in New England*, first published in London in 1653.[5]

Johnson's book is essentially a defense of the Puritan project in the New World. It begins with the failure of post-Elizabethan England to realize the vision propounded by John Foxe and his contemporaries and proceeds to exalt the Puritan mission in America through the spiritual biography of leading "pilgrims," through typology connecting the New England churches to scriptural Israel, and through a thoroughgoing military rhetoric not bashful about declaring who soldiers for Christ and who for Antichrist. Johnson is clear about the missionary intentions of the colony: "[F]or *England*'s sake they are going from *England* to pray without ceasing for *England*, O *England*! thou shalt find *New England* prayers prevailing with their God for thee." The history itself is a piece of education, mixing narrative, moralizing, and versified elegies for great men into a spiritual-historical sermon, filled with edifying anecdotes demonstrating both the miraculous protection of God's elect and the supernatural judgment upon those who reject His ways. The entire work is an attempt to define and plot a course for a unified New England by reconfiguring its history into a story of the progress "from purity to peace to plenty to participation in Armageddon." It particularly strikes the modern reader, accustomed to looking for continuities between English and colonial civilizations, just how abrupt and comprehensive the break between the two appears in Johnson's work.[6]

But it is also a history of education proper, the first of its kind in the Western Hemisphere. Johnson repeatedly focuses in classic Puritan fashion upon the importance of education for perpetuating the religion and virtue of the current generation in the next. Where education thrives, there thrives right doctrine, pure preaching, and faithful living. The Israelites of old had been instructed by Moses to educate their children ceaselessly to understand and follow the commands of God, and it was clear that any holy people must do the same if their fervor was to be passed on to the next generation. The establishment of schools, then, is the fruit of holiness, and it is in such a context that Johnson places the founding of Harvard.

To introduce Johnson's account, we must first know what precedes it. He has been chronicling the fate of several groups who either left or were forced out of Massachusetts because of religious heterodoxy. After being informed of the fact of false doctrine, the reader learns of the divine consequences such thinking precipitates:

> Yet was not this the first loud speaking hand of God against them; but before this the Lord had poynted directly to their sinne by a very fearful monster, that another of these women brought forth they striving to bury it in oblivion, but the Lord brought it to light, setting forth the view of their monstrous Errors in the prodigious birth.

The lesson is clear: unfaithfulness to God in matters of religion leads to impure fruit, in this case to the birth of a "monster," which through the intervention of God was allowed to live and remain as a testimony against its mother and her community. If this is the result of impiety, what is the fruit of piety? Johnson follows the preceding quotation immediately, not even breaking the paragraph, with an account of Harvard College:

> This yeare, although the estates of these pilgrim people were much wasted, yet seeing the benefit that would accrew to the Churches of Christ and Civil Government, by the Lords blessing, upon learning, they began to erect a Colledge, the Lord by his provident hand giving his approbation to the work, in sending over a faithfull and godly servant of his, the reverend Mr. *John Harverd* who joining with the people of Christ at *Charles Towne*, suddainly after departed this life, and gave near a thousand pound toward this work; wherefore the Government thought it meet to call it *Harverd* college in remembrance of him.

The moral is clear. Prosperity and the founding of noble institutions are the issue of orthodoxy, whereas calamity and chaos are the fruits of heresy.[7]

Johnson's work achieves a sense of unity through its continual refrain celebrating the "wonder-working providences" of God. In his world, all events are orchestrated by God and serve as messages from God, be they commendations or warnings. He reports that in 1650, a disease carried away many of the colonists, particularly the children. Why?

> Yet were these pilgrim people minded of . . . the little regard had to provide means to train their children up in the knowledge of learning, and improve such means as the Lord hath appointed to leave their posterity an able Minister; and also to stir them up to prepare for the great work of the Lord Jesus in the overthrow of Antichrist, and calling of the Jews which in all likelyhood is suddenly to be performed.

We see in this passage the significance of schooling for Johnson, not only as a method of securing ministers for the next generation and for spreading learned piety among the children but also as a key factor in God's redemptive plan in history, a plan in which the Puritan outpost in the New World played the key role. Although his words to the rank and file of Massachusetts carried a firm warning to them to attend to the education of their children, he is confident that obedience will be swift and glorious, that transhistorical results will follow as schools are founded and funded to bring the virtues associated with Harvard College to every hamlet and village in New England.[8]

But the ink had scarcely dried on Johnson's paper when momentous changes began to occur both in England and in the colony that would soon make his vision of a millennial victory for Protestant forces led by New England seem impossible to realize. Upon the restoration of Charles II in England, New Englanders went from seeing their community as prototype for English reformation to seeing it as "the last, isolated outpost of light in a world of darkness." In the 1650s and 1660s the first generation of leadership died off, the halfway covenant was created as an unhappy expedient to maintaining Puritan control of the colony, and a disappointed millennialism was recast in the form of the jeremiad—New England had forsaken her first love. Michael Wigglesworth's long narrative history poem, "God's Controversy with New England" well illustrates the shift, for whereas Johnson had been able to turn the failings of the settlers into a vision of historical progress and millennial triumph, Wigglesworth is not so sure of success. Thus was born what the self-designated "second generation" termed "declension." Given the assumption that deaths of leaders were visitations of the displeasure of God, it became the historian's role to discern where the colony had gone wrong.[9]

A final blow to the millennial aspirations of Puritan New England was the revocation of its charter and the issue of a new one in 1691 nullifying the old Puritan commonwealth and establishing in its place a royal province under direct control of the Crown. This revised political situation made it all but impossible to envision how the pilgrim experience in America could be related to the apocalyptic understanding of world history shared by most Puritan divines. The second generation of historians, men such as Wigglesworth, John Norton, and Increase Mather, failed to conceive an account that could synthesize recent political events with their understanding of the "last days" and were left with only a vague sense of the degeneracy of present times and a nostalgia for the New England of their parents. If the Protestant utopia was the standard against which empirical events were to be judged, it was clear to everyone that New England was no New Jerusalem. The dawning of this revelation was the most important development to occur between Johnson's day and that of our next Puritan educational history, Cotton Mather's *Magnalia Christi Americana*. "For Cotton Mather, the event that 'killed' New England was the imposition of the new royal charter in 1691. . . . the *Magnalia* is not so much a defense of the new charter as an attempt to restore the spirit or life of the old charter in the days of the new." Mather's effort, by far the most ambitious New World history of its time, was at root an attempt to use history to reverse historical trends. "Whether New England lived or no depended on his audience's agreement with his assessment of the past, and on its willingness to keep alive the spirit of that past as it was refracted through the pages of that history."[10]

Throughout Mather's two-volume work the reader can detect a profound awareness and celebration of education, not only in the material but also in Mather's prose itself, which is laced with Latin, Greek, Hebrew, and French quotations on nearly every page. The period between 1650 and 1750 have been termed an "age of erudition" in Western historical writing, as great men writing great narrative were replaced by scholars expending enormous energy investigating, criticizing, and publishing their results. Mather was such a scholar, and the *Magnalia* was his finest work.[11]

In Edward Johnson's day, it was still an open question whether nonconformity would be the victor in England's struggle for religious self-definition. By the time Cotton Mather was writing, it was clear that the nonconformists had lost and that their last hope for future victory, New England, was no longer even a viable independent political entity. As a result, there was a shift in emphasis in Mather's historical account. No longer would colonial distinctiveness from the mother country be emphasized, but *continuity with* English Protestant institutions as opposed to *divergence from* them would mark his treatment.

This approach explains the structure of Mather's account of Harvard College and its graduates. Books 3 and 4 are both concerned with biographies of prominent, orthodox Puritan ministers, and their juxtaposition demonstrates just how continuous was the tradition between the English-trained (chapter 3) and the Harvard-trained (chapter 4). "[The second generation of ministers] were not come to an age for service to the church of God, before the wisdom, and prudence of the New-Englanders did remarkably signifie it self, in the founding of a COLLEGE, from whence the most of their congregations were afterwards supplied. . . . From that hour *Old* England had more ministers from *New*, than our New-England had since *then* from old."[12]

But Mather's Harvard account, despite its now canonical tale of the origins and development of the institution under its first presidents, is not the most important contribution to educational history that Mather makes. Puritan historiography, as has been explained, took as its organizational paradigm the individual pilgrim's experience, which itself was modeled after the experiences of Israel. All this makes biography the most promising of genres for expressing the national story and for encouraging contemporaneous readers to follow in the path blazed by the historical subjects. The strong biographical focus of Mather's history allows his reader in particular to discover in story after story just how profound an influence the right sort of education could have in making the right sort of man. It likewise demonstrates that the man rightly made would thereafter expend no small labors attending to the education of others. In life after life Mather brings these lessons home, as a sampling from his account of John Eliot's educational endeavors makes clear:

> A grammar-school he would always have upon the place, whatever it cost him; and he imported all other places to have the like . . . with what fervor he uttered an expression to this purpose: "Lord, for schools every where among us! That our schools may flourish!" . . . God so blessed his endeavours, that Roxbury could not live quietly without a *free school* in the town. . . . Roxbury has afforded more scholars—first for the colledge, and then for the publick—than any town of its bigness. . . . From the spring of the school at Roxbury there have run a large number of the "streams which have made glad this whole city of God."[13]

This allusion to the "streams which have made glad this whole city of God" is the continual refrain uniting Mather's treatments of educational institutions. Harvard is a "river, without the streams whereof, these regions would have been mere unwatered places for the devil." Again, it is "a river, the streams of whereof made glad the city of God." It was Mather's goal to ensure that the entire land would be watered after the fashion of Eliot and his successful scholars. If the reader would not understand him through the medium of institutional history or even biography, Mather would spell out his message clearly, which he did at the end of the work:

> Where *schools* are not vigorously and honorably encouraged, whole *colonies* will sink apace into a degenerate and contemptible condition, and at last become horribly *barbarous*: and the first instance of their *barbarity* will be, that they will be undone for want of men, but not see and own what it was that *undid* them.[14]

As it turned out, however, even Mather's scholarly and sparkling prose was insufficient to rouse his fellow colonists to reformation, and so this the last gasp of the Puritan effort to build of the New World a New Jerusalem, to connect America to the line of progress that began with Abraham and would culminate in the defeat of Antichrist and the installation of Christ as king of the earth, failed to achieve its ends. But to the south, in Virginia, there were emerging other, more humble understandings of America's educational history and its place in the American story. Although it was the generation that fought and thought about the Revolution that made the decisive break, even in the colonial period hints of alternative models of educational history could be discerned. Many attitudes would emerge to fill the void created by the collapse of the Puritan millennial vision, and one of the most enduring would be a spirit of collective harmony forged by a strong economic prospect and a coherent political system. It was Virginia, rather than New England, that first embodied the spiritual ethos responsible for such a vision, and Virginia's most characteristic and colorful colonial historian was Robert Beverley.

Beverley's *History and Present State of Virginia* was completed in 1705 and enjoyed a relatively wide readership in both Virginia and England. His text is remarkable chiefly for its informal style and literary candor—qualities that make it substantially easier reading than the Puritan histories and mark Beverley as closer than any of New England's historians to the modern American type. In Beverley we do not exactly have a cowboy or a democrat, but we do have a uniquely New World personality. "I am an Indian and don't pretend to be exact in my language" he said, and though we know him to be in reality a planter, with large holdings of land and the requisite slaves, he does strike the reader as more American than English.[15]

Virginia, it needs to be recalled, had none of the first-generation heroism that marked the settlement of Massachusetts. Early Virginia was the domain of the starving time, of cannibalistic famine, of the foolish and futile search for gold to the neglect of farming, of unbridled greed, organizational ineptitude, and frequent massacres. Such a history itself did little to suggest the narrative of linear progress and pilgrimage that came so naturally to Puritan New England. The mindset of Virginia's planter class, in addition, was thoroughly conformist in religious sentiment and little disposed to a biblicist self-understanding. It was a predominantly this-worldly society, and to people like this,

> it made far more sense . . . to downplay the early failures and concentrate instead on Virginia's potentialities. Hence the prevalence in Virginian historiography of reportage and description and the relative absence of historical synthesis. . . . While Puritan historians acted like preachers in disguise, Virginia's historians put on the mantle of the press agent.[16]

Beverley, in fact, seems to have hardly any sense of Christian theological categories in his history. Virginia is no Canaan for him, but rather an

Eden of verdant fields and fecund valleys, of playful streams and charming native cultures. His historical account chronicles the early catastrophes to be sure, but manages to do so in a manner that suggests no providential oversight in the matter whatsoever. While not exactly exonerating the natives of responsibility for the massacres they performed, it attempts to explain their actions in a surprisingly sympathetic fashion. To Beverley, Virginia should have had more Pocahontas and less purity: intermarriage would have increased population, reduced animosities leading to warfare, and made for lasting peace between Indian and European. But most Virginians did not partake of this charitable attitude and conflict was the result.

Beverley's history is dominated by two concerns, concerns that befit a profiteer in his situation. He focuses fairly exclusively on the political and agricultural history of the colony. Other elements of his story are only significant inasmuch as they illuminate either of these domains. Educational history, therefore, is only present when it is important for understanding the political situation of a given moment. Thus we first read of educational endeavors in the colony when an assembly was convened to petition for a charter to begin a college: "It was proposed that three things should be taught in this college, viz. languages, divinity, and natural philosophy. They appointed a certain number of professors and their salaries. And they formed rules for the continuation and good government thereof to perpetuity." It was as a political event that the founding of the College of William and Mary deserved mention, and the fortunes of the college are subsequently discussed only as they relate to the successes and (more often) failures of Virginia's royal governors.[17]

Although Beverley's tone and style are uniquely American, his history is not. This becomes clear when we compare his account of William and Mary's founding with the more thorough account offered by the school's first president, James Blair, in the tract he wrote with Henry Hartwell and Edward Chilton in 1697, titled *The Present State of Virginia, and the College.* Although Blair's story is considerably more detailed—tracing the school's origins in 1691 in the General Assembly, its financial backing by the Crown, pecuniary squabbles with the royal governor and key planters, and finally its modest beginning as a grammar school—his agenda is substantially that of Robert Beverley. Blair's goal for the college was to use it as a tool in rehabilitating an authentic Anglican clergy. His enemies are also the royal governers. For Blair, as for Beverley, the college "is honestly and zealously carry'd on by the Trustees, but is in Danger of being ruin'd by the Backwardness of the Government."[18]

Works such as Blair's were few, however. On the whole it may be safely asserted that other colonial historians, from Virginian William Stith to Massachusetts Royalist Thomas Hutchinson, tended, like Beverley, to stress political and military history to the near exclusion of social developments such as the education of the people. Hutchinson, for example, though he wrote what is unquestionably the most thorough history of Massachusetts composed in the eighteenth century, only mentions Harvard when matters relating to its charter or internal organization transpire, and he provides no account at all of the now famous school laws passed in 1642 and 1647. The assiduous reader can find him quoting sources that acknowledge such events, but he gives them no deliberate discussion in any of his three volumes. It is perhaps ironic given the debates in the twentieth century regarding the significance of these laws for future public education in the country that no historian in the colonial period so much as mentioned them.[19]

And so as the political ties between England and her belligerent colonies grew increasingly strained, the most powerful historical vision of the New World, that of the Puritan divines, was struggling for survival in the mercantilist and pluralist society that was in the making. Beverley's *Virginia*, with its colloquialisms and worldliness, foreshadowed a potential replacement of the Plymouth tradition with that emanating from Jamestown, and eighteenth-century historians began to compile more detailed political accounts stripped of the dominant narrative pattern derived from the history of Israel. But with the coming of revolution and the new republican and federalist ideas that found embodiment in American constitutional government, educational history was once again to find a narrative structure, a teleology, that allowed it at one and the same time to retain the Puritan story of progress and to relocate the apex of that story given the new economic and political circumstances.

FROM PURITAN TO WHIG

Historians of the latter half of the eighteenth century were faced with the difficult task of drawing connections between the past and the rapidly changing political and social situations in which they found themselves. If we are to make any sense of their efforts, we must, while acknowledging that it is we who do the making, impose some sort of order on their thoughts. The order I would like to impose consists of a series of ideologies that, with considerable overlap, gradually transformed the way historians told their stories about the past, so that by the 1820s we may detect a modern historical consciousness among American historians where we could not a century before, though the contours of that consciousness certainly bear the marks of their seventeenth- and eighteenth-century predecessors. Thus the most profound development in educational historiography during the revolutionary period is to be found *not* in works of educational history but in the subtle shifts in thought that occurred as Puritan history became republican, liberal, federalist, millennial, or Scottish Realist history—*all* of which promoted an interpretation of American education that would eventually be appropriated by nineteenth-century Whigs such as Henry Barnard. Such categories as republicanism, liberalism, and millennialism might not exhaust the meaning of the early eighteenth century, but they are the categories we need in order to explicate clearly the shift in historical consciousness that produced what Herbert Butterfield labeled the Whig interpretation of history. Butterfield's metaphor sought to describe a tendency in historical studies to reify the present and to cast it as the culmination of a long process of development, a tendency he associates with the English Whig Party. I am using the term in a similar fashion. The Whig view means for me not whatever the American Whig Party happened to think about history but instead a philosophy of history that recognizes in the past a gradual unfolding of the present in a pattern marked by material improvement, moral progress, and a richer and fuller life. That this view of history was in fact held by the American Whigs has been amply demonstrated by historians of the party.[20]

If Cotton Mather's *Magnalia* was something of a last gasp of the Puritan vision in the New World, it did not signal the end of the influence of the Christian interpretation of history. Christian faith was revived through the ministries of such European imports as George Whitefield and the Wesley brothers and homegrown ministers such as Jonathan Edwards. The revivals left their mark not only on the souls and moral lives of the colonists, but also on their understanding of history and the role of their society in it. The revivals were transcolonial in scope; disassociated from the traditional centers of intellectual, ecclesiastical, and political power; profoundly popular in appeal; and essentially individualistic in focus, yet at the same time they fostered community, thanks to their ability to unite classes, denominations, and factions in one emotional and spiritual experience. Jonathan Edwards, chief among many observers of the Great Awakening, interpreted the phenomenon just as his Puritan fathers would have:

> 'Tis not unlikely that this work of God's Spirit, that is so extraordinary and wonderful, is the dawning, or at least a prelude, of that glorious work of God, so often foretold in Scripture, which in the progress and issue of it, shall renew the world of mankind.

For Edwards, the millennium was at hand, and it was beginning in America.[21]

But sooner than anticipated, the Awakening languished. The *Christian History*, Thomas Prince's organ for broadcasting testimonials of lives changed by the Awakening so as to stir millennial fervor, was by the early 1740s lamenting the seeming lapse in enthusiasm and spiritual visitations. Deep disappointment set in as the anticipated culmination of history seemed slow in coming. In 1745, the *Christian History* folded and George Whitefield's tour of the colonies went scarcely noticed amid growing preoccupation with emerging political troubles with France. Some clergymen, such as Aaron Burr, Edwards's son-in-law, turned to a millennialist vision that was starkly pessimistic, almost premillennial in its interpretation that things would get worse before they got better. Others, however, turned their attention from the remarkable providences showcased in revival settings to acts of God in the realm of politics. In July 1745, New England militiamen seized Louisbourg from the French, and a new focus for millennial fervor was found to fill the gap left by a listless Awakening.

For the New England clergy, the French and Indian War could be interpreted in no other way than apocalyptically. Catholic France was the literal embodiment of the forces of Antichrist, and the war was one of God's elect against the forces of sin and Satan. As historian Nathan Hatch explains:

> Clergymen at mid-century manifested an intensity of interest in Antichrist's overthrow unknown since the time of John Cotton and Edward Johnson. . . . When the long-awaited news of French downfall in Canada reached New England, millennial optimism knew no limits. In sermon after sermon ministers celebrated the removal of the last and greatest obstruction to the coming kingdom.[22]

The French peril altered the way American Protestants pursued their millennialism in several ways that are crucial to our story. First, a common enemy united Old and New Light factions in a common cause, thereby healing in a large measure a rift caused by the Awakening while building on its millennialist emphasis. Second, the progress toward the millennium increasingly became wedded to the political situation of colonial America as opposed to the pietistic focus on individual morality in the Awakening. So on the eve of the Revolution, we find a Protestant culture more or less united in a self-understanding that knew the present politics of America to be the key to unlocking the meaning and timing of the kingdom of God.

At the same time, another intellectual tradition was at work among the colonial elite to bring the more secular, Enlightenment-oriented thinkers of the time to an interpretation of history very similar to that of the dogmatic Protestants. With a pedigree that extended from classical civilization through cinquecento Italian civic humanism and seventeenth-century English political theory, republican thought became a powerful interpretive paradigm for the colonists of the 1760s and 1770s as dissatisfaction with royal governance grew feverish. Republican theory pitted "masculine" political liberty against a "feminine" monarchial system, positing civic virtue as the only refuge of free men against the enfeebling decadence associated with unlimited power. The concept of civic virtue derived from that of Roman *virtu*, this latter term used to describe a courageous devotion to the public good, irrespective of personal considerations, self-interest being the bane of the republic.

Republicanism tended to view history as cyclic. A pattern of rising and falling was consistently repeated as a civilization mounted to greatness through virtue and then fell, as a result of internal collapse through the spread of self-interest and greed. Out of the chaos of the American Revolution, those whose task it was to construct a nation were to a great extent influenced by this conception of history, popularized both in great works such as James Burgh's *Historical Essay on the English Constitution* and in countless dissenting Whig pamphlets. This Whig republican influence goes far in accounting for both patriot zeal against the Crown and fear of impending declension should the virtue of the American citizen become corrupted by naked self-interest and demagoguery.

The cyclic theory of history is itself an early version of the recapitulation theory, seeing the development of societies as an organic process analogous to human development. Harvard professor David Tappan summarized this view in 1798:

> Experience proves that political bodies, like the animal economy, have their periods of infancy, youth, maturity, decay, and dissolution. In the early stages of their existence their members are usually industrious and frugal, simple in their manners, just and kind in their intercourse, active and hardy, united and brave. . . . The practice of these virtues gradually nourishes them to a state of manly vigor. They become mature and flourishing in wealth and population, in arts and arms, in almost every kind of national prosperity. But when they have reached a certain point of greatness, their taste and manners begin to be infected. Their prosperity inflates and debauches their minds. It betrays them into pride and avarice, luxury and dissipation, idleness and sensuality, and too often into practical and scornful impiety. These, with other kindred vices, hasten their downfall and ruin. [History teaches that] virtue is the soul of republican freedom; that luxury tends to extinguish both sound morality and piety; and that the loss of these renders men incapable of estimating and relishing, of preserving or even bearing the blessings of equal liberty.[23]

Such a view would seem to land one consistently in a pessimistic stoicism regarding the inevitability of degradation, but in the years following the Revolution, American republicans, conscious that their nation was still on the youthful side of history, made a profound move that fundamentally altered the republican interpretation of history, in the process rendering it amenable to the Protestant millennialist vision of American destiny. It was the hope of the founders to create *institutions* that would stave off the process of decay, to use the lessons that history teaches time and again to avoid the error common to all previous civilizations. For some, among them James Madison and John Jay, these would be political institutions such as the bicameral legislature or the system of checks and balances; for others, such as Thomas Jefferson, a wide distribution of property ownership and cultivation of the soil would be our salvation; and for some, such as Noah Webster, the answer would lie in a system of education.

In Webster's famous and oft-anthologized essay "On the Education of Youth in America," we have a clear illustration of both the cyclic interpretation of history and the hope that an institution forged from the lessons of past historical failures will stave off the inevitable. "While nations are in a barbarous state," says Webster,

> they have few wants and consequently few arts. . . . the education of a savage therefore extends little farther than to enable him to use with dexterity a bow and a tomahawk. But in the progress of manners and of arts . . . artificial wants multiply the number of occupations, and these require a great diversity in the mode of education. Even the civilities of behavior in polished society become a science; a bow and a curtsy are taught with as much care and precision as the elements of mathematics. Education proceeds therefore by gradual advances, from simplicity to corruption. Its first object, among rude nations, is safety; its next, utility; it afterwards extends to convenience; and among the opulent part of civilized nations it is directed principally to show and amusement.

All Webster's recommendations, from the stress on English over Latin, to the preference for towns over cities as locations for schools, to his censure of novelistic fiction, are ultimately related to his hope that a system of education built on republican virtue will enable the republic to escape this inevitable procession from simplicity to corruption. To fail to establish a system of common schools whereby the citizens of the republic can become educated is nothing less than to hasten the demise of the republic itself. But to succeed would mean a new thing in the world:

> Mankind cannot know to what degree of perfection society and government may be carried. America affords the fairest opportunities for making the experiment and opens the most encouraging prospect of success.[24]

It is the prospect of such a success, the dream that America might become the great exception to the general rule of the decline and fall of civilizations, that best accounts for the astonishing consensus regarding American history that was produced during the Revolutionary period, for rationalistic republicans (who had imbibed an Enlightenment understanding of history that tended to strip God of active agency in its processes) came to share with millennially minded Protestants (with their supernaturalist understanding of God's invasive role in history) the same basic orientation to America's role in the future and hence its historical derivation. "The republic," asserts historian J. G. A. Pocock, "was the true heir of the covenant and the dread of corruption the true heir of the jeremiad."[25]

We lack only one piece of the puzzle to account for the overwhelming presence by the 1830s of what has come to be known as the Whig interpretation of history. That piece has often been dubbed Enlightenment liberalism. It is difficult to generalize about liberalism as an ideology, for its sources were so varied and its impact so diverse upon population segments that any singular account risks gross oversimplification. Educated Americans were conversant with Lockean empiricism, Hobbsean pessimistic market forces, Scottish Common Sense Realism, French theories of social contract, and Adam Smith's economics. Thus we would do well to see along with Henry May not a singular Enlightenment but a whole series of "enlightenments" occurring in overlapping succession as political and social events interacted with intellectual movements. But whatever the source and whatever the impact, the point that needs to be made here is that the vague entity called liberalism that was emerging in the eighteenth century brought with it a view of history that only reinforced the philosophy of history present among millennialist Protestants and republican statesmen.[26]

For one, the Enlightenment did not transmit itself to Western shores unaffected by the American context. European Enlightenment figures were often culturally marginal and cosmopolitan in outlook. In America, especially after the Revolution, Enlightenment ideas were mainstream and profoundly nationalistic. "The effect" of the Revolution, according to Arthur Shaffer, "was a turn away from the Enlightenment ideal of the universality of human experience to a preoccupation with a distinctly national experience." Thus if we wish to speak of a liberal interpretation of history in the eighteenth century, it will be, like its millennialist and republican counterparts, that of a national history.[27]

Yet the liberal mood did make a singular contribution to historical interpretation in the eighteenth century. The notion of progress was present among Protestants and republicans, to be sure, but the means of progress could differ. For millennialists, progress could be detected in the advance of Christian piety and public morality. For republicans, progress was to be found in institutions rightly ordered and a polity prepared to think and act according to the dictates of civic virtue. But for the dawning liberal mind, progress could be charted by the advance of science and especially in its offspring, technology. One can detect such a perspective in Benjamin Franklin's writings, even in such an offhand comment as his infamous line about Native Americans: "[I]ndeed, if it be the Design of Providence to extirpate these Savages in order to make room for Cultivators of the Earth, it seems not improbable that Rum may be the appointed Means." Franklin's career as printer and inventor may be interpreted chiefly as an attempt to realize the promise of progress through scientific achievement. So also Jefferson, who in earlier years had held a distinctly cyclic view of history, in his later days began to sense the possibilities the new science held for civilizations yet to be born:

> Science had liberated the ideas of those who read and reflect, and the American example had kindled feelings right in the people. An insurrection has consequently begun, of science, talents and courage against rank and birth. . . . Science is progressive, and talent and intellect on the alert.[28]

What bears repeating, however, is that while a thinker of Jefferson's stature may have been able to keep his philosophical perspectives straight, for most educated Americans, Enlightenment ideas blended unconsciously into their religious and political perspectives in complex and, to our perspective today, seemingly contradictory ways. This jumbling of sensibilities explains in good measure the perennial disagreements that historians have had in trying to interpret the period. Gordon Wood, arguably the greatest historian who has studied these times, is clear at least about the muddle:

> It seemed indeed to be a peculiar moment in history when all knowledge coincided, when classical antiquity, Christian theology, English empiricism, and European rationalism could all be linked. . . . To most of the Revolutionaries there was no sense of incompatibility in their blending of history, rationalism, and scripture.[29]

Historians writing during this period of immense ideological cross-fertilization were characteristically eclectic, and this is especially true of the group of writers who first sought to chronicle the American Revolution. Consider the following remarks by Mercy Otis Warren, taken from the final chapter of her three-volume *History of the Rise, Progress, and Termination of the American Revolution* (1805):

> Notwithstanding the advantages that may be derived, and the safety that may be felt, under so happy a constitution, yet it is necessary to guard at every point, against the intrigues of artful or ambitious men, who may subvert the system which the inhabitants of the United States judged to be most conducive to the general happiness of society. . . . There has been a conspiracy formed against the dissemination of republican opinions, by interested and aspiring characters. . . . [The United States] have now to maintain their well-earned fame, by a strict adherence to the principles of the revolution, and the practice of every public, social, and domestic virtue.

In this passage Warren is clearly rehearsing a characteristic republican theme: fear of declension as a result of a lapse in civic virtue among the citizenry.

The solution she looks to is the "dissemination of republican opinions," and she is hopeful, noting, "Colleges and academies have been reared, multiplied, and endowed with the best advantages for public instruction, on the broad scale of liberality and truth." But immediately following this paean to republican virtue and its institutions she strikes what to us seems a more liberal note:

> The effects of industry and enterprise appear in the numerous canals, turnpikes, elegant and well constructed buildings, over lengths and depths of water that open, and render the communication easy and agreeable, throughout a country almost without bounds. In short, arts and agriculture are pursued with avidity, civilization spreads, and science in full research is investigating all the fources [*sic*] of human knowledge. Indeed the whole country wears a face of improvement.

And this seemingly liberal ode to scientific and technological progress blends seamlessly into this her culminating and closing statement of three dense volumes of history:

> This last civilized quarter of the globe may exhibit those striking traits of grandeur and magnificence, which the Divine Economist may have reserved to crown the closing scene, when the angel of his presence will stand upon the sea and upon the earth, lift up his hand to heaven, and swear by Him that liveth for ever and ever, that there shall be time no longer.[30]

So we see in a few short pages all three of the ideologies we have traced at work. Warren's reader is likely, if not careful, to be swept up in her language, because the result of the combination of all of these seemingly discordant philosophies is not dissonance but, astonishingly, a glorious harmony akin to the counterpoint of a Baroque fugue. The three distinct melodies together produce a singular effect that is intellectually satisfying and rhetorically appealing: they produce the Whig interpretation of history.

HISTORIES OF EDUCATION IN THE REVOLUTIONARY ERA

Ideological shifts were not the only significant development of the Revolutionary period. There was actual history written during the time as well, and some of it was educational history. Three genres in particular—state histories, historical fiction, and biographies of George Washington—addressed educational topics in a manner that is both instructive of the temper of those days and vitally important for understanding the development of educational historiography.

Comparatively speaking, there was little history written during the Revolutionary era. Many of the best educated of the American colonists had been royalist sympathizers who left the colonies as soon as revolution was proclaimed. The respect for bookishness among patriots might be appreciated as we recall the treatment royal governor and standout historian Thomas Hutchinson received at their hands in Massachusetts: his library was sacked and his manuscript history of Massachusetts scattered to the wind.

But despite the Revolutionary era brain drain and the rather anti-intellectualist cast of much of the patriot mind, four historical genres managed to win a readership. Most obviously, many patriots tried their hands at composing a history of the late Revolution itself, and where these authors say anything at all about education it is sweeping and celebratory, as fits the spirit of such works composed during the first blush of nationalism. If anything is remarkable in these accounts it is that the very school systems that the following generation will berate as inadequate and in need of replacement are lauded to the heavens. From 1793, when David Ramsay enthused that "from the later periods of the revolution till the present time, schools, colleges, societies, and institutions for promoting literature, arts, manufactures, agriculture, and for extending human happiness, have been increased far beyond anything that ever took place before the declaration of independence," to 1828, when Timothy Pitkin declared that the fine colonial system of education "has been greatly improved, since the American Revolution," nation-building historians of the Revolution found only praise for American educational history.[31]

But the Revolutionary histories were in fact minority documents. More representative of their day were histories of a particular state. This may seem surprising given the retrospective stress on nation building that historians since the Civil War have imposed on the period. But "to the man of that day, inhabitant of a particular State, and little accustomed to 'think continentally' as the phrase was, the thought that his colony had become an independent and sovereign state was often quite as prominent, and was a source of pride and inspiration to a degree difficult for us to conceive." The state histories were themselves products of the most significant development in historical scholarship during this generation, the creation of state historical societies. Beginning in 1791 in Massachusetts and expanding nearly as rapidly as did the union itself, every self-respecting state had to have a historical society, and to have a society was to collect the resources necessary for composing a state history. Scholar David Van Tassel finds herein the most significant development in American historiography of the time, for the societies "originated as a weapon in the battle to dominate the writing of national history. . . . The most powerful states set out to dominate the nation's historical writing, just as they sought to control its politics and economics."[32]

The first and, in the view of most critics, greatest of these state histories was Jeremy Belknap's *History of New Hampshire*, the first volume of which appeared in 1784, with two more to come over the following eight years. Volumes 1 and 2 take the reader from the first American settlements to the founding of the nation and exhibit for the first time in North America a self-conscious historiographical tradition, with frequent citations from previous secondary works and even occasional rebuttals of a predecessor's judgment. Belknap's history has won such high marks from recent appraisers not only for its lucid language and elegant use of sources but also for its scope. Unlike many of its successor state histories, it not only chronicles military and political affairs but also provides clear expositions of religious matters, vivid portrayals of social settings and human interactions, and a good deal of educational history.

Although Belknap is a lively narrator of battles and political disputes, his disposition clearly favors times of peace and prosperity. This tendency is manifest in his exaltation of toleration in religious matters, his evenhanded treatment of border squabbles and the Indian character, and his relish for internal improvements. One such improvement was the founding of Dartmouth College, which Belknap details from its origins as a missionary school for natives under Eleazar Wheelock to its growth via transcontinental philanthropy into a legitimate degree-granting college. The reader learns along the way that the subversion of the original purpose of training Indian youth was in fact an "improvement on the original design" because of the positive example that European youths would set and because of the unfortunate tendency of Indian boys to lapse back into their "savage life" and "barren dialect."[33]

Volume 3 of Belknap's history is a fine example of that lost "interdisciplinary" study formerly termed geography. In addition to a survey of the state's natural features and topography, Belknap's geography includes sketches of "productions, improvements, and [the] present state of society and manners, laws and government," one of which is the education system. "The old laws of New-Hampshire required every town of one hundred families to keep a grammar school," he begins, describing the colonial curriculum and the ambiguous feelings settlers had about such laws. As settlement thickened, the laws were increasingly ignored, clear evidence "of a most unhappy prostration of morals during that period," which "excited some generous and philanthropic persons to devise other methods of education."[34]

Such methods included the founding of academies, most notably Exeter by John Phillips in 1781. In his discussion of this trend in education, Belknap is at pains to counter arguments that the academies draw interest and business away from Latin grammar schools. New Ipswich's academy, for instance, "is so far from discouraging town schools, that the sum of one hundred pounds is annually raised in the same town for that purpose." The point, for Belknap, is that any and every mode of education is to be encouraged, from "social libraries . . . established in several towns" to medical societies, to the capstone of the state's system, Dartmouth College. Initiating an interpretation of war that will continue for at least 150 years in educational historiography, Belknap tells us that Dartmouth "during the late war, like all other seminaries of literature, . . . lay under discouragement," but since peace has come the college, "is in a more flourishing situation," a situation Belknap describes in fascinating detail and with no irony, even as he notes that as of 1790, 252 men had graduated, "among whom were two Indians."[35]

While state histories were a mark of distinction that no self-respecting sovereign territory could well do without, they did not sell particularly well. Belknap's was one of the most readable of the lot, and his lost money. The public, if it wanted history at all, wanted to read tales that reinforced their emerging national self-concept, created for them a mythology, edified their religious sensibilities, and excited them with the romance of the increasingly popular novelistic fiction. There were two ways to meet this demand: biography and historical fiction. And no biographical subject was in stronger demand than George Washington.

But one must pitch Washington just right to reach the reader. The first and authoritative biography of Washington was Chief Justice John Marshall's ponderous five-volume set. In addition to being expensive and dull, it did not promote the mythos sought by the American people. Washington the man is not even introduced until the second volume, and when he finally takes the stage, anyone still reading has exactly two pages of the young man but four more volumes of the life and times of Washington the soldier and president. Washington's education is described by Marshall in this one sentence: "He lost his father at the age of ten years, and received what was denominated an English education, a term which excludes the acquisition of other languages than our own."[36]

In colorful contrast, Mason Locke Weems's *The Life and Memorable Actions of George Washington* is still in the public memory thanks not only to Parson Weems's exaggerated claims regarding his clerical assistance to the first president, but especially for its educational history. No one remembers the parson's treatment of the French and Indian War, but the story of the founder of the country with his hatchet and his honesty still brings a smile to many Americans. Weems himself was inspired to market his own text as he beheld firsthand how poorly Marshall's biography (which Weems was peddling around the country) was selling but how eager the public was to read about Washington. Knowing his audience, Weems hunted down anecdotes from Washington's early days in Virginia, embellishing them with a moralism calculated to appeal to the common reader, and he marketed the product with perfect timing and compelling new techniques, such as the bulk discount and the school rate. His instincts produced a work that "ranks as one of the most successful books in publishing history," seeing twenty-nine editions by 1825.[37]

Parson Weems was engaged in the same project that had inspired Noah Webster and countless others of the founding generation. He was creating a national mythology, with the education of the young George Washington as his central figure and the schoolhouse as his chief market. Washington's formal schooling is discussed in some detail, but stress is placed on the moral training the boy Washington receives from his father. The father-son relationship is the context for most of what remains compelling in the Weems biography, from the cherry tree anecdote to the story of cabbage seeds spelling *George Washington* as a sort of cosmological argument for the existence of the Deity. Marshall devoted one sentence of five volumes to Washington's education and fell into debt. Weems gave it four chapters out of sixteen and produced a bestseller.

The parson's Washington is of course a good republican, from his early childhood, leading his comrades in mock battles and prohibiting fighting or animus, to his dying moments, when he set aside large sums of money for educational purposes. Given what we have said concerning the hope so many republican theorists placed in educational institutions, we are not surprised to find Weems stressing Washington's educational contributions throughout his public life:

> Sensible that a republican government, that is, a government of the people, can never long subsist where the minds of the people are not enlightened, he earnestly recommended it to the United States, to promote . . . institutions for the general diffusion of knowledge. . . . He established a charity-school in Alexandria, and endowed it with a donation of *four thousand dollars!*[38]

But at the same time, in Weems we see reflected on the popular level a literary phenomenon that had very little to do with republicanism and was actually opposed to the focus that republicans placed on moderation and sobriety. Although Weems's morality was republican, his style was romantic. German Romanticism was popularized on this continent largely through the works of the English historical novelist Sir Walter Scott. Scott was "by a large margin, the best-selling author in the United States until the Civil War," and he bequeathed to many nineteenth-century historians a sense of novelistic device, of plot, setting, character, emotion, and morality. Weems was able to capture this sensibility, if not its substance, in his biography, which George Callcott has called "the first 'Romantic' history published in the United States," and more serious writers were able to create an American historical fiction that not only satisfied a popular demand for national mythology and story but also helped mold the consciousness of the greatest of nineteenth-century historians: writers such as George Bancroft, William H. Prescott, Charles Gayarré, and Francis Parkman, all of whom declared their indebtedness to Scott. In short, for a brief time in America, from roughly 1790 to 1820, historical fiction, painting, sculpture, plays, and biography were all the rage. As Callcott aptly quipped, "[H]istory was fun."[39]

No American more successfully appropriated this romantic novelistic sensibility than Washington Irving. Irving's own corpus well illustrates the significance of the various genres discussed in this chapter. His first success was the *History of New York* (1809), a wild romp through the Dutch past of that colony-turned-sovereign-state, narrated by Irving's famous character Diedrich Knickerbocker. Later in his career he would try his hand at a biography of George Washington, and of course he is still widely read today for his charming historical fiction. But Irving also gives us a glimpse into why the romantic sensibility, though powerful in its contribution to early American literature of the genteel variety, was not in the end of lasting influence in educational historiography. Irving, like other Romantics, had just enough respect for the integrity of the past and just enough of the aristocrat in his disposition to approach the present with something close to cultural snobbery and, what is worse, political cynicism, though the resulting opinions were often only semiconscious and usually combined with the cant of the day in ways that defy tidy classification.[40]

In "English Writers on America," for example, Irving offers what seems commonplace Enlightenment hubris:

> What have we to do with national prejudices? They are the inveterate diseases of old countries, contracted in rude and ignorant ages, when nations knew but little of each other, and looked beyond their boundaries with distrust and hostility. We, on the contrary, have sprung into national existence in an enlightened and philosophic age; when the different parts of the habitable world, and the various branches of the human family, have been indefatigably studied and made known to each other; and we forego the advantages of our birth, if we do not shake off the national prejudices, as we would the local superstitions of the old world.

Yet even as he declares himself, one cannot really trust Irving's words, for most of his best work is interesting precisely for its fascinating portrayal of local superstitions and prejudices. Irving officially is glad to be rid of the past, but dispositionally his affections are all on its side. And thus his *History of New York* lovingly lampoons Dutch old ways. And thus his most memorable characters are the slob Rip Van Winkle and the superstitious Ichabod Crane. Irving is at heart a Romantic, and this allows him a vantage of critique that doesn't entirely fit with his ostensible Americanism. This most American of early writers, it turns out, is a chronicler of ancient myth, as one can see in his fascination with forgotten Christmas traditions from the feudal ages:

> One of the least pleasing effects of modern refinement is the havoc it has made of the old holy day customs. It has completely taken off the sharp touchings and spirited reliefs of these embellishments of life, and has worn down society into a more smooth and polished, but certainly a less characteristic surface. . . . Society has acquired a more enlightened and elegant tone; but it has lost many of its strong local peculiarities, its homebred feelings, its honest fireside delights.[41]

This tendency, what I shall call Irving's romantic check, is a rare presence in the early historiography of education, or indeed in American letters generally, and it leads him into some remarkable interpretations of American history. Perhaps most astonishing is his ribald treatment of the very idea of the utility of history. Knickerbocker is nothing if not a caricature of the contemporary historian, painstakingly compiling authorities and citations. Irving later explained, "To burlesque the pedantic lore displayed in certain American works, our historical sketch was to commence with the creation of the world; and we laid all kinds of works under contribution for trite citations, relevant or irrelevant, to give it the proper air of learned research." Irving's original full title tells it all: *A History of New York from the Beginning of the World to the End of the Dutch Dynasty . . . Being the only Authentic History of the Times that ever hath been or ever will be published.*[42]

But there are serious results from the romantic check as well. In his *New York* Irving had wickedly satirized European exploitation of American natives at the very time that frontier soldiers were waging war against Native Americans, and later writings continue this concern:

> Society has advanced upon [the Indians] like one of those withering airs that will sometimes breathe desolation over a whole region of fertility. It has enervated their strength, multiplied their diseases, and superinduced upon their original barbarity the low vices of artificial life. . . . How different was their state while yet the undisputed lords of the soil. Their wants were few, and the means of gratification within their reach. They saw every one round them sharing the same lot, enduring the same hardships, feeding on the same aliments, arrayed in the same rude garments.

Irving continues, suggesting to his reader the true motive for historical study:

> If, perchance, some dubious memorial of them should survive, it may be in the romantic dreams of the poet, to people in imagination his glades and groves, like the fawns and satyrs and sylvan deities of antiquity. But should he venture upon the dark story of their wrongs and wretchedness; should he tell how they were invaded, corrupted, despoiled . . . and sent down with violence and butch-

ery to the grave; posterity will either turn with horror and incredulity from the tale, or blush with indignation at the inhumanity of their forefathers.

Such sentiments are a far cry from those with which this chapter began, all of which conspired to create a version of history that was optimistically progressive. In Irving, though he wavers at times, one finds an early and remarkable expression of dissent that stems from no other source than an instinctive appreciation for "the world we have lost."[43]

One component of that world to which Irving was especially attuned was the old country school. Irving's "Legend of Sleepy Hollow," his most successful piece, contains what is perhaps the best history of education written in the early nineteenth century. Schoolmaster Ichabod Crane has come to Sleepy Hollow from Connecticut, "a state which supplies the Union with pioneers for the mind as well as for the forest, and sends forth yearly its legions of frontier woodmen and country schoolmasters." Irving's description of Crane's one-room schoolhouse and what went on there has become the default popular understanding of this era's educational facilities and classroom activities, with "the windows partly glazed, and partly patched with leaves of old copy books." Crane, no pedagogical faddist, believes the golden maxim "spare the rod and spoil the child: Ichabod Crane's scholars certainly were not spoiled." The teacher's pay was small, but "according to country custom in those parts," he was "boarded and lodged at the houses of the farmers, whose children he instructed." Irving's portrait continues with lavish descriptions of the social situation surrounding the old country school, from the subtle interpersonal and interfamilial politics associated with the schoolmaster's presence in the village to witty accounts of the actual intellectual apparatus of the hero, complete with examples of musical instruction, quotations from the *New England Primer*, and as befits the story, copious reference to Cotton Mather's writings on witchcraft.[44]

It is unclear to what degree Irving's sketch is based on actual historical observation and how much of it is imaginative. However, other works suggest how he may have gone about producing this one. Just as Mason Weems scoured the Virginia countryside drumming up anecdotes from locals who had known George Washington as a boy, so Irving was fond of tripping through villages and towns to talk to the elders. Consider this example from his essay "Stratford-on-Avon":

> In the course of my rambles I met with the grey headed sexton, Edmonds, and accompanied him home to get the key of the Church. He had lived in Stratford, man and boy, for eighty years. . . . His dwelling was a cottage, looking out upon the Avon and its bordering meadows. . . . In one corner sat the old man's grand daughter sewing, a pretty blue eyed girl,—and in the opposite corner was a superannuated crony . . . who, I found, had been his companion from child-

hood. I had hoped to gather some traditionary anecdotes of the bard from these ancient chroniclers; but they had nothing new to impart. The long interval during which Shakespeare's writings lay in comparative neglect has spread its shadow over his history; and it is his good or evil lot that scarcely anything remains to his biographers but a scanty handful of conjectures.

Irving's interview method was a commonplace in the nineteenth century, and indeed today, when it is given the noble designation *oral history*, but it bears remarking that carrying out interviews was a gentleman's occupation, scarcely the sort of historical method that a man without the requisite financial backing could undertake. Irving himself made more money than any other pre–Civil War historian, and even he could not support himself by his pen alone. What motivated his historical endeavors was above all a romantic fascination with the past in all its colorful and human details, and this fascination, together with the gentleman's wanderings it precipitated, bore fruit in his treatment of early national education in a sleepy New York community.[45]

Most significant, Irving's "Legend of Sleepy Hollow" provides us with the first example in American letters of something like a social history of education. All previous accounts had focused nearly exclusively on institutional beginnings, on political and philanthropic work dedicated to the cause of fostering schools, on the theory of schooling as Christian duty or republican necessity. But Irving's romantic check allows him to escape for a moment the all-pervading paradigm of progress and see glimpses of what life was like in the past on its own terms. Irving himself was never able to harmonize his impulsive love for the simpler past with a reformist spirit, and so his reader is left with the sense of double-mindedness that has tended to accompany Arcadian dreamers, from Rip Van Winkle to Miniver Cheever, who wake from their reverie to find themselves, alas, in the modern world.

But not all Romantics were as dichotomous in their sensibilities. Most of them were able to reconcile their fascination with the otherness and colorful particulars of the past with a deep and mystical sense of world progress. It must be recalled that the doctrine of evolution was entrenched in the literate English-speaking mind well before Charles Darwin put pen to paper. Here is John Keats, for example, in 1819:

So on our heels a fresh perfection treads,
A power more strong in beauty, born of us
And fated to excel us, as we pass
In glory that old Darkness.[46]

We have seen how the evolution and progress of material institutions were the hallmark of the Enlightenment interpretation. As the nineteenth century matured, American intellectuals were increasingly affected by the spirit of Romanticism emanating from both Germany and Britain. Romantic poets and philosophers believed in progress just as deeply as did their Enlightenment predecessors, only this progress was redefined away from material entities and toward matters of spirit, of *Geist*. Writers operating with this assumption, often from the genteel classes, would thus be able all at once to deplore the excessive Mammonism and the hustle and bustle of the modernizing world while at the same time maintaining the broad outlines of progressive history that were fashioned in the Reformation and Enlightenment. Washington Irving, as we have seen, was very close to such a synthesis, but a more consistent early example on the American continent is the Presbyterian minister Samuel Miller, to whose underappreciated *Brief Retrospective on the Eighteenth Century* we now turn.

Miller was thirty-four years old when his *Brief Retrospective* was published, and his youthful enthusiasm for Jeffersonian democracy enlivens many of its pages, a vital force that Miller would later come to regret when Jacksonian democracy gained the ascendency, and intellectual currents akin to Jefferson's deism increasingly threatened to overthrow Christianity's intellectual dominance in America. The scope of Miller's work is enormous—unquestionably the most all-encompassing tour of knowledge thus far attempted by an American. The contents of the two volumes he was able to complete are described in his subtitle—"*A Sketch of the Revolutions and Improvements in Science, Arts, and Literature*"—and conceived on a broad pan-nationalist scale that was rare for his time. One might even interpret the book as the first American history of "Western Civilization," and most certainly it was the first to integrate the story of the United States into European intellectual affairs. It is Miller's *Brief Retrospective on the Eighteenth Century* that deserves first place in the long line of histories of education that took as their subject matter the entire civilized world.[47]

Driving the account is the motif of progress, but progress of a very particular sort. Progress for Miller, the enlightened yet orthodox Protestant clergyman, is not the same thing as perfectibility, and this distinction must be understood if we are to properly interpret his educational history. For Miller, human perfectibility is impossible because of the constraints necessity places upon the species. It is not surprising that for him the greatest philosopher of the eighteenth century is the American theologian Jonathan Edwards:

> This gentleman wrote on the side of moral *necessity*, or against the self-determining power of the will. . . . Though all Calvinistic writers before his time were characterized by a firm adherence to the doctrine of *Predestination*; yet they seem, for the most part, to have adopted a kind of middle course between his creed and that of the Arminian *contingency*.

As the predestination of God limits the extent of human freedom, so a human escape from the condition of sin in which we exist is impossible. Thus the doctrines of such thinkers as Helvetius, Concordet, and Godwin cannot be sustained:

> The advocates of this doctrine maintain the *Perfectibility of Man*. . . . They suppose that . . . by means of the diffusion of knowledge, and the adoption of better principles and modes of education, the improvement of man in intellect, in virtue, and in happiness, will go on to an illimitable extent, that, at length, mind shall become "omnipotent over matter," perfect enjoyment assume the place of present suffering, and human life, instead of being bounded by a few years, be protracted to immortality, or at least to an indefinite duration.[48]

So we see that what we might for the sake of consistency call Miller's Calvinist check has kept him from the sort of faith in education's powers for social transformation that would soon become a hallmark of educational historiography. In fact, Miller's essentialist understanding of human nature leads him to consider the doctrine of the "*omnipotence of education*" to be "pregnant with mischief." For Miller there is a fundamental division between God's hand in human history and the advancement of knowledge, a division that would soon melt away in the great heat of revival religion's stress on the freedom of the individual will. But Samuel Miller cannot predicate the millennium upon the progress of educative institutions alone.[49]

Perhaps because his expectations for education's contribution to human society are not so grand, Miller is able to interpret the history of education during the eighteenth century as one of remarkable progress:

> [S]o far as respects the extension of its benefits in a greater degree to the female sex, and to almost every grade in society; the multiplication of seminaries of learning, of popular elementary works for the use of youth, and of the various means and excitements to the acquisition of knowledge; and the decline of that despotic reign which the dead languages held for three preceding centuries, we may look back on the period under consideration as a period of honorable achievement.

Above all, progress is defined in terms of the quantity of literature produced, and in this respect America had made remarkable advances during the eighteenth century. The concluding section of Miller's volumes is a fascinating and comprehensive look at the literary progress of three countries that had only during the eighteenth century risen to a stature comparable to that of Britain and France—Germany, Russia, and the United States. Educational history for Miller becomes the study of those trends and institutions responsible for creating in emerging nations a penchant for literate production and consumption. As such he is able to consider a wide array of organizations, from academies and colleges, to libraries and learned societies, to printing presses and textbook writers. But the criterion of literacy also limits his examination. If a location has not produced books and pamphlets, it is backward and unworthy of consideration: "Neither in New York, New Jersey, Pennsylvania, Deleware, nor Maryland, had anything taken place, in favor of literature, worthy of notice, prior to the eighteenth century."[50]

Given this literary bias, Miller's appraisal of the history of education in America demonstrates unmitigated progress in every colony during the eighteenth century. This is a critical point to notice at this stage in our study, for we will soon see such a view not only challenged, but completely reversed, in the wake of the common school movement of the 1830s and 1840s. For Miller, however, education has exploded since the Revolutionary War: "Academies, during this period, were multiplied almost without number"—so much so that he wonders if there might now be *too many* schools. Textbook sales have taken off since the Revolution thanks to "that disposition to attend to the education of children, which has long characterized the Eastern States, and which, during the last ten years of the century under review, rapidly extended itself through every part of the Union." Educational attainments were so great during the eighteenth century that he can say of New England schools in 1803:

> These establishments have been carried to such a degree of perfection, that in New England . . . scarcely an individual can be found, of either sex, who has not been instructed in reading, writing and arithmetic, and who does not habitually read more or less in newspapers, and a few of the best books on religion and morality.

Recent studies using both quantitative and literary data have concluded much the same thing, of course. It is now a textbook commonplace to attribute near universal literacy to eighteenth-century New England and to assert that the rise in school attendance antedated the common school reforms. Long before cliometrics, Miller got it right, and this fact alone would recommend him as worthy of more consideration in the annals of educational historiography.[51]

But rectitude is not Miller's only virtue. He was also a pathbreaker, presenting what was far and away the most comprehensive treatment of American educational history yet to appear. When one considers that his definition of literature allowed him to include in his account such institutions as the church, the library, the club, and the press, his position in the history of educational historiography takes on an ironic significance, for here at the turn of the nineteenth century is a fine example of just the sort of history Lawrence Cremin advocated as the antidote to generations of narrow educationist writing: it is transcontinental, embedded in two volumes of intellectual context, and driven by a definition of education broad enough in scope to encompass all sorts of institutions.

In addition to covering what had by 1800 become the standard educational landmarks—the founding of Harvard and the colonial school laws—Miller also includes much that would not receive coverage again for many decades. He chronicles with great felicity such heady topics as the shift from the classics to belles lettres at Yale in the 1760s and 1770s and the introduction of Scottish Common Sense Realism at Princeton under Witherspoon. He describes the "schools of the prophets" emerging from the Great Awakening, the "Log College" of William Tennet, the significance of textbooks such as Noah Webster's *Grammatical Institute*, and the development of academies in many states. He chronicles the development of schools and colleges in every English colony of North America. Although Miller does not rely on archival research, he is able to advance knowledge on these and other topics both in his consolidation of materials gleaned from many state histories and through his reliance on the personal correspondence of such notables as Noah Webster, Jr., David Ramsay, and Hugh Williamson. But despite its suggestive interpretive paradigm, its rich intellectual apparatus, and its comprehensive content, Miller's history of education was within one generation all but forgotten. Why?

The Whig Tradition

Our age is retrospective. It builds the sepulchres of the fathers. It writes biographies, histories, and criticism. The foregoing generations beheld God and nature face to face; we, through their eyes. Why should not we also enjoy an original relation to the universe? Why should not we have a poetry and philosophy of insight and not of tradition, and a religion by revelation to us, and not the history of theirs? . . . Why should we grope among the dry bones of the past?

—Ralph Waldo Emerson

On the eve of war in early January 1812, Daniel Sheffey, a wary Virginia federalist, sounded a cautious note regarding America's prospects:

We have considered ourselves of too much importance in the scale of nations. It has led us into great errors. Instead of yielding to circumstances, which human power cannot control, we have imagined that our own destiny, and that of other nations, was in our hands, to be regulated as we thought proper.

After two and a half years of political mismaneuvers, military bungling, expenditures estimated at 158 million dollars, and the death of twenty thousand men, Sheffey's prognosis was beginning to sound prophetic. But almost three years to the date of Sheffey's remarks, on January 8, 1815, Andrew Jackson's forces delivered a blow to the British that would provoke amazement across the land: at the Battle of New Orleans, the British lost more than two thousand men while Andrew Jackson lost thirteen. Almost immediately, the sordid history of the conflict was lost in the thrill of victory, made stronger by word that the Treaty of Ghent had already been signed. By January 1817, New Jersey congressman Henry Southard could exclaim:

The glorious achievements of the late war have sealed the destinies of this country, perhaps for centuries to come, and the Treaty of Ghent has secured our liberties, and established our national independence, and placed this nation on high and honorable ground.[1]

For many Americans, the War of 1812 was the clear signal of an emerging national destiny, a destiny manifest to all who would but investigate the matter. Tecumseh was killed and with him the last hope of Native Americans for defense against further westward expansion of the Europeans. The already flagging Federalist Party, symbol of old New England, suffered a mortal blow as their Hartford Convention became synonymous with treason. Perhaps most important, the establishment of peace and the expansionism it promoted liberated the forces necessary to produce in antebellum America what historian Charles Sellers has termed "the market revolution," the gradual replacement in the American interior of an agrarian, land-based economy of subsistence with a mercantile, profit-driven, capitalist order. Cities emerged to consolidate economic output. Canals and rails were constructed to transport goods. Capital, goods, and labor thus became increasingly mobile, and the entire process was abetted by promarket legislation and court decisions.[2]

But movements in opposition to the expanding commercial order emerged as well. Some looked for a political solution in Andrew Jackson and democracy's return to governmental localism and a prebanking economic order. Others sought release from the world of mammon and vice in the penetrating preaching of Charles Finney and other prophets of the Second Great Awakening. What is of importance for this study is that both the Jacksonians and those affected by religious revival, many of whom would later become Whigs, shared a concern that American progress was being threatened by either the commercial or the moral implications of market revolution. But definitions of that progress could vary considerably.

Progress for Jacksonians was quantitative and spatial: it was about land acquisition. And land acquisition is accomplished through war. America was born complete and needed only to be extended westward and southward to progress. For Whigs, however, progress was qualitative and temporal: it was about improving public morality and building a national consensus upon past precedent. War was thus a liability. Horace Greeley captured the contrast, in the process explaining why educational historiography has tended to equate war with regression:

> Opposed to the instinct of boundless acquisition stands that of Internal Improvement. A nation cannot simultaneously devote its energies to the absorption of others' territories and the improvement of its own. In a state of war, not law only is silent, but the pioneer's axe, the canal-digger's mattock, and the house builder's trowel also.

One perspective produced the astonishing expansionism that has come to be known as Manifest Destiny; the other, the intense reform impulse that created so many societies and organizations for human betterment in the antebellum world. Both were millennial in their fervor, Anglo-American in culture, inclined to an easy synthesis of scientific and religious truth, and generally supportive of the reforms in public education that brought about the first great revisionist movement in American educational historiography.[3]

For Democrats, education and land acquisition were two sides of one coin. Cheap land would provide an individual's livelihood, and education would ensure an equality of condition and opportunity for offspring. The ownership of property was itself the first step toward virtue, for ownership imparted responsibility, and Democrats as well as Whigs maintained the profoundest respect for the sanctity of private property. Although there was an occasional urban dissenter to the education-and-property-as-opportunity thesis, on the whole the ideology of common school reformers transcended party lines, and the politically successful took advantage of this situation.

Thus when we speak of a "Whig interpretation" of educational history, we should understand that there is no contrasting "Democrat interpretation," for both groups in the main supported the reform movement that gave birth to Whig revisionsim. We call it Whig only because Whigs were more interested than Democrats in the internal development of schools over time: they were the ones who wrote the history. One might imagine a "democrat" educational history that regretted the loss of local control or resented the imposition of bourgeois culture upon urban workers and rural farmers, but nothing of the kind was ever written until after World War II. That the "Whig" interpretation of educational history was never challenged, even by Democrats, is itself strong evidence for the consensus on this issue between parties. When it came to public schooling, most Democrats were Whigs.[4]

Perhaps the major factor unifying the parties on the issue of school reform, and hence on the history of education as interpreted through the lens of such reform, was the religious function of schools. The Second Great Awakening had transformed American Protestantism's demographics and theology. Before the Awakening there were about three hundred Methodists in the country. When the indefatigable Francis Asbury died in 1816, there were two hundred thousand. By 1812 there were also two hundred thousand Baptists, and both groups continued to grow exponentially: by 1850 there were more than a million Baptists in the United States. Theologically, the Awakening popularized a shift in American Christianity from a focus on God's sovereignty and human degradation to God's benevolence and the possibility of human agency in personal spiritual regeneration and in social transformation. This shift combined with the emerging doctrine of post-millennialism—the belief that Christ will not return until the church has established the millennium through evangelism and social reform—to set off an explosion of Protestant missions, organizations, and societies for moral reform, what Charles Foster has aptly termed "the Evangelical united front."[5]

The enthusiasm for moral reform, for Arminian individualism, and for child nurture generated by the Awakening's invocations of a millennial kingdom in the New World led to a wide-ranging coalition of support for common school reform. Egalitarian-minded idealists, labor radicals, middle-class advocates of social order, and industrialists all supported government schooling for their various reasons. The only real opposition, aside from isolated (and debatable) working-class objections, was from Roman Catholics. Perhaps nothing consolidated the Evangelical front so much as the perceived threat to free American institutions posed by the immigration of thousands of Roman Catholics. Common schooling was the pan-Protestant answer to this problem, an issue over which Democrats and Whigs, not to mention their Know-Nothing successors, would set aside their differences to beat down the Catholic menace. The result, as Rush Welter has argued, was that "in spite of obvious disagreements, workingmen and Democrats, Whigs and educational reformers established universal public education as the indispensable institution of the American democracy."[6]

But there was another source of opposition to common school reform: the opposition of the historical record. As we have seen, previous historians who treated the subject were very positive in their evaluations of what they took to be a straight line of educational progress in this country from colonial days into the nineteenth century. If Whig reformers were to sell their ideas, they would have to come up with a rival account of America's educational past. Such an account was first developed by James G. Carter.

WHIG REVISIONISM

The first great revisionist movement in American educational historiography began in the sleepy town of Leominster, Massachusetts. There, on September 7, 1795, James Gordon Carter was born to a poor farming family, only nineteen years after the birth of that town's most famous son, the peripatetic orchardist John Chapman, alias Johnny Appleseed. Carter's modest circumstances made schooling a difficult attainment, though he was able to work his way through Groton Academy and eventually Harvard College by teaching in district schools, giving instruction in vocal music, and lecturing on the history of freemasonry. He was graduated with honors from Harvard in 1820 and immediately embarked on the customary apprenticeship for young men of his means as a common school teacher in Cohasset and then at the academy in Lancaster.[7]

But keeping school was not the only vocation of this ambitious young man. In 1821, Carter began what was to be a successful career in journalism by composing a series of papers on the state of education in Massachusetts for the *Boston Transcript*. These papers were collected and published in pamphlet form in 1824 under the title *Letters to the Hon. William Prescott, LL.D. on the Free Schools of New England*. Two years later Carter published a second pamphlet, again composed of essays he had written for a Boston newspaper, titled *Essays upon Popular Education*. Together these books offer the first revisionist account of American educational history, an interpretation emerging directly out of the difficulties of Carter's own struggle to obtain a formal education.[8]

The *Letters* is the more detailed historical account, but its main argument is restated with greater directness in the *Essays*. In both texts Carter's history provides the crucial backdrop for understanding his calls for reform. The history of education thus is appropriated as a weapon in the political struggle for the reform of Massachusetts common schooling, and it is this social function that accounts for the revisionism. Historiography was born in the late Renaissance as politically motivated nationalists and religious reformers sought self-consciously to overcome conventional views of the past propagated by humanists and ecclesiastics, and ever since then shifts in historical interpretation have correlated closely with political and ideological rivalries. Carter's revision was no different.[9]

Carter knew that for his reform suggestions to be heeded he would have to debunk a deeply ingrained understanding of educational history as one advancement after another. In fine rhetorical form, he begins by granting a measure of plausibility to this convention:

> The system of free schools in New England, has long been the subject of almost unqualified praise. . . . New England may well offer her most hearty congratulations, that the system of free schools, originating with her, has been introduced into most of the States of the Union. . . . I am, certainly, not disposed to detract any thing from so good an establishment. It is, indeed, the richest inheritance, we enjoy from our ancestors.

Although Carter is forthright in his disdain for the motives of the Puritans and their "*zeal* to propagate a blind and bigoted *faith*," nevertheless he compliments their love of free institutions and the tradition of universal education that their questionable motives created. In what is certainly the most complete treatment that had yet been produced, Carter provides detailed assessment of the various colonial laws that created Harvard College and the district system of free schools, not only in Massachusetts, but in Connecticut, New Hampshire, and Rhode Island as well. To this point he is well within the contours of previous interpretation. The colonial schools produced a liberty-loving, prosperous, intelligent, and virtuous citizenry who in turn supported their schools.[10]

But then came the Revolution. Carter has to be careful here, for the American Revolution was by his time already sacrosanct. So he hedges nobly, but still makes the point that "[d]uring the strong excitement . . . the attention, which had been paid to the subject of education, was, probably, for a time somewhat diverted." Thus the beginnings of a great declension are announced, caused by that nettlesome foe of educational progress, warfare. After the war the citizenry was poor and individualistic materialism ascendant, so concern for schooling was on the wane. Such a condition was reflected in the "alarming relaxation" of standards captured in the 1789 Massachusetts School Law. Whereas previously towns of one hundred families were required to hire a grammar school teacher, now it takes two hundred. Whereas previous legislation had required towns with five hundred families to support two writing and two grammar schools, now this category is not even mentioned. And above all, whereas in the past the law had called for constant instruction, now the school year is reduced to six months.[11]

Subsequent history was one of dreadful decline, so that by 1824 "the free schools, strange as it may seem, had received almost no legislative attention, protection, or bounty, for nearly forty years." Popular demand for education, however, had not similarly declined, and so local citizens took it upon themselves to provide what the legislators would not. They chartered academies.[12]

The year 1780, when Phillips Academy was chartered and given support in the form of land grant by the Massachusetts legislature, was the critical transition point, for "before this time, all public schools, it should seem, were also free." As academies spread they drew the best people of the towns in which they were located away from the management of common schools and set up invidious distinctions between citizens, since "for the rich and those in easy circumstances, these schools answer the same, and probably a better purpose, than the grammar schools . . . but they are out of the reach of the poor." Academies, out of financial necessity, charge tuition, and thus "not one in twenty, if one in fifty, throughout the State, will ever find their way to any of them. It is the poor who are to suffer."[13]

Carter, the one in fifty who did find his way, has become the champion of the forty-nine. So while he must acknowledge that the growth of academies has been an actual improvement in education by absolute measures, his contention is that such progress pales in comparison with population and economic growth. And what is worse, though academies were not free, they were at least officially public, with government charters and boards of over-seers. But as the academies themselves proved ineffectual, a new class of wholly private schools has emerged to threaten the very social fabric of the republic. Republics, according to hallowed theory, cannot survive class distinctions, and if private schools continue to enable the rich to "secede from the whole" the result will be catastrophic:

> Then will the children of the higher classes be contaminated by contact with those of the lower; then will general and public interest yield to particular and private interest[;] . . . then will the several classes, being educated differently and without a knowledge of each other, imbibe mutual prejudices and hatreds, and entail them upon posterity from generation to generation.[14]

To avoid this cataclysm, Carter recommends state-supported teacher training and better textbooks. But in 1824 his suggestions fell on deaf ears. It would take more than a revisionist account of educational history to change public opinion. It would take legislative activism and propaganda. So while his anachronistic employment of the concept of the "free school" to rewrite American educational history encountered no opposition, his reform platform did.[15]

In 1835 Carter was elected the Lancaster representative to the Massachusetts House, where he immediately became chair of the Committee on Education. He lobbied hard for surplus revenues to be allocated to teacher training institutes and was the driving force behind the creation of the state Board of Education and its salaried secretary. Carter himself, the veteran educator and propagandist, was the frontrunner for the position until two considerations conspired against him. The first was his demotion from the deaconship of the Congregational Church, thus potentially jeopardizing the delicate coalition supporting the board, of which the orthodox Congregational element was a key component. The second, eerily prophetic of future struggles between educationists and other academicians, was Edmund Dwight's backroom suggestion to Governor Edward Everett that "the reform of the common schools was too important and difficult an undertaking to be placed in the hands of a mere educator." As such the position went to Horace Mann, and James Carter gradually faded from prominence in the Massachusetts school reform community. Not everyone was satisfied with this turn of events, however, as comments from Carter's local following in Leominster reveal. "It was the opinion of some, I think I may say not a few," claims the region's historian in 1852, "that Mr. Carter was by far the most suitable person to have been appointed to the first Secretary of that Board."[16]

But Carter's hope, voiced in the introduction to his first pamphlet, that his work "may be a remote cause of interesting minds more commensurate than my own, with the magnitude of the object" was true in a double sense.

Ultimately his recommendations concerning normal schools and inductive textbooks received institutional embodiment, as "more commensurate" minds followed his lead. But just as successful was his historical revisionism once the opposition, mild as it was, was swept away by legislative savvy and by the homely propaganda of the revision's most successful popularizer, Warren Burton.[17]

Warren Burton's life is something of a microcosm of antebellum New England's intellectual history. Whatever the latest ideas might be, Burton was to be found championing them on the lyceum circuit and in publication. He lived for a time at Brook Farm, was at various moments attracted to transcendentalism, phrenology, or Pestalozzianism, and ultimately became a disciple of that champion of conjugal love Immanuel Swedenborg. But his greatest success came not from association with any of the period's fashionable schools of thought but from his investigation of the decidedly unfashionable old country school. Beyond question, the most widely read of this popular author's many writings was his *District School as It Was by One Who Went to It*, first published in 1833.[18]

Burton was born in 1800. The memoir recounts his experiences in schools from 1803 until 1816, after which time he attended Harvard, graduating with distinction just a year after Carter, and proceeded to teach school himself. As a piece of propaganda for the common school reform movement his book is nearly flawless. Its tone is conciliatory, whimsical, and thoroughly engrossing. Using the first person to describe the old district schools largely through anecdote and personal recollection, Burton succeeds in his double purpose of providing a nostalgic look at the past even as he condemns it. The reader becomes intimately acquainted with the daily routines and local struggles that together made the district school "what it was." We learn of petty disagreements over the location of the school, of the politics of teacher selection and retention, of student curricular progress (if it can be so called) in reading, writing, and arithmetic, all taught, indeed, to the tune of the hickory stick. Yet throughout the breezy descriptions are peppered constant criticisms of the whole system. The "accommodations, or rather dis-accommodations" of the old schoolhouses were trumped only by the teachers, who "were remarkable for nothing in particular." The lessons were tedious, the seats hard, the temperature either frigid or stifling. The pedagogical wisdom was that "there should be no more sound and motion than was absolutely necessary," and physical response to noncompliance was usually swift and severe. In short, Burton's account of the district school is the locus classicus of what has ever since been the popular understanding of the schools of the period.[19]

That Burton's book is the source for a folk understanding of the period is tribute to his success as a strategist, for the book "was written in the hope

that it would be a trifling aid to that improvement which is going on in respect to common schools." Burton expressly intended to write a book that
would influence the historical understanding of generations of Americans,
and his program was to market the product to the young so as to convince
them, more by atmosphere than by argument, how things were:

> It is hoped that [the book] will be deemed particularly appropriate to School
> Libraries, and not unsuited to others; that it will be sought as an agreeable gift-
> book from Teachers to Pupils; and lastly, that it will ever be of historical use
> to rising generations, educated under better auspices, as exhibiting a true and
> graphic picture of "The District School as it Was."[20]

The strategy proved a stunning success. The book was received with high
praise in Boston in 1833 and was republished in New York to equal acclaim.
Later it was reprinted in London, where it was lauded for "giving a faithful
description of one of the Institutions of New England." Henry Barnard, who
himself had briefly kept a district school, purchased several hundred copies
of the book and distributed them "for the purpose of suggesting ideas of
reform." This venerable reformer later remarked that Burton's book, more
than anything else, "helped to revolutionize public sentiment and public
action in rural school edifices and management," largely because it "was
widely read in quarters where more formal expositions would not have been
listened to or heeded." Barnard was intense in his admiration for Burton's
work and adamant about its continued relevance, in his characteristically
self-congratulatory way:

> It should never be out of print, nor be wanting in any of our public or private
> libraries, but kept at hand, that the children of this and coming generations
> may be informed, how many more, and how much greater, are the advantages
> provided for them, than were enjoyed by their parents and grand-parents, when
> young; so that they may be prompted to inquire who have been their benefac-
> tors, that they may do them honor.[21]

Emerging from the works of Carter and Burton was a view of American educational history strikingly different from that offered by Samuel Miller
in 1803. The new story stressed decline after the Revolution on two fronts:
first in terms of legislation and second in terms of actual quality of education. In addition, the concept of "public school" had been narrowed to include only schools that charged no tuition, thus making the academy the bête
noire of the story. Midcentury reformers were hereby able to solve the dilemma articulated by Emerson in this chapter's epigraph: they could compose "biographies, histories, and criticism" even as they forged their own

"poetry and philosophy of insight and not of tradition." Horace Mann himself provides a fine summary of this synthesis on the second page of the first issue of his 1838 *Common School Journal*:

> That the general interest once felt in regard to our common schools has subsided to an alarming degree of indifference, is a position not likely to be questioned by any one who has compared their earlier with their later history. This is not to be attributed to any single cause, but to the cooperation of many. First, perhaps, in the series, came the life-struggle of the Revolution. . . . The revolutionary struggle was one for self-preservation, and, of course, it condensed the future into the immediate and the present. After that epoch passed, the fiscal condition of the country, the momentous questions connected with the organization of a new government . . . and, at a later period, the agitations of party, have engrossed the time and enlisted the talents of men most competent to do it. It cannot be denied too, that for years past the public eye has been pointed backwards to the achievements of our ancestors, rather than forwards to the condition of our posterity; as though the praise of dead fathers would provide adequately for living children.[22]

Mann's declension thesis blends seamlessly into his own efforts at revival. As economic conditions improved, private philanthropy channeled educational funds away from common schools into academies. Well-intentioned philanthropists supporting academies have shone their light "rather on the solitariness of the summits of society than through the populousness of its valleys." To compound matters, Mann finds at work in American society a pernicious penchant to favor material well-being over spiritual, to support the body rather than the mind. The solution to all this neglect, misplaced generosity, and Philistinism is of course the state-supported common school system:

> Of all the means in our possession, the common school has precedence, because of its universality; because it is the only reliance of the vast majority of children. . . . Whatever advances the common school, then, will enhance individual and social wellbeing for generations to come. History must be written and read with different emotions of joy or grief, as they rise or decline.

In Horace Mann's rhetorical dazzle and personal authority the revisionist view of early American educational history gained a powerful advocate. But were there no challengers? Was there no rival interpretation produced?[23]

In fact there was. Horace Mann's struggles against his various enemies have been described many times and have become the stuff of legend among students of educational history. But they have never been viewed as a debate over historiography, which to some degree they were. This is not so much the case with his struggles against certain book publishers and orthodox clergymen, for the debate there was one of principle. But in the cases of his Democratic opponents and the Boston schoolmasters, this revisionist historical account was in fact challenged.[24]

In 1839, the Democratic legislature, together with Democratic governor Marcus Morton, made the case that education had always been decentralized in New England and should remain so, that it was not the academy that was the innovation but the Board of Education and its Prussian ways. State oversight was in this view a dangerous novelty and a historical aberration. Implicit herein is the essentially ahistorical understanding of the country's institutions that Democrats tended to hold. American institutions were born perfected and all that was left to be done by government was to keep them that way. Development was not something to be sought, but feared. Given the long and bitter struggle between forces advocating centralization and those supporting subsidiarity, these Democratic arguments, while coherent and compelling on their own terms, simply found themselves on the wrong side of history. The march toward the Leviathan state that began with antebellum reform efforts became irresistible after the Civil War made manifest the superiority of northern industrial and urban organization. It would not be until the post–World War II disillusionment with centralization and scientific management that this alternative conception of educational history would garner a significant following.[25]

The extended controversy that followed publication of Mann's *Seventh Annual Report* is even more suggestive of a rival historiography that might have been but was not. Mann's report had been sharply critical of the pedagogical methods used by Massachusetts's schoolteachers, and he made no exception for the schools of Boston. In addition, he loaded his report with suggestions for improvement, including such novel practices as the word method of reading instruction, the curtailment of corporal punishment, and substitution of interest for fear as a motivator for learning. Like the Democratic challengers, the Schoolmen pointed out that it was Mann who was the historical innovator, stressing the continuity between their methods and that past that all parties were fond of venerating. Since they did not interpret the academies as a historical discontinuity, they were able to argue for a strong and steady progress from colonial times, such that the educational situation was "*never more prosperous than at the time the Board of Education was formed.*"[26]

Thus there was the potential for a rival historical tradition. But the rival proved to be stillborn, for two reasons. First and foremost it needs to be remembered that when we speak of a Democratic opposition, we really only mean a minority of the Democrats. There were more Democrats for Mann, his board, and the cause of common schools generally, than against them. This is clear not only from the resounding defeat in the state legislature of the General Court majority report advocating the abolition of the board, but also from the fact that several prominent Democrats played key roles in advancing the common school cause in Massachusetts. Likewise, the Boston schoolmasters were a very small minority in the profession, and their stance was not generally supported by the public or the press. The very organization the schoolmasters founded to consolidate Massachusetts teachers' opposition to the board was quickly commandeered by Mann's many supporters in the profession.

The second and more decisive reason that the rival tradition had no chance of life was the overwhelming success of the common school movement itself. Although Mann highlighted his opposition to great political advantage, often seeming to believe in a vast conspiracy against him, by the time the smoke had cleared and a sense of proper proportion had returned, he was able to recognize that

> [t]he Common School cause in Massachusetts was so consolidated . . . that I felt sure nothing could overturn it. It was only annoyances and obstructions, that we had to look after, and these had dwindled away until they had fallen into the hands of some of the meanest spirits with which God suffers the earth to be afflicted.

The "incipient bureaucracy" Mann and others created scored a victory so complete, established such an overwhelming ideological hegemony, that after what meager opposition there was had been routed there was no one left, neither Democrat, orthodox clergyman, nor partisan of the academy, to refute the historical account written by the winners. After Mann's triumphs all educational historians were Whig historians.[27]

That this was the case is evident from the immense collaboration with education reform prosecuted by the leading historians of the day. John Gorham Palfrey had an active career in school reform long before he composed his works on New England history. He chaired the Massachusetts House Standing Committee on Education in 1842 and 1843, working in close collaboration with Horace Mann to successfully procure increased expenditures for common schools, teacher training, and colleges. Jared Sparks, the inspiration behind the famed Library of American Biography and editor of Washington's papers, served from 1838 to 1841 on the Massachusetts Board of Education. Local historical societies similarly joined in, as historian David D. Van Tassel explains:

> During the [18]20's and 30's, with growing support of the public school movement, evidence of the early recognition of the importance of education was cherished as a mark of superiority, and local historians avidly copied every mention of the founding of schools in their area. Massachusetts might boast of her common school law in 1649 [sic], but a Pennsylvanian historian declared

that in 1683, before our ancestors covered themselves from the weather, a school was opened in the city of Philadelphia.[28]

But there is perhaps no better illustration of the consensus of the Whig view than the work of the nineteenth century's most famous American historian, Democrat George Bancroft. The first volume of his monumental *History of the United States* was published in 1834, and "up to its completion in 1885, it still continued, as our phrase is, to vote for Jackson." Bancroft's Democratic credentials are impeccable. He came out firmly against the Bank of the United States in 1831, campaigned for Democratic governor of Massachusetts Marcus Morton in 1835–36, started and edited the *Bay State Democrat* as a party organ, was a key player in getting James K. Polk nominated for the presidency, and even ran (unsuccessfully) as Democratic gubernatorial candidate in Massachusetts. Much of the income and travel necessary for composing his history was provided by the American people in the form of Democratic appointments as secretary of the navy, acting secretary of war, and ambassador to England and then Germany.[29]

Back in 1823, however, Bancroft's politics were ambiguous and his goals were generally pecuniary in nature. At the very time that James Carter was denouncing them on the printed page, Bancroft and Joseph Cogswell opened an academy in Massachusetts, on Round Hill, near Northampton, catering to elite families. But schoolmastering was not to Bancroft's taste, so he soon left it for banking, politics, and historical study. This episode in his life needs to be remembered as we investigate his appraisal of the common school movement. If ever there was a historian in the position to challenge the Whig view of American educational history, it was Bancroft. A Democrat with experience in academies might have been expected to dispute the claim that the common school movement represented the continuation of an original colonial design that had been obfuscated by the emergence of novel private educational ventures. But Bancroft did no such thing.

The first volume of his *History of the United States*, published in 1834, met with immediate acclaim both in America and abroad. It is significant that this volume concludes with an assessment of the Puritan character and contribution to American life. One of his strongest arguments for including such extensive treatment of the Puritan heritage is the spread of New England culture westward:

> To New York and Ohio, where they [in 1834] constituted half the population, they carried the Puritan system of free schools; and their example is spreading it throughout the civilized world.

For Bancroft it was the Puritan system of "free schools" that was the chief cause of the conversion of American society from the bigotry of religious persecution to the "charity of intelligence." In the laws of 1642 and 1647 and the support of Harvard by all the people can be found the source of America's strength:

> In these measures, especially in the laws establishing common schools, lies the secret of the success and character of New England. Every child, as it was born into the world, was lifted from the earth by the ordinance of the country, and, in the statutes of the land received, as its birthright, a pledge of the public care for its morals and its mind.[30]

Although the remainder of Bancroft's famous *History* is largely an interpretive military and political chronicle, concluding with the ratification of the Constitution, it is possible to get a glimpse of his perspective on the subsequent history of American education elsewhere. We have seen already his adoption of the slippery terms *common* and *free* to designate and so to praise colonial schools. In one of the most powerful statements of his philosophy of history, delivered before the New-York Historical Society in 1854, Bancroft situates the common school reforms of his day within an ambitious context, which he named in his title: "The Necessity, the Reality, and the Promise of the Progress of the Human Race."

The history of Man, says Bancroft, is always one of movement, a movement either toward growth or decay. Happily, the first half of the nineteenth century has been a history of unparalleled growth, of the gradual unfolding of the Divine mind in human affairs. And historical necessity suggests that further progress toward the benevolent ideal is inevitable. The evidence is overwhelming—"the proofs of progress are so abundant, that we do not know with which of them to begin." But Bancroft, ever the man of his time, begins with the advances of science, describing the enlargement of the boundaries of knowledge in physiology and astronomy. He proceeds with a chronicle of expansionism and internal improvements, from the great explorations to the harnessing of steam and its extension via canal and rail. After a self-consciously insecure and unconvincing attempt to portray the relegation of the female sex to the private sphere as another great advance, Bancroft moves to social reform, to the progress of the rights of labor, to the seemingly imminent abolition of human servitude, and to the marshaling of press and school as the "controlling agency in renovating civilisation." Prophetically, Bancroft announces:

> The system of free schools, though still very imperfectly developed, has made such progress since it first dawned in Geneva and in parishes of Scotland, that we claim it of the future as a universal instituion.

Thus we see in George Bancroft, the preeminent Democratic historian of the nineteenth century, nothing less than the Whig view of educational history.[31]

FROM REVISION TO TRADITION

Clearly, by 1854 Carter's claim on the publicly supported free school as the essential instrument of human advancement along scientific lines had taken the field. Itself a continuation of the colonial and early nationalist interpretation that understood the founding of colonial schools to be illustrative of the progress of the American people, it added to this tradition its own conception, born of the reformist spirit, of subsequent American educational history as a decline and rebirth in his own day. Thus Carter's conception both takes its place in a long tradition and is itself the point of origin for a more comprehensive tradition. His account was able to displace its rivals because it seemed to provide a compelling explanation for where things stood at present in the field of education—it made sense of the reform buzz that was in the air. It was able to incorporate the insights of previous accounts, to continue the story of educational progress from the Pilgrims' first days, while overcoming the difficulties such accounts had in explaining the remarkable surge in common school reformism. If progress in schooling had been so great, why was New England astir with cries for reform? Carter's explanation, that Massachusetts had suffered a grave declension, not only made sense of the cries, but also cast those who did the crying as heroes. This flattering interpretation was so overwhelmingly successful that we are justified in seeing it as the starting point of the Whig tradition of educational historiography.

Traditions begin with creative inquiry into the nature of reality. Any number of impulses may initiate such an inquiry: curiosity about the physical world, reaction to some sort of religious experience, the need to solve a practical problem. The discoveries one person makes become a tradition when they are passed on to other people. When a tradition is young and vital, the problem or situation that spawned the original discoveries is fresh in the community's consciousness. Energetic advances continue to be made and the tradition grows. But eventually two problems emerge for any tradition. First, the context that first initiated the tradition tends to become obscured by the passage of time, with the result that "what survives from a tradition is most often phrase and form." Second, the body of knowledge the tradition has produced grows so large that it becomes necessary to formalize it somehow so that new initiates can acquaint themselves with the tradition's past in hopes of advancing inquiry the next step. This attempt at formalization we might call *encyclopedia*.[32]

By 1850 the interpretation initiated by Carter and popularized by Burton was so widely accepted that encyclopedic treatment became conceivable. The first generation of common school reformers had enjoyed great success and were anxious to pass on their vision and experience to the next generation, but they feared that their successors, not personally acquainted with the struggles they had endured to accomplish what they did, would lack an appropriate historical appreciation for the work of reform. No one exemplified such tendencies better than Henry Barnard, and his *American Journal of Education* became the encyclopedia of this first great revisionist tradition.

Barnard himself was more than an encyclopedist, however. He was, after all, a key player in the common school movement, usually awarded second place after Horace Mann in overall importance. He early on showed a penchant for the historical side of reformist agitation, taking the main outlines of Carter's thesis and adding to them a much more rigorous historical method to produce in 1834 a complete history, the *History of the Common Schools in Connecticut*, from colonial times to his own administration. Significantly, it is a history only of common schools, not of the entire educational complex of Connecticut society, though Barnard's impeccable research does allow him for the first time to place the school laws that were passed in their appropriate setting, showing how "the first law on the subject did but little more than declare the motive, and make obligatory the practice which had grown up out of the character of the founders of these colonies, and the circumstances in which they were placed."[33]

Perhaps the most important element of this study is the facility Barnard shows with Carter's declension thesis, which becomes his organizing principle in making sense of the debates over management and allocation of the Connecticut school fund and the switch from town control of schools to that of school societies. In this regard, however, Barnard does not follow Carter's argument for the novelty of academies. While Carter saw academies as upstart rivals to the historic free schools, Barnard understands that "[colonial free schools] were the predecessors of the incorporated Academies which do not appear under that name until a comparatively recent period." Finally, though his work appears only a decade after Carter's, he is able to end on a positive note by chronicling the successes of great reformers such as Thomas H. Gallaudet, Walter R. Johnson, DeWitt Clinton, William and Bronson Alcott, Josiah Holbrook, and of course James Carter himself, interpreting them all as merely tending separate plants in the same reform garden. Although in its original form Barnard's history of the Connecticut common schools had only limited circulation, it was republished serially in several volumes of the *American Journal*, and its basic outline of the history leading to and including common school reform became the template for countless similar stories by Barnard and other writers.[34]

Barnard is a fine example of the set of historians whom David Van Tassel has labeled the "critical localists," a transitional group appearing between the romantic historians and the professionals who "not only raised the general standards of scholarship but also improved the current methods of collecting, evaluating, and editing documents." He was largely responsible for the revival of the Connecticut Historical Society, serving for many years as its corresponding secretary or president. Through this outlet and in correspondence with such leading historians as George Bancroft and John G. Palfrey, Barnard became sensitive to the need to preserve the raw materials of the past so that future historians would have them to build their interpretations. Experience in school reform, moreover, convinced him of the need for a strong body of nationally oriented literature that could serve as texts for training teachers in their professional heritage, the proper pedagogical philosophy, and the principles of organization that, once institutionalized, would ensure the perpetuity of the reforms his generation had initiated. It was thus the twin goals of historical preservation and practical instruction that led him to conceive the *American Journal of Education*, and both goals must be kept in mind if sense is to be made of its contents.[35]

The first issue of Barnard's *Journal* appeared in August 1855. The final volume, number 31, was issued in December 1881. Altogether it totaled twenty-four thousand pages and twelve million words. Although the *Journal* was never the popular success Barnard hoped it might be, it has been praised by generations of educators as the first great encyclopedia of education in the English language. This judgment is correct in terms of content and interpretation, though all would admit that organizationally it is a very unencyclopedic nightmare. But leaving aside this major impediment, interpreting the journal as an example of encyclopedia allows us to understand its larger significance in the historiography of education. Those familiar with the *Journal*'s advertisements will recall that Barnard had intended to publish a separate "Encyclopedia of Education," but as this project never materialized, he attempted to realize it through the *Journal* itself, publishing therein pieces originally earmarked for the encyclopedia whenever he had occasion to complete them.

It needs to be understood that an encyclopedia is not a neutral compilation without an interpretive framework. Although some scholars have read Barnard's *Journal* this way, to do so masks the underlying ideology that informs virtually every page of the text. Encyclopedias flourish in times of ideological consensus, for consensus enables a comprehensive interpretation of events, ideas, persons, and institutions to accumulate without morbid preoccupation with first principles. By Barnard's day, for example, it was a universal maxim that schools before the reforms of the 1840s were backward. The journal reflects and reinforces this view in nearly every issue, with its regular feature offering the recollections of old-timers concerning the schools of the past. It is never suggested that the sample, made up as it is of Barnard's cronies and other school reform advocates, might be biased in favor of this interpretation. No voices pining for the lost virtues of simpler days are heard, and on that rare occasion when a classic statement such as in

W. Winterbotham's 1796 *View of the United States of America* or Noah Webster's 1806 *Historical and Geographical Account of the United States* appears in the journal to praise the prereform schools, no recognition of the discontinuity is ever registered, so deeply ingrained is the dominant view. Only after the consensus has been shattered can readers uncover some of the unspoken assumptions guiding an encyclopedic project, and the consensus infusing Barnard's work had a long life ahead of it. But it needs to be understood that such a retrospective as we are now able to make, in uncovering some of the hidden assumptions guiding the *Journal*, can exonerate just as certainly as it can condemn. Unmasking need not always mean debunking.

What first strikes the reader sensitive to the Bailyn/Cremin discussions is the breadth of Barnard's definition of education. This is a critical point to make clear, for it has not been correctly understood before. Since Bailyn wrote, most historians have considered all pre-1960 educational historiography to have been narrowly focused on schooling without reference to the broader social context within which educational institutions are situated. Yet here is Barnard a full century earlier, in his introduction to an 1860 work by Linus Brockett (alias Philobiblius), tellingly titled *History and Progress of Education*:

> The education of a people bears a constant and most pre-eminently influential relation to its attainments and excellences—physical, mental, and moral. The national education is at once a cause and an effect of the national character; and, accordingly, the history of education affords the only ready and perfect key to the history of the human race, and of each nation in it,—an unfailing standard for estimating its advance or retreat upon the line of human progress.

World history is the history of the gradual progress of civilization, and a record of that progress is preserved in the educational institutions and ideas of the various nations that led the world at key moments in history. To equate education with civilization and to examine civilization from the perspective of the entire world provides Barnard room for an expansive encyclopedic scope.[36]

In the first place, he is not limited to schools. The stage of civilization a particular people has reached is always revealed in that people's institutions, of which schools are only one example. One could hardly conceive of a broader definition of the history of pedagogy than that provided by the *Journal*:

> the successive developments of human culture, both theoretical and practical, under the varying circumstances of race, climate, religion, and government, as drawn from special treatises of teachers and educators in different languages, or as embodied in the manners, literature, and history of each people.

The most accessible embodiment of the manners, literature, and history of a people are its institutions. All cultures, even primitive ones, reveal their natures in the institutions they create:

> Scarcely a trace of even the form of charity is visible amongst the ante-Christian nations. Much more expressive of the general heathen hard-heartedness, is the prevalence of legalized child-murder or exposure, slaughter of the old to be rid of them, and such other institutional abominations.

In the pages of Barnard's journal one meets with the history of museums, art galleries, exhibitions, scholarly societies, and lyceums, as well as all sorts of schools, including high schools, academies, schools for girls, and normal schools. For Barnard, the Whig tradition of educational history was meant to apply not only to schools, but to all formal institutions created and sustained by benevolence and goodwill. That later generations narrowed the focus has more to do with the needs of teacher training institutions than with departures from this fundamental outlook.[37]

A second illustration of Barnard's scope is in his transcontinental focus, expressed in various ways. Worth special mention given Bailyn's strictures, Barnard was keenly sensitive to the transmission of culture from England during the colonial period. In what is surely his most compelling historical production, the biography of Ezekiel Cheever printed in volume 1, Barnard describes in precise detail the origins of the grammar school in English precedent, understanding that

> [t]he names, by which the various educational institutions in the colonies were designated in the early records and laws on the subject, were adopted with the institutions themselves from the fatherland, and must be interpreted according to the usage prevailing there at the time.

Because of his sensitivity to the impact of British Protestant culture on American systems, Barnard regularly includes in the *Journal* reprints of classic works by such English writers as John Milton, John Locke, Roger Ascham, and Thomas Elyot, even when the ideas reflected are not republican or progressive.[38]

But not only was Barnard a recorder of European precedents, he was also an *agent* of cultural transmission. Like many another well-heeled Yankee, Barnard as a young man had embarked on the *Wanderjahre*, the grand tour of Europe, developing a firsthand acquaintance with and fondness for English and especially German society. His *Journal* features a regular section where foreign periodicals and publications from various European nations (and occasionally from even farther afield) are culled for experiments, trends, and ideas that might be of interest to his American readers. In keeping with his ideas of world progress in civilization, the *Journal* provides readers with accounts of educational systems of ancient peoples, modern nations, the various states of the union, and most especially, historical and contemporary Germany.

One of the most significant components of Barnard's *Journal* was its publication in translation of Karl Von Raumer's *Geschichte der Pädagogik*. Raumer had studied with Johann Pestalozzi and was heavily influenced by Fichtian Prussianism. He, like Barnard, wrote history with the practical instruction of teachers in mind, seeking always to highlight progress but to steer it in pan-Protestant directions. Thus Raumer would praise the critiques of thinkers such as Michel de Montaigne and Jean-Jacques Rousseau but censure their godless novelties, substituting instead the ideas of more Christian theorists such as Martin Luther, Johann Comenius, and Pestalozzi. The translation of Raumer's work introduced these and other Germans to many American educators in a manner that suggested the importance of German innovations in the development of civilization and recommended their experiences to the American context. Most important, Raumer practiced Barnard's own historical method: a focus on the progressive development of the national soul as embodied in its institutions and as reflected in the ideas of its great men. Raumer synthesized for Barnard the "great man" history he admired in his friend Thomas Carlyle and the institutional focus dictated by his understanding of civilization.

In Barnard's *Journal*, then, the great individual and the institutions that he (and it is nearly always he) founded were considered together as a reflection of national progress. Subsequent historians, however, would tend to bifurcate into two traditions. One group would write a progressive intellectual history, focusing on the canonical list of "great educators" established largely by Raumer and later German writers, and explicating the development of their ideas, perhaps adding on a contemporary name or two as the culmination of all this progress. Another group would chronicle the evolution of Western institutions—public schools and universities. Both would find the same theme of progress animating their studies, and both would trace their disciplinary origins to Henry Barnard, seeing him as their trailblazer.

But for Barnard himself, the focus on great educators was no pioneering venture; it was contemporary historical fashion. The romantic historical tradition had matured to the point where compendiums and encyclopedias were embodying its tenets, and Barnard's *Journal* took its place beside such other biographical compilations as John Livingston's 1853 *Portraits of Eminent Americans Now Living*, Lucius M. Sargent's 1856 *Dealings with the Dead*, the 1856 Appleton *Cyclopaedia of American Biography*, and Evert Duyckinck's 1855 *Cyclopaedia of American Literature*. Like the authors of some of these works, Barnard was not above having the subjects of the biographies themselves compose their own essays, which explains why so many of these pieces appear under anonymous authorship.

What is remarkable about his biographies, however, is that Barnard's selection was largely responsible for creating the canon of reformers that subsequent historians would lionize. And this occurred according to plan. Barnard, honestly believing in the advance-of-civilization interpretation of history, could not but see his own service and the work of his fellow reformers in this light. Barnard's friend J. W. Bulkley captured this point in correspondence: "Our successors will bless us for leaving on record, well-defined '*land-marks*' of our labors." It is at this level that Barnard's genius and interpretive framework become most apparent, for his *Journal of American Education* not only consolidated in encyclopedic form the Whig interpretation of the past, it also virtually guaranteed its perpetuation into the future as a result of his deliberate choice of materials on contemporary school reform. Subsequent historians would raid Barnard's *Journal*, so they thought, only for the information it contained. In fact what they also carried with them, even if unintended, was Barnard's historical interpretation as reflected in his editorial choices regarding what to include and in his overarching design to both preserve the raw materials of the past and to load these materials with lessons for the rising generation of educators his own reform efforts had done so much to create.[39]

Educational History as Professional Science

The idea of duty in one's calling prowls about in our lives like the ghost of dead religious beliefs.

—Max Weber

FROM CHRISTENDOM TO CIVILIZATION

The Civil War has long been understood as a crucial turning point in American history. The war consolidated northern industry, decimated its rival form of productivity, and assured the future sovereignty of wage labor. It liberated the African slaves and made them, if only for a brief moment, Americans, at least politically. It necessitated an increased public role for women whose husbands, brothers, and fathers were away on the front and whose consciences were piqued by slavery and the conditions of the freedmen and -women and their children. It provided an opportunity for recent immigrants to prove themselves and their people through demonstrations of bravery and loyalty, even as they were Americanized in the process. It vindicated claims of the supremacy of the national interest over local interests, amplified the role of the federal government in public life, and set precedents for dramatic increases in federal expenditures. It taught people about other regions of their nation, facilitating postwar migration and relocation, especially into urban areas. Finally, and most important for this study, the war signaled the beginning of the end of Protestantism as the guiding national ideology, thus creating a crisis of authority that was resolved by an increasing reliance on the religion of science and its clerisy, the professionals.[1]

The sectional political disputes of the 1830s and 1840s had their parallels among the major Protestant denominations. In 1837 the Presbyterians split over, among other issues, sectional conflict regarding slavery. Schism came for the Baptists in 1845 when the denomination could not agree on the propriety of missionaries owning slaves. The Methodists, the largest organization of any kind save the federal government at the time, similarly split over the issue of slaveholding bishops. Sectionalism thus dovetailed with the historic Protestant conception of America's millennial role in history to produce *rival* versions of the millennium. Although both North and South drew on the same historical and intellectual traditions of republican virtue and commonsense realism, the results of the war proved that "armies, not arguments" settled conflict, and ironically, neither the Northern vision of a Christian society where the cancer of slavery was abolished nor the Southern vision of a Christian society free from subversive northern busybodies actually emerged. Historian Mark Noll summarizes the outcome: "The War, which had been fought on both sides to defend republican Christian virtue, led to a world in which that kind of virtue was not nearly as important as it had been before."[2]

What became increasingly important were struggles Americans faced in reconciling their inherited "island community" value systems with the newly emerging national, corporate, urban-industrial complex that was rapidly being constructed by commercial speculation, its centers of production being connected by miles and miles of railroad. Said differently, Gilded Age America was experiencing the fragmentation of ideologies, as Christian republicanism began to part ways with the market liberalism that was emerging as the dominant cultural force, producing what Daniel Bell classically called "America's un-Marxist revolution": the shift from a property-based economy to one founded on managerial control and technical expertise. In the fallout from this revolution, all sorts of social fissures moved to the foreground: class struggles completely unnoticed by such antebellum commentators as Alexis de Tocqueville became a daily reality as a result of the extension of the wage-labor system in the cities and the consolidation of transport ownership in a few hands; racial tensions mounted to new heights in the North as homogeneous communities were replaced by ethnically mixed populations with limited material resources and in the South as redemption politics and supremacy movements militated for keeping the black populace from realizing the fruits of liberation; relations between the sexes became increasingly problematic as concerned women began to respond to the social ills unleashed by the new economic order in ways that threatened the Victorian convention of separate spheres. "America in the late nineteenth century," says historian Robert Wiebe, "was a society without a core. It lacked those national centers of authority and information which might have given order to such swift changes."[3]

This authority vacuum appeared at a historic moment in which it was becoming impossible for America's traditional Protestant civic religion to provide stability. The war's destruction of both northern and southern Christendoms was followed by two crises for American Protestants. As more and more Americans traveled to Germany for graduate education, the German historical criticism of the Bible became generally known, causing a good number of Protestant leaders both public and private turmoil as they wrestled with the implications of subjecting the sacred text to scientific scrutiny. At the same time, Darwinism was gaining converts among American naturalists, and by the 1870s Protestant leaders were on the defensive. Although some ministers were able to construct harmonizations of various versions of Darwinism with a reworked scriptural account, for many American Protestants, the combination of German biblical criticism and scientific evolution proved too difficult to incorporate into their religious tradition, and as such that tradition became increasingly marginal to intellectual debate (as the postwar secularization of colleges around the country attests) and subsequently to public policy.[4]

But policy was in desperate need of being made. The Civil War itself provided a model for future directions that was seized upon with avidity by the one group of Americans positioned to benefit from the new economic order—the middle class. During the war, the Sanitary Commission had pioneered the process of expert oversight of benevolent concern. These "sanitary elites" positioned themselves as representatives of an unorganized and at times misinformed populace that was in need of guidance if suffering was to be relieved efficiently. The model proved successful, and after the war a number of organizations adopted the commission's methodology. Women's groups particularly, as Lori D. Ginzberg has shown, had by the 1850s been narrowing their vision from that of a moralistic triumphalism to that of a more moderate legislative agenda of restraint and so were primed for the new ideas of benevolence. After the war they increasingly divested themselves of the rhetoric of femininity that had characterized antebellum movements and replaced it with a more businesslike, rational discourse modeled after that of the Sanitary Commission. Ginzberg observes that, "increasingly, male values were viewed as necessary to control and limit a female effusion of emotion, sensibility, or passion."[5]

A vigorous masculinity was in the air after the war. With peace declared, the U.S. War Department ordered the assembled federal armies to pass through Washington under a final review, and the nation was captivated by the symbolic strength of so many thousands of uniformed soldiers moving in consort. With the antebellum millennialist mentality largely discredited, moralistic reform and romantic notions of social transformation gradually gave way to a more collaborative, institutional approach modeled on the successes of the Sanitary Commission and the awe-inspiring vision of the victorious Union Army marching through the streets of Washington. The future was with the national organization, and that organization would only be successful if, like the commission and Sherman's army, it was managed by competent experts on the basis of scientific principles.[6]

The professional applying scientific principles to an ever-widening domain thus became the arbiter of progress, and the institution wherein this progress was envisioned, where the expert was produced, was the modern research university. Variously funded by public monies, land grants, or private philanthropy, the research university was the most conspicuous institutional sign of the new scientific order. In 1870 there were 52,000 undergraduates in the country. In 1890 there were 157,000, and by 1900 there were 238,000. The first generation of university managers therefore was faced with the daunting task of creating ad hoc a system that could accommodate such growth and establish standards of excellence in the various new academic fields that were emerging. Most important for our study are the efforts of the architects of the discipline often called the "science of education."[7]

Modern professions have tended to achieve self-definition by a process of rationalization along three separate but connected lines. First, a profession must stake out a field of knowledge of which it is the sole possessor and cultivator. Second, it must formulate exclusive standards of admission so as to ensure quality control by determining who has access to this privileged knowledge. Finally, it must develop an ethic of professional behavior that will demonstrate to the public the disinterested service provided in its behalf. All this was attempted by the schoolmen who were responsible for converting teacher training from the normal/model school type to that provided by the new teacher-training institutions situated within research universities.[8]

A primary concern of these educational leaders was the creation of the body of knowledge required if claims to professional status were to be taken seriously. Thus was born the science of education. But educational science, as Bruce Kimball has shown, could mean different things to different professionals. For the earliest professionals, the science of education was akin to the German study of *Pädagogik* that they picked up on their tour as graduate students. It tended toward idealism, toward metaphysical notions of human progress as revealed through institutional configurations. Later education scientists sought a more disciplinary, empirical conception of education, taking the findings of psychology or sociology and applying them to educational issues. Still other schoolmen tended to reduce science to management principles, seeking to apply Frederick Winslow Taylor's techniques of scientific management to school systems bursting at the seams.[9]

Educational history, interestingly, was able to embrace all three definitions, though it found its primary raison d'être under the first, for it provided historians with a theoretical base for constructing a coherent narrative of world events. History became the preferred method of accounting for social phenomena not amenable to experiment. If the progress of species could be unearthed from the geologic record, the progress in morality could be extracted from the historical record. Like so much else in the middle-class professional world, old patterns of thought were not so much changed as rationalized. Much as antebellum prejudice was reformulated as race science, so antebellum Whig historiography was dressed up by professional historians as evolutionary science. One can see this clearly in an examination of the first full-scale world histories of education that were produced both before and after the Civil War.

H. I. Smith's *Education* (1842), Linus Brockett's *History and Progress of Education* (1860), and Robert H. Quick's *Essays on Educational Reformers* (1868) were each considered by their respective authors to be the first global history of education to be penned in the English tongue. Save one key element, all of them are remarkably similar. Their authors all rely heavily on the same Germanic sources and thus import the same basic canon of key events and figures. All arrange their material in a straight line of progress that begins in the Far East and culminates with the Anglo-Saxon achievement in western Europe and especially in America. But Smith's book, significantly published before the Civil War, equates human progress with that of Christianity.

H. I. Smith was professor of German languages and literature at the Theological Seminary in Gettysburg, Pennsylvania, and he readily acknowledged his indebtedness to German scholarship and ideas:

> While the Germans possess voluminous works of the greatest merit from such authors as Jean Paul Fredr. Richter, Niemeyer, Schwarz, and others, no work, covering the whole ground of education, has, within our knowledge, appeared in the English language. . . . the Germans have long used the words "pædagogik" and "pædagogisch," and it is time that the terms were domesticated among us also.

The German periodization thus becomes the English periodization as Smith presents a narrative sequence that will be reproduced time and again. Although he begins with antediluvian times, unlike some of his German sources but in keeping with his abiding Protestantism, he quickly finds the German groove as he works his way from Asia westward through Babylon, and then Phoenicia, detouring to Egypt, and returning to Israel, Greece, Rome, and medieval Europe. Real progress begins with the Italian Renaissance and the transalpine Reformation that led to the rise of Baconian science and the birth of modern civilization.[10]

Throughout the table of nations, education history is most frequently the history of theory produced by the intellectual elite, from Plato and Aristotle; through Cicero and Quintilian; down to Rousseau, Pestalozzi, and Johann

Fichte. Thus far, Smith is merely abridging the work of his German sources. Original with Smith, however, is an element of his text that also marks it out from all subsequent works covering the same ground: Smith, writing before the crisis of knowledge brought on by Darwinian science, still believes that the history of Western civilization is the history of Christendom. Vaguely aware of the winds of doctrine stirring around him, he often interrupts his otherwise orthodox account of steady and assured progress with a note of pessimism:

> We have reason to rejoice at the zeal and energy with which the Protestant churches of our country have engaged in the establishment and improvement of Sabbath-schools. As an omen for good we would regard the extent to which Christianity is allowed to influence our institutions of education: they are, indeed, for the most part, monuments of Christian effort for the improvement of mankind. . . . The future true, healthy, and beneficial development of our system of public education, which is yet in its infancy, the permanent existence of our free institutions, and the true greatness, and progressive culture, and abiding glory of this rising nation, all depend on this one thing: the religion of Christ must preside over, direct, and pervade the entire education of the free people of this mighty realm, otherwise we can but add another to the list of republics in which public corruption achieved national ruin.

Smith's fear of ruin is no mere republicanist commonplace. He has legitimate grievances with the course of recent events:

> Above all, when we consider the progress of demoralization and irreligion throughout the civilized world, let us take heed that we boast not of advancement where there is retrogression, and remember that "pride cometh before destruction, and a haughty spirit before a fall"; and let all who labour for the improvement of human education take for their motto that word of unchanging truth, *the fear of the Lord is the beginning of wisdom.*"[11]

To postwar writers such sentiments would seem quaint at best. W. N. Hailmann, for example, writing in 1874, predicts that the civilization founded by Christ "must henceforth live and grow, even if it should lose its name." What is remarkable is that while the biblical tropes of Smith's work were jettisoned, the structure of his narrative remained virtually unchanged for a century. What was needed by writers living in an age having experienced the end of Christendom was a replacement concept to allow the center to hold, lest the entire narrative on which their budding professional self-image was built fall apart. They needed a new name. That center, that name, was found in the idea of civilization.[12]

The idea itself has a venerable pedigree, extending back to Voltaire, one of the first Europeans to seek an alternative to Christendom. In his *Essay on*

General History (1756), the great philosophe posits a concept of civilization embodying "good government, sane philosophy, material welfare, good taste, refined manners, and the agents of cultural dissemination" and then evaluates the societies of the past by these criteria. For Voltaire, civilization was a singular phenomenon capable of objective description, and the various kingdoms of the world more or less approached it. But when the German Romanticists began to work with the concept, it was transformed into the notion of *Volksgeist*, the idea that different nations have their own particular culture. Under F. G. Guizot these folk cultures were arranged chronologically in a progressive fashion, and this formulation was picked up and perfected by Georg Willhelm Friedrich Hegel in Germany, Auguste Comte in France, and Herbert Spencer in England. By the time Americans began arriving en masse at German research universities, the progression had become commonplace.[13]

The doctrine of civilization, though often preceded by the term *Christian* in the literature of the nineteenth century, proved adaptable to the Darwinian notion of natural selection and the race science it promoted. And social Darwinism itself needed a telos, for natural selection by species survival provides little by way of edifying historical schemata. The doctrine of civilization conflated social evolution with social progress in a creative synthesis that allowed the late-nineteenth-century West to discard its Christian teleology yet keep its self-understanding as agent of world progress. Civilized nations were no longer characterized by Christians fighting infidels but by "superior races outsurviving inferior races." Thus late-nineteenth-century Americans, after the fashion of Voltaire, constructed a definition of the highest civilization yet achieved and then used it to evaluate past societies and to construct a persuasive account of the history that produced their own. If, for example, Victorian America separated the sexes into two distinct spheres, this was found to be a hallmark of civilization. So Spencer rationalizes, "[U]p from the lowest savagery, civilization has, among other results, caused an increasing exemption of women from bread-winning labour, and . . . in the highest societies they have become most restricted to domestic duties and the rearing of children."[14]

But the descriptor *civilization* could be appropriated by any number of ideologues. Feminists could and did employ the term to argue for their own notions of woman's place in society. Black intellectuals did the same, as attested by Ida B. Wells's campaign against lynching. What is notable here is that despite differences in the specifics employed to flesh out the doctrine, all parties assumed the value of the concept itself. Thus, as we shall see in this chapter, the doctrine of civilization perpetuated for the late nineteenth and early twentieth centuries the underlying narrative of progress that had been imported by the first colonial educational historians. In this process, however, historians set themselves up for tremendous backlash by those who would come to resent their cultural construct. Some opponents would use civilization's own guns against it by articulating a contrarian's version of civilized society. Others would reject the notion of civilization entirely, or at least seek to limit its application. From manly men celebrating the culture of boxing as they sought after "a saving touch of honest, old fashioned barbarism!" to American youth moving courtship "from front porch to back seat," components forming the Victorian consensus of moral civilization that undergirded the dominant version of progress in educational history would soon encounter growing opposition. This would lead to ultimate rejection, less among anachronistically genteel middle-class academicians than in the recreational world of the working and leisure classes and from those groups placed by the concept at the margins of public life.[15]

NATIONAL IDENTITY AND GLOBAL CONSCIOUSNESS

While the doctrine of civilization was a useful substitute for concepts of Christendom now embarrassingly outmoded by evolutionary science, its synthetic capacity was not the only reason for its longevity in educational historiography. To understand its other, more practical functions, we must understand the social uses to which the blossoming postwar educational historiography was put. There were two predominant social functions for educational history in the late nineteenth century. The first was to aid in the professional formation of American schoolteachers; the second, to contribute to the recovery of a positive sense of national identity in a populace weary of sectional conflict and anxious that its centennial retrospective provide just cause for optimism.

In his centennial year message to Congress in 1875, President Ulysses S. Grant made this surprising recommendation:

> We are a republic whereof one man is as good as another before the law. Under such a form of government it is of the greatest importance that all should be possessed of education and intelligence enough to cast a vote with a right understanding of its meaning. . . . As the primary step, therefore, to our advancement in all that has marked our progress in the past century, I suggest for your earnest consideration, and most earnestly recommend it, that a constitutional amendment be submitted to the legislatures of the several States for ratification, making it the duty of each of the several States to establish and forever maintain free public schools.

Although the general's recommendation never became law, it is striking evidence of the increased concern for schooling at the federal level. The United

States Bureau of Education was created by the Reconstruction Congress in 1867 with the explicit task of providing a national voice in educational affairs. The present-day student, mindful of the neglect that current policy makers tend to show toward educational history, is struck by how central the creation of a national history was to those to whom this task had been delivered. Its first commissioner, Henry Barnard, was the preeminent historian of education in the country, a man who had long been preaching the national idea in education and providing it with a useable past. Subsequent leaders would be equally concerned with propagating a national history of education, seeking in particular to give Americans something to look back on with pride at their centennial celebration and at the World's Columbian Exposition of 1893.[16]

Lawrence Cremin has described well the extent to which late-nineteenth-century educational historiography, from the Bureau of Education–sponsored thirty-six-volume series, *Contributions to American Educational History,* edited by Henry Baxter Adams, to the immense proliferation of state histories, was an outgrowth of the "spirit of '76." In both sets of monographs the essential thesis was the same: the transition of the management of schools, be they primary, secondary, or tertiary, from control by "religious denominations" to oversight by "private benevolence" to, finally and gloriously, the highest stage, wherein schools are "founded and maintained by the State." Bureau commissioner N. H. R. Dawson summarized the motive for such state-level studies:

> To bring the work of several States in comparison tends toward unity of sentiment and unity of design in education, and these make for patriotism and nationality. . . . A constant and persistent publication of the history of higher education in all its phases will do more to harmonize our educational systems than almost any other thing.[17]

The result of this attempt at normalizing the various state histories was that the Whig interpretation of educational history was expanded into a national story, formulated to bolster the postwar quest for American self-confidence. That quest was embodied nowhere more explicitly than in the fairs held to celebrate national accomplishment. Commissioner William T. Harris, Dawson's successor at the Bureau of Education, recognizing this fact, proclaimed of the Adams series:

> I desire to complete it in time for exhibition at the World's Columbian Exposition in 1893. A cooperative history of American higher education, with due regard to common and secondary schools, would be a noble and worthy contribution from this Bureau to the United States Government exhibit.[18]

It would be difficult to assess the influence of Adams's series and the various state histories emanating from these celebrations. Tucked away as they were in government circulars or produced by local presses with little advertisement or circulation, it is doubtful that very many of these monographs were widely read. But there is another genre that was widely read, and it offers us a more direct access to the grand narrative underlying even the most specialized of the monographic studies. Every state history of education produced during this period was arranged according to a preordained notion of progress, even if this conception was not clearly described in the text. To get at that conception we would do well to attend to the broader understanding of educational history assumed by all these writers, and to do that we must examine the textbooks.

To a degree that marked it out from other fields, educational science was continually faced with the requirement that it prove useful to practitioners. The student teacher was the primary consumer and disseminator of its findings. As such the textbook became the most pervasive genre of educational scholarship by the 1880s. Prominent educators produced multivolume textbook series, such as William Torrey Harris's International Education Series, Nicholas Murray Butler's The Great Educators, M. G. Brumbaugh's Lippincott Educational Series, and Ellwood Patterson Cubberley's Riverside Textbook Series, all of which sold extremely well thanks to the immense growth of the professional ideal in teacher education, both within normal schools, desperately trying to stay abreast of the most recent developments, and at the universities, slowly consolidating their position as brokers of legitimate credentials.[19]

This drive to produce textbooks to meet a pervasive market demand had a profound impact on educational historiography for three reasons. First, combined with the national trend discussed above, it dramatically increased the volume of production. Second, it increased the audience that such books could claim: more people read them than had read previous histories of education. Advertisements of the day demonstrate publishers' keen awareness that a lucrative and captive market was being made available. "The price paid for the sample copy," promises a Scribner's broadside for Nicholas Murray Butler's The Great Educators series, "will be returned, or a free copy inclosed, upon receipt of an order for TEN or more copies for introduction." One successful textbook author understood market forces perfectly, skillfully covering all his bases:

> This book is designed to furnish all the material that can be reasonably demanded for any state, county, or city teacher's certificate. It also provides sufficient subject-matter for classes in normal schools and colleges and for reading

circles. The material offered can be mastered in a half-year's class work, but, by using the references, a full year can be well employed. . . . Every investigator knows the labor involved in finding suitable material. To spare the reader something of that labor, the literature is given at the beginning of each chapter. By following the collateral readings thus suggested, this book will be found suitable for the most advanced classes.[20]

Finally, the impetus to produce textbooks affected the content of educational history in important ways. Successful history of education textbooks would have to inspire as well as instruct, providing teachers with a sense of historical tradition, a continuity with a past of which they might be proud. E. L. Kemp's 1899 textbook powerfully explains:

> To the teacher the study of the history of education brings three valuable results. It widens his professional horizon and makes him feel the dignity of his calling. It gives him true pedagogic perspective and enables him to estimate accurately the value of courses of study and methods of teaching. It inspires him, for the great teachers with whom it makes him acquainted were sacrificial high priests who mediated to the world its higher life, and they themselves were the sacrifices.[21]

Textbooks must also be informative, of course, reinforcing with historical argument the same scientific principles of pedagogy that students were learning in their other classes and were expected to practice once they joined the profession. Professional science needed method and content, and history proposed to provide both. The doctrine of civilization was just the thing to unify the teacher preparation curriculum, as Charles De Garmo explains in his treatment of the culture-epoch theory of Tuiskon Ziller:

> If, therefore, we are to regard this principle as substantially true, if there is in reality such a parallelism between the successive stages of the child's mental growth and the culture epochs of the race as this theory claims, then, as Ziller and Rein declare, a striking advantage at once comes to view, the psychological principle coincides with the historical one of the material of study, so that without further search we have a common guide to the development of the several culture branches.

Evolutionary psychology and evolutionary history are thus mutually constitutive—their findings support one another. Even more important, historical investigation prosecuted according to the evolution-of-civilization thesis turns out to be the social science equivalent of the experimental method in the physical sciences, as John Dewey, writing in 1902, explains:

> There is an exact identity, between what the experimental method does for our physical knowledge, and what the historical method in a narrower sense may

do for the spiritual region: the region of conscious values. . . . History offers to us the only available substitute for the isolation and for the cumulative recombination of experiment. The early periods present us in their relative crudeness and simplicity with a substitute for the artificial operation of an experiment: following the phenomenon into the more complicated and refined form which it assumes later, is a substitute for the synthesis of the experiment. . . . history does for moral matters, for matters of conscious value, what experimentation does for physical things: it gives control by furnishing relative isolation.[22]

Dewey's assumption that history proceeds from the simple to the complex undergirds the argument that it is the equivalent of experimental method, allowing us to study social phenomena in isolation. This is of course the evolutionary assumption, and it was the fashion in other social science disciplines as well. Thorstein Veblen, for example, writing in 1898, was impressed with the idea of "evolutionary science," defined as "a theory of a process, of an unfolding sequence." He sought to reconceive economics as "the economic life history" of a community construed along evolutionary lines.[23]

All social disciplines were to be recast in evolutionary terms, and thus all would tell the same tale, a historical tale. Thus they all can be ordered and rationalized by the history of education, and it is this rationalizing power that explains the brief dominance of historical courses in professional teacher preparation from roughly the late 1890s to about 1920. Likewise, as we shall see, when after World War I these assumptions come into question, criticism of history of education as a subject for teachers began to mount. But these decades witnessed the high-water mark of the idea of civilization's influence in the United States, and so books reinforcing these assumptions were embraced. "The history of education begins with the childhood of the race, and traces its intellectual development step by step to the present time," asserted one such book, and so long as the doctrine of the advancement of civilization proved tenable, the book could be read profitably.[24]

Leading educators, then, were simply reflecting the cultural moment when they sought to unify the teacher preparation curriculum by saturating it with evolutionary histories of education as demonstrations of the progress of civilization. "It is generally conceded," wrote one textbook author in 1899, "that the plan of a historical work should be based upon the evolution of civilization." Another successful textbook explains this orientation's utility:

It is evident that a knowledge of the history of education, an acquaintance with the thoughts of earnest men that have gone before us, a familiarity with the results of faithful laborers in similar fields, an intimacy with their struggles, their martyrdom, or their triumph, will do much to enhance our efficiency, as well as our professional self-respect.

In the age of the research university when "knowledge" was multiplying and new disciplines developing, some organizing concept was needed to make the universe cohere. The principle of the progress of civilization provided the framework necessary to meet both the scientific needs of the profession and the functional needs of student teachers.[25]

This professional and pedagogical utility explains in good measure why the German idealism of the earliest textbooks continued to inform those written by professionals operating under different understandings of educational science. Whereas Bruce Kimball sees a changing succession of definitions regarding exactly what schoolmen meant by *educational science*, historical textbooks tend to show a remarkable continuity maintained by accretion. That is, the philosophical, the empirical, and the organizational were not alternative views, but partners in the task of constructing a viable tradition of educational science, each one absorbing the findings of its predecessor and adding to it in the same spirit. A more detailed examination of their contents will demonstrate this process.

Whereas Smith's 1842 work was the first global history of education in English, Linus Brockett's *History and Progress of Education* was the first such work explicitly intended as a textbook for normal schools. At the time of its composition, Brockett was a man in transition. A graduate of Yale Medical School, he found practice to be tedious, and the lure of a literary life led him to a Hartford publishing firm, where his encyclopedic and historical interests brought about a long-standing friendship with Henry Barnard. Readers of Barnard's journal will find Brockett's contributions frequent and his perspective congenial to the renowned editor. But while Barnard was able to carry on as if the sectional conflict were irrelevant to the high calling of education, Brockett became fascinated by the war and its heroes. The year 1860, when Brockett's book on education came out, would prove to be a turning point in his life as he became a father and moved from Connecticut to Brooklyn, New York, beginning a long and successful career as an author. All told, he published around fifty books, most on Civil War themes. Even in these later works, however, one can find some of the same impulses detectable in his *History and Progress of Education*, most notably his preference for focusing on great individuals and his interest in women's history. As was his wont, Brockett often employed a pseudonym for these later works, just as he had for the *History and Progress*. When writing about the Civil War, Brockett was Capt. Powers Hazelton. When writing about educational history, he became Philobiblius.[26]

Brockett's scope, like Smith's before him, was universal. Here, indeed, is what Peter Bowler calls "Whig history on a cosmic scale." Brockett begins with antediluvian times and proceeds through India, Egypt, China, Japan, Babylon, and Persia to Greece, Rome, and Christianity. Much of this material is directly lifted from a French work by Theodore Fritz titled *Système complet d'instruction et d'éducation*, and Brockett, trailblazer that he is, occasionally chases side roads that later textbook authors would consider irrelevant to the story: we read about Persian fire god rituals, Antoninus Pius's school for orphans, Druidism, Mexican poetry, and Peruvian agriculture. But his focus sharpens as the Middle Ages are finally put to rest and the light of the Renaissance begins to shine.[27]

In a fine reversal of the Christian interpretation of Haggai 2:7, Brockett declares, "Two events hastened the upheaval for which the nations were looking: the invention of printing, about 1450, and the discovery of America, in 1492." This upheaval is central to his text and is important for two reasons: first, it exemplifies an attention to the broad social forces that were driving educational progress over and above the theories of leading pedagogues. Second, it introduces the heart of Brockett's history, for in the sixteenth century we find the origins of the ideas that have led to the school systems of the nineteenth. With the introduction of Baconian science, Brockett's dependency on Germanic sources becomes apparent. He takes the reader through Comenius's application of Baconian inductivism to educational concerns and through the usual cast of Germanic theorists and philanthropists, with a few French and English figures thrown into the mix. Anticivilization man Rousseau receives strong criticism, while Pestalozzi is cast as the hero of the entire drama: "The man who has exerted the most influence over the education of the race, in the last hundred years, is J. H. PESTALOZZI." All this is merely prolegomena—or, if you will, context—for the main event, however, which is the history of education in the New World.[28]

What immediately strikes the contemporary reader about Brockett's treatment of American education is the extent to which he foregrounds the Old World roots of American ideas and systems. "The colonies. . . . brought with them not only the manners, customs, and culture of their native land, but the determination to rear here educational institutions." From the beginning of professional educational historiography, the transmission of civilization across the Atlantic has been recognized and put into a nearly overwhelming European context that interprets these English and Dutch traditions as the fruit of two thousand years of educational theory and experimentation. One might certainly fault the interpretive grid of slow and steady progress in Brockett's account, but it must be acknowledged that his narrative of the founding of institutions and the ideas informing their growth is situated in a broad European context.[29]

Once established, it was New England that took the lead with its early school laws and university. "But little was done" elsewhere, save perhaps New York, which made modest steps toward educational progress. It was not until the 1830s when Horace Mann, Henry Barnard, and "other eminent friends of education" began to work that much was accomplished "for the diffusion of right views on the subject of teaching" and measures adopted "which render our common school system the glory of our country." Despite appearances, one ought not see vainglory in this construal of history. Barnard commissioned and introduced this text with a powerful and much cited argument for the utility of educational history for schoolteachers. His own reform efforts are the culmination of the entire global story from before the Flood to the very moment Brockett is writing. This may seem an egregious case of narcissism, but it was not. Faith that they were merely the agents of human destiny drove these reformers. They believed their version of history, and so naturally they saw themselves as being on the right side, confident that future generations would rise up and call them blessed, would "do them honor."[30]

And rise up they did. A fairly reliable mark of the extent to which subsequent generations of American historians accepted the idea of civilization can be seen by attending to the assessment of Mann and Barnard offered by biographers. From Mary Peabody Mann's 1865 chronicle of how her husband revived a Massachusetts school system that had "degenerated in practice from the early theoretical view of the early Pilgrim Fathers" by instituting "new measures" that assured the "rise and progress" of the "idea of universal education," to B. A. Hinsdale's rich 1898 account of the "great educational work that Mr. Mann accomplished" to E. I. F. Williams's 1937 effort to "do honor to the one who, more than any other, was responsible for the common-school revival of a hundred years ago . . . who deserves to be ranked with Washington and Lincoln in his influence upon the development of a democratic America," Mann's many biographers sought to outdo one another in praising their subject for his contribution to national progress. He was "born to be a champion. Fearless of consequences to himself, he had the stuff that martyrs are made of."[31]

The tone Brockett set was followed by a host of successors who sought to present the same general outline, only embellishing his story with a more streamlined chronology and hence a more compelling presentation of the advance of civilization. At times, however, they sacrificed his combined emphasis on institutional and theoretical progress for the sake of clarity and continuity. The similarity of style and content in these works would make full individual treatment a tedious affair, but taken as a group they provide us with some insightful clues regarding the understanding of civilization on which they were all based.

It is important to reiterate that these works, taken as a whole, are richly contextual and by no means limited in scope to the history of school systems. They all situate their American subject within a massive, even stultifying, global context, as befits their rise-of-civilization thesis. This very thesis leads them to broad definitions of educational history. S. S. Laurie, for example, is convinced that "the history of education of a people is not the history of its schools, but the history of its civilisation." F. V. N. Painter makes the case for a focus on the physical, moral, intellectual, and religious nature of humankind, holding that "it has been reserved for the nineteenth century, so distinguished for its many-sided advancement, to realize an education which leaves no part of man's nature neglected" and thus to a definition of education as "an exhibition of what has been thought and done in all ages and countries in reference to training the young." Gabriel Compayré, whose translated work *History of Pedagogy* was one of the most widely used of these books in America, proclaims, "What would a complete history of education not include? It would embrace, in its vast developments, the entire record of all the intellectual and moral culture of mankind at all periods and in all countries. It would be a *résumé* of the life of humanity." And William Torrey Harris, perhaps the key architect of fin de siècle educational historiography through his influential tenure as U.S. commissioner of education as well as numerous other strategic professional positions, tells us with his characteristic philosophical precision, "In a history of education, therefore, we should sharply discriminate between the unconscious education acquired from the four cardinal institutions—family, civil society, state, and Church—and the education in the school." Elsewhere he even intimates that this broader perspective is in fact the superior approach: "The history of education is best studied when taken in that large sense in which nations are said to be teachers, each people bringing its ethnical [*sic*] contribution to the civilization of the human race."[32]

Broad definitions lead to expansive interpretations, both in terms of institutions considered as players in a history of education and in terms of transcontinental context. Richard G. Boone, whose *Education in the United States: Its History from the Earliest Settlements* is the first book-length treatment of its subject, is worth considering in this respect. In addition to covering an amazing breadth of institutions, from reading circles and libraries to the Smithsonian Institution, reformatories, and industrial/professional training, he provides a nuanced discussion of the colonies' European heritage as well as the unique environment presented by the New World. He explicitly poses and seeks to answer the big question that Bailyn so strongly recommended to his generation's attention. "How far," he asks of colonial traditions of schooling, "was it a natural evolution from the social usages and laws of England? How far from those of Holland?" He answers that "the true parent of the current system of teaching was the Reformation," but it was a Reformation transplanted to a land where there "was to be found the more favorable conditions, freedom from established customs and precedents, and an absence of fixed public institutions, giving room for invention."[33]

Neither the question nor its answer was original to Boone. The very wording of the question Boone asked concerning the extent to which colonial education was imported or autochthonous came directly from Daniel Coit Gilman's 1876 centennial retrospective sketch of American educational progress. And Boone's answer is substantially that of Brockett and the other universal historians, though his formulation, displaying his cognizance of such macro factors as "the invention of printing, . . . the consequent and rapid multiplication of books, . . . [the] increase in the facilities of commerce, [and] the extension of geographical discoveries," is a notably complete synthesis. What we have here is precisely a history seeking to place the development of American education in its transatlantic context yet mindful of the changes wrought by a New World environment. To take another example, Elsie Clews's doctoral dissertation under Nicholas Murray Butler and Herbert Levi Osgood similarly makes the case for a combination of the imported and the domestic:

> All colonial institutions are in major part imitative, and as the character of the colonists is the result of inheritance as well as of adopted environment, the social histories of England, Scotland, Holland, Sweden, France, Germany must lie open to the student of American colonial education. But, in fact, the social history of those parent countries, or that part at least of their social history which may properly be called their educational history, is still unburied treasure.[34]

In short, every synthetic educational history written by an American during the nineteenth century, whether by an amateur or a professional associated with a school of education, sought consciously to connect the American story to the larger European context implicit in the notion of the progress of civilization. If they were not so successful at this as later scholars were perhaps to be, it was not for want of asking the right questions. It was, as Clews notes, because these sorts of questions were only beginning to be entertained by anyone at all, inside or outside of the schools of education. "The story of American civilization," asserts this soon-to-be anticivilization anthropologist, "as well as that of its educational phase, remains untold."[35]

A second point to be made concerns what is perhaps the most compelling thesis offered in these books. It is implicit in all of them but spelled out in some with great power. Here is F. V. N. Painter's formulation:

> Asia is the birthplace of the human race. The march of progress, following the course of the sun, has been westward through Europe to America, which completes the circle of the globe. Here the great problems of religion, science, government, and education will probably receive their final solution.

Taking the long view, the advancement of civilization has been ever westward, and this progress is that of the entire "human race." The instability of the one word *race* in this construal makes for a fascinating study in itself. Painter clearly believes that the entire human family is united in a single human quest:

> It is a profound thought of German philosophy that God is leading the world, through a gradual though not uninterrupted development, to greater intelligence, freedom, and goodness. Like the individual, our race as a whole has to pass through the successive periods of childhood, youth, and maturity. . . . Human progress is an evident fact.

But in another context the same term could take on a profoundly different meaning:

> It is proper to say a word here in reference to the Teutonic race, which received the precious boon of civilization and Christianity from falling Rome, in order to purify, preserve, and disseminate it throughout the world. The Teutonic tribes, the noblest branch of the great Aryan family . . . it is the Teutonic nations that are chiefly to claim our attention hereafter. They are the great leaders in education, as they are in every other weighty human interest.

Harmonization would make it seem that it is the Aryan race's burden to lead the human race to higher civilization through science and especially education. It is left unresolved whether all races are capable of inclusion in the human race or whether some are biologically unable to achieve civilization. S. S. Laurie believes at once in "the human race" and chastises Classical education for not developing a human ideal to replace its ethnic parochialism, but at the same time he wonders about just how far to extend the human boundary: "The human possibilities of such tribes may be, in germ, as high as those of many more favored races; but this is doubtful."[36]

Historically, the march of racial advancement has always taken a westward course. But by 1890 there was no more West. The western frontier of the United States had closed. Frederick Jackson Turner in his famous essay "The Significance of the Frontier in American History," first read to the American Historical Association in Chicago on July 12, 1893, assessed the implications of this fact for the American national story, closing with these words:

> And now, four centuries from the discovery of America, at the end of a hundred years of life under the Constitution, the frontier has gone, and with its going has closed the first period of American history.[37]

Turner's talk was given in the context of the World's Columbian Exposition being held concurrent with the American Historical Association convention in Chicago. The exposition itself exemplified the shift in periods Turner had in mind: it was a celebration of America's transition from isolated agrarian communities to an integrated, planned society, to national order. But Turner was not the only academic at the Expo to appreciate its significance. James A. Skilton, a strong advocate of scientific social theory and cooperative national planning, presented a frontier thesis of his own; his, however, was epochal in perspective, proposing a frightening dilemma for advocates of continual westward progress. Skilton, after proffering the idea that "the center of civilization and empire had moved steadily westward from Mesopotamia, making the ascending West always the lively, innovative, and upward-bound area and leaving the East with ordered, well-settled, but stagnant civilizations," ominously reports:

> Just now this westward march of empire and freedom during the ages comes to an abrupt end. The Cherokee strip marks the spot, where, after ages of continuous advance, this movement, during the current month, has dashed itself into pieces. . . . [The] Columbian Exposition of 1893 celebrates both the beginning and the end of the Columbian epoch. It also, but not intentionally, celebrates the end of one epoch of characteristic modern Western Civilization and the beginning of a new epoch, in which the race is again to be tested as to its capacity to advance toward those higher possibilities from which it has always heretofore recoiled.

The closing of the American frontier, then, not only was the terminus of one phase of American history, but also threatened to be the curtain call to the entire pageant of civilization on which the self-image of American teachers and the professional claims of their professors were based.[38]

Two possible solutions presented themselves to this problem. The first was Turner's answer, that America would have to exchange the frontier mentality that "produces antipathy to control, and particularly, to any direct control," for a well-organized, institutionalized democracy supported by state universities and public schools:

> By training in science, in law, politics, economics and history the universities may supply from the ranks of democracy administrators, legislators, judges, and experts for commissions who shall disinterestedly and intelligently mediate between contending interests.

This solution, a professionalized version of the Whig emphasis on internal improvements, was second nature to an educational profession keen on constructing "the one best system," and so the metaphor of the western frontier was quite naturally appropriated by the keepers of that institution whose presumed role it was to advance the frontiers of social democracy. Civilization was seen not so much in quantitative as qualitative terms, as one educational historian noted:

The general progress of civilization is from small and simple organizations of men among whom there is but little differentiation of thought and occupation, but little freedom of the individual, to large national unities which protect and foster the individual in the enjoyment of almost unlimited scope for the development of his personal endowments. A clan is at one end of the line, a great republic at the other.[39]

But there was also another solution suggested by educational historians to the crisis of the frontier's closing. This was the solution that had animated railroad financiers as early as the 1840s and that became official American foreign policy from 1898: American expansion need not be landlocked. Beckoning from across the Pacific were the huge markets and "primitive" cultures of Asia. While recent scholars have justly attended to the economic motivations driving the open-door policy, its cultural opportunity was of primary concern to educational historians anxious lest civilization should stagnate.[40]

For global educational historians, civilization need not end at California's western coast. "No civilized nation now fails to make provision, to a greater or less degree, for the instruction of the peoples. Even the unprogressive nations of the Orient are affected by the Christian education of the West." An export of American school systems to the ancient Eastern peoples would complete the global cycle of westward advancement. If Eastern schools could be "fertilized by occidental progressiveness," then the Mongolian races could "become thoroughly humanized—a truly free and happy people." In this sentiment we find the resolution of the protean term *race*: only with the added benefit of progressive civilization could the various races of the world obtain access to full humanity. The human race consists, then, of all races that have become human through civilization. Linus Brockett perhaps best captures the sentiment, offering at the same time another example of the intimate connection in the work of these writers between education and other marks of civilization:

Ere long, the teeming millions of China, Japan, and India, driven from their slumber of three thousand years by the impulses of the electric wire and the rush of the locomotive, will join with the enlightened nations of the West, in seeking a higher intellectual development, and the beneficial results of a purer science.[41]

EDUCATIONAL HISTORIOGRAPHY ON THE MARGINS OF CIVILIZATION

Up to this point we have seen how the idea of civilization replaced that of Christianity as the dominant, some would say hegemonic, social construct of the late nineteenth and early twentieth centuries. We have assessed the impact of this idea on two sorts of mainstream educational historiography, both the nationalizing monographic state histories and the panoramic world history textbooks. But the same thesis that offered a compelling interpretive paradigm allowing society's organizers to construct a usable past for themselves also left others on the margins of the organization these men were building. To approach the educational historiography of such marginal groups we would do well to return to the 1893 Columbian Exposition.[42]

George Santayana famously described fin de siècle America in gendered terms:

> The American Will inhabits the sky-scraper; the American Intellect inhabits the colonial mansion. The one is the sphere of the American man; the other, at least predominantly, of the American woman. The one is all aggressive enterprise; the other is all genteel tradition.

Henry Adams, inclined to agree with this analysis, was therefore stunned by the World's Columbian Exposition. "Chicago asked in 1893 for the first time the question whether the American people knew where they were driving," Adams mused. It was "the first expression of American thought as a unity; one must start there." At Chicago the "aggressive enterprise" and "genteel tradition" met each other in an overpowering homage to civilization, an attempt to bring American scientific inventiveness and the American artistic Renaissance (then in full Classical bloom) together, all financed by free-market speculation. Electric lighting, the Corliss engine, Krupp's 130-ton cannon, Edison's kinetoscope, and other inventions and gadgets were housed in stately Romanesque buildings laden with neoclassical sculpture. The result was a bizarre blend of sensibilities, summarized in the motto "Make Culture Hum!" The fair was both "a vision of strong Manhood" and of the "perfection of society," and few were those who saw any contradiction between the two.[43]

But for the efforts of Chicago socialites, most notably Bertha Honoré Palmer, whose husband donated two hundred thousand dollars toward construction of the Women's Building, the "perfection of society" as embodied in "woman's work" may not have made an appearance at all. The fair was organized into two essential parts: the first and most glorious was the formal White City, whose centerpiece was the Court of Honor. It contained building after building celebrating all aspects of modern technology, manufactures, commerce, communication, and, with less fanfare, education. At the end of this magnificent tribute to civilization was the Women's Building. The *New York Times* situated it in this way: "[T]he achievements of man [are] in iron, steel, wood, and the baser and cruder products . . . [while] in the Woman's Building one can note . . . more refined avenues of effort which culminate in the home, the hospital, the church, and in personal adornment."[44]

After visiting the Women's Building, the fairgoer was to exit the White City and proceed to the Midway, a sort of national bazaar where scenes from so-called uncivilized nations were arranged for display in hierarchically descending order, from charming, romantic, "semi-civilized" Germanic and Irish villages through "barbarous" Turkish, Arab, and Chinese hamlets to the "savage" constructions of American Indians and African Dahomans. "What an opportunity was here afforded to the scientific mind to descend the spiral of evolution," gushed the *Chicago Tribune*, "tracing humanity in its highest phases down almost to its animalistic origins."[45]

We see in this one spectacle a *précis* of Victorian assumptions regarding civilization. Progress belongs to the white man. It is, after all, the *white* city. Woman, however, is the doorkeeper of civilization. Without her contribution, the progressive nations are likely to slip back into the barbarism and even the savagery of the Midway. Most significant, "the Exposition's logic of constructing manly white civilization in opposition to savage swarthy barbarism made it impossible for the white organizers to recognize the existence of fully civilized African-Americans."[46]

Thus blacks were faced with the dilemma of either rejecting entirely the white notion of civilization or accepting it and trying to alter its racist assumptions by proving that blacks too could be civilized. Booker T. Washington, of course, would choose the latter path:

> The Indian refused to submit to bondage and to learn the white man's ways. The result is that the greater portion of American Indians have disappeared, the greater portion of those who remain are not civilized. The Negro, wiser and more enduring than the Indian, patiently endured slavery; and contact with the white man has given the Negro in America a civilization vastly superior to that of the Indian.

Remarkably, the first African American educational historians, Carter G. Woodson and W. E. B. Du Bois, chose this same approach. Although their historiographical battles are those of a later time and hence will not be treated in this chapter, it is worth remarking that the cultural climate in which they formed their strategies was on display in 1893 in Chicago. Here is Du Bois, for example, in 1897:

> The history of the world is the history, not of individuals, but of groups, not of nations, but of races, and he who ignores or seeks to override the race idea in human history ignores and overrides the central thought of all history.

In the same way that Frederick Douglass and Ida B. Wells by their very presence (and clandestine activities) at the fair challenged the prevailing assumption that civilization was the exclusive domain of the white man, so Woodson and Du Bois would scour American history to discover the "great men" of African extraction who proved that the black race too was capable of civilization.[47]

Educational historiography written by women also benefits from comparison with the Expo. The Woman's Building by definition was a sort of ghetto, a tiny outpost reinforcing the separation between women's work and the male world of steam, wire, and steel. There were correspondingly very few women writing educational history around the turn of the century, but an examination of even two figures allows us access to the differences arising among women concerning what to say with their slowly maturing public voice. There were ultimately two choices: one could accept essentialist notions of woman's nature and pursue a scholarly agenda wedded to issues that were ostensibly feminine in nature, or one could reject the very assumptions about woman's nature that were embedded in such professional choices and seek to enter masculine territory. Alice Morse Earle chose the former path, and Elsie Clews the latter.[48]

No American historian at the turn of the century so prolifically and successfully collected tidbits of early American social life for presentation in winsome publications as did Alice Morse Earle. In an age when history was becoming the venue of dreary professionalism prosecuted according to the strictest Rankean methods, Earle was composing history that people actually read. Her depictions of early American social life became the basis for innumerable efforts at twentieth-century public history, as museums, pageants, and redramatization projects used her as their authority. As late as 1969, publishers were reproducing colorful abridgements of her work for the nation's schoolchildren.[49]

Earle was immensely prolific—publishing eighteen books and forty articles in the span of fourteen years—but this was problematic for her. Like many of her peers, she was seeking to navigate the turbulent waters of public life on the margins of domesticity. She gave only one public interview (and regretted even that), never explicitly stated the reformist implications of much of her historical work, and persisted in upholding the myth that she had merely fallen into her career as author when in fact it had been a deliberate and aggressive effort on her part. Biographer Susan Reynolds Williams has demonstrated conclusively just how proactive Earle was in her career: wrangling with publishers, managing finances, negotiating publicity, and utilizing networks of female associations to forward her work. If Alice Morse Earle's topics were domestic and private, her methods often belied separate spheres.[50]

At the turn of the century, many middle-class white Protestants were captivated by what has been dubbed the "colonial revival," a nostalgic reappropriation of the past for the sake of providing a sense of psychological well-being in the face of a society over which they were losing control. Earle's publications "did much to make the colonial revival a genuinely popular phenomenon" through her literary charm, innovative source material, and use of visual illustrations to secure for her readers the assurance that her research offered them no mere imitation of the past, but access to "the real thing."[51]

Concerned as she was with domestic affairs and material culture, Earle's research often led her into educational topics. Her methodology was that of the hoarder and sorter: she would gather into voluminous scrapbooks all the facts and evidence she could on daily life in the past and then arrange this material topically for her publications. Often material that had formed a chapter in one book would later be augmented until there was sufficient material for a book of its own, as is the case with her most comprehensively educational book, *Child Life in Colonial Days*, published in 1899. As early as 1894, she had compiled enough data for an opening chapter on child life in her *Customs and Fashions in Old New England*, and a good bit of the material for *Child Life* had appeared just the year before in one of Earle's most impressive efforts, *Home Life in Colonial Days*. In these and other works, notably her 1894 *Diary of a Boston School Girl*, and her article for the *Chautauquan* titled "Schools and Education in the American Colonies," educational history is gracefully situated within the overall social history of early America and even in its transatlantic context, all for the purpose of bolstering the self-image of the anxious New England middle class that was her audience.[52]

Earle's history is a fascinating mix of reverence and disdain, a double thesis in which she is quick to point to the superiority of Puritan society over the English civilization they left behind but also the inferiority of the former to that developed by the Puritans' offspring. "Let us thank God for having given us such ancestors," she intoned, immediately adding, "and let each successive generation thank him not less fervently, for being one step further from them in the march of ages." "I have freely compared the conditions in this country with similar ones in England at the same date," Earle explained,

> both for the sake of fuller elucidation, and also to attempt to put on a proper basis the civilization which the colonists left behind them. Many statements of conditions in America do not convey correct ideas of our past comfort and present and liberal progress unless we compare them with facts in English life.

The transit of civilization, then, was for Earle evidence of American improvement. But improvement did not end with the first settlers:

> No greater contrast of conditions could exist between the school life of what we love to call the "good old times," and that of the far better times of to-day.

Poor, small, and uncomfortable schoolhouses, scant furnishings, few and un-
interesting books, tiresome and indifferent methods of teaching, great severity
of discipline, were the accompaniments of school days until this century.[53]

Earle is sensitive to the present situation of her readers. Noting the "large
share which child study has in the interest of the reader and thinker of
to-day," she is curious about "how little is told of child life in history." And
when the telling is done, the New England reader cannot help but be both
entertained and encouraged. After dwelling at length, for example, on the
harsh tradition of infant baptism in severe winter conditions, in which ice
had to be broken through in christening bowls, Earle points out:

> This religious ordeal was but the initial step in the rigid system of selection
> enforced by every detail of the manner of life in early New England. The mor-
> tality among infants was appallingly large; and the natural result—the survival
> of the fittest—may account for the present tough endurance of the New England
> people.

Although Susan Reynolds Williams is right that, in general, Earle's work taken
as a whole "presented a vision of an ideal society, a golden age that had
reached its zenith during the years of the early republic and had been wan-
ing ever since," when it comes to educational history and child life, Earle is
as much convinced of progress as the most orthodox schoolman. Despite her
sensitive portraits of children in the schools and homes of early America, her
readers would likely have concurred with her sentiment that "I am glad I
never was a child in colonial New England."[54]

If Alice Morse Earle was by disposition a premodern Romantic who
accepted on the whole late-nineteenth-century notions of separate spheres
and achieved popular éclat largely because she was representative of "white,
Anglo-American, middle-class culture," the other significant female educational historian of the turn of the century was her diametric opposite. Elsie
Worthingham Clews was born into the highest strata of American society,
but from her earliest days she kicked against the goads seeking to prod her
in the direction of Victorian gentility. From rough childhood play and un-
chaperoned swimming with boys, to college and graduate academic work,
to her eventual career as a pioneer ethnographer and architect of female sexual
liberation, the string of continuity in her life was the pursuit of a modernist
autonomy through a challenge to convention wherever she found it.[55]

One must understand her personality in this way to make sense of
Clews's doctoral dissertation, which was her only significant piece of educational history. As a senior at Barnard College in the spring of 1896, Clews
had taken Nicholas Murray Butler's seminar on the history of education, at

which she had presented a paper on the relationship between education and government. As her funding and the patience of her family for graduate study was wearing thin, she was anxious to complete her doctorate, and an enlargement of her earlier work seemed appropriate. In 1899, her dissertation, *Educational Legislation and Administration of the Colonial Governments*, was completed and subsequently published.[56]

With the notable exception of the introduction, in which, as has already been noted, she ably posits the need for a transatlantic perspective, Clews's study is German historical scholarship through and through. The body of the work itself is the most spiritless litany of legislation imaginable. There is no interpretation whatsoever, just five hundred pages of bills, acts, statutes, and charters, organized chronologically by state. Useful as it is as a reference resource even today, the study does little historiographically other than to illustrate the sort of professional scientific scholarship then coming into vogue, and this is precisely its significance. From a woman at the turn of the century, a charming, anecdotal account of home and hearth would have been an expected and welcome contribution. The men, on the other hand, were writing dispassionate institutional histories. Clews would go on to show the world how spirited her prose and how original her ideas could be, but for her doctoral dissertation she needed to prove that women could write history just as colorlessly and about the same subjects as did men. Given her specialization in history of education, she might have written about the higher education of women or the softening ideals of child nurture, but she chose instead to focus on the aspect of that history that was most closely associated with masculinity: public legislation. The fact that her study blends seamlessly into the literature of the professional male historians—the work's very unremarkability—testifies to the success of her attempt to transgress the boundaries set for her sex in academia and to deconstruct by her own actions the dominant account of civilization on which those boundaries were built.

One final point needs to be made concerning educational historiography on the margins of civilization. There were moments when the civilized cosmopolitan white man showed himself to have but lately arrived at civilization. Although the rhetoric of national purpose and system was dominant, on the margins residual provincialisms were often ready to break the surface should an affront present itself. And in 1892, Andrew S. Draper felt the slap of George H. Martin's Massachusetts boosterism strongly enough to initiate a decidedly unprofessional feud.

The story really begins with Washington Irving's irreverent *Knickerbocker's History of New York*, against whose caricatures of the colonial Dutch subsequent historians, most notably John R. Brodhead and John L.

Motley, devoted many pages. In his *Rise of the Dutch Republic* and his four-volume *History of the United Netherlands*, Motley sought to rehabilitate the Dutch and credit them with originating much that was considered best in American institutional life, including American schools. Brodhead's work contained particularly suggestive passages regarding New Dutch education, none more often quoted than this one:

> Neither the perils of war, nor the busy pursuit of gain, nor the excitement of political strife, ever caused the Dutch to neglect the duty of educating their offspring to enjoy that freedom for which their fathers had fought. Schools were everywhere provided, at the public expense, with good schoolmasters, to instruct the children of all classes in the usual branches of education.

By 1891, George Martin had heard enough of such "glittering generalities." He cast his own scholarly work in terms of a competition between Massachusetts and the rest of the country, particularly New York, for honors in initiating educational progress. His thesis in a paper read before the Department of Superintendence of the National Education Association in 1891 was the first statement of a claim that will be recognizable to readers of his later *Evolution of the Massachusetts Public School System*:

> Reviewing the evolutionary process from the beginning, we note that there have been six steps: compulsory education, compulsory schools, compulsory certification of teachers, compulsory supervision, compulsory taxation, compulsory attendance; and it seems that Massachusetts took each of these steps in advance of the other States—a little in advance of her sister States in New England, far in advance of all the others.[57]

To Draper, this seemed more than a bit overstated. In a respectful, circumspect rebuttal in the *Educational Review* in April 1892, he presented his counterclaim that:

> *America is indebted to the Dutch rather than to the English for the essential principles of the great free-school system of the country, and that in the several most important steps which have marked the establishment and the development of that system, New York, and not Massachusetts, has led the way.*

Draper first deconstructs Martin's argument by contrasting English society with that in Holland during the early seventeenth century, finding in England only aristocratic schooling assuming the unity of church and state, but in Holland widespread popular education deriving from its Reformation heritage. Interpreting New England school laws in this transcontinental context, he finds that "for certainly more than sixty years of Massachusetts colonial life, and probably much longer, elementary instruction was held to be only a family duty for the attainment of a religious end. A few of the brighter boys were sent to a Latin school commonly kept by the village pastor."[58]

In contrast, from 1633, when, according to Draper, the first schoolmaster came over from Holland, the New Netherlands provided widespread popular education until it was captured by the English, who imposed their own notions of education on it, destroying all current efforts and curtailing all future attempts at popular education. Draper concludes by contrasting subsequent development according to Martin's six categories, finding each time save one that it was in fact New York that was ahead of Massachusetts, which, after all, was still bogged down in governance by locality rather than by the state.

The following June, Martin replied to Draper's criticism with notably more rhetorical steam. "Mr. Draper," he tells his readers, "has the courage of his convictions, possibly beyond them. . . . A modern Van Tromp, flying Dutch colors and with broom nailed to his masthead, he sails exultantly over all the Massachusetts seas. . . . Had he gone a step further and denied the existence of Massachusetts altogether, he would have done no more violence to history." And so it goes. Martin himself deconstructs Draper's claims for the Dutch schools, demonstrating that the 1633 school was "*only a parish dame-school taught by a man.*" Doing his own bit of cultural transmission spadework, Martin finds that the very concept of individual political liberty was foreign to the Dutch colonists. Concluding that "the Free Public School system—the American system—in New York is just twenty-five years old," Martin goes on to amass more evidence to support his claims for Massachusetts, the essence of which is that "Massachusetts enjoyed a rounded century of absolutely free public schools, elementary and secondary, before New York had reached the same goal."[59]

The gauntlet had been thrown down, and Andrew Draper was eager for the fight. Nicholas Murray Butler once remarked of Draper: "[I]t is red blood that flows in his veins and an indomitable will that executes the policies concerning which his intelligence is convinced." Of his rectitude in this matter Draper was convinced, as he was of Massachusetts hubris:

> It is the habit of Massachusetts to claim everything in sight educationally. The habit has fed and fattened upon the fact that no one has felt disposed to contest such claims. . . . Regardless of popular conceptions, the work of fervid orators and alleged historians, nothing becomes clearer to the mind of the investigator than that the common school idea was not of English origin, and that Massachusetts, which was exclusively of English origin, was slow in taking the steps which led to its complete development.

Draper adds little substantively to the discussion in this his second reply, but he does cite a new volley of secondary authorities and conclude with a vicious reference to the "dense superstition and the misguided, even bloody, religious intolerance" of the early Massachusetts settlers.[60]

To Draper's reply Martin added his final statement, which, stripped of personal offense at Draper's jabs at Massachusetts's founders and some over-blown bombast, is reduced to a repetition of his original claim and a pro-found insight into his philosophy of historical development:

> I reaffirm the statement made at Philadelphia, that each of these six steps was taken by Massachusetts in advance of the other States. . . . The whole future of the system was in the first enactment. Let any State decree that every child shall be educated up to a standard which it sets, and all the rest must inevitably follow—public schools, public taxation, public supervision, authorized teachers, and compulsory attendance. . . . As early as 1647 Massachusetts had a complete educational system, elementary schools, secondary schools, and the college, related to each other precisely in the same manner as similar schools are related to-day.

This statement was answered by Draper's final reply, which, while certainly the grand finale of the rhetorical fireworks, again is reduced to a restatement of his original contention:

> Accordingly it is confidently submitted that it is abundantly established that the essential elements of the public school system were first developed in the Netherlands, and had their first exemplification in America among the Dutch at New Amsterdam, and not among the English in Massachusetts.[61]

Thus ended the controversy, though its ripples could be detected for many years to come. Martin's book-length treatment was published in 1894 and reiterated his arguments, characterizing those of his opponent rather unchari-tably, we might add. This work, as Lawrence Cremin noted, is something of a summarization of the Whig view of educational history, complete with early glories, declension, and revival at the hands of the common school reform-ers. Other writers amplified the claims of one or the other locale, as C. W. Bardeen did in ascribing to New York "the earliest educational journal pub-lished in English," or as Seth Low and A. Emerson Palmer did in their 1905 recapitulation of Draper's arguments.[62]

Some later writers added complexity to the picture, among them George LeRoy Jackson, writing in 1909:

> It must be admitted that these facts point to the conclusion that town schools previous to 1647 were maintained by voluntary and by compulsory contribu-tions. . . . the law of 1642 made elementary education compulsory and—for the poor—made it free as well. . . . the cost of the education of such children was borne by the community.

Others sought a synthesis of the two perspectives, as did Edwin Grant Dexter in 1904, arguing both the Draper thesis—"[t]he Puritans in New England recognized at first only a need for higher education for the maintenance of a learned clergy, the Dutch began at the bottom, with their own children. In the matter of popular education they were the leaders"—*and* the Martin thesis: "[t]he sturdy settlers upon the New England coast played a much more important part in the making of our school system than had their predecessors."[63]

Still others sought to destabilize the debate by taking a closer look at the evidence. A young William Heard Kilpatrick, examining colonial sailing records, discovered that the first Dutch teacher had come to the New Netherlands not in 1633, as had been universally assumed, but in 1638. Robert Francis Seybolt concluded from an exhaustive study of all the available records in the city of Boston that there were more schools than Draper had assumed, that these were "fairly well administered and supervised" and "were not established or maintained as preparatory schools for Harvard College." Finally, Paul Monroe, at the end of a long career of following these developments, abandoned the dichotomy altogether and declared, "[T]his educational ideal belonged to no nation. It belonged to a religious group or sect and was rooted in fundamental religious and moral and political principles."[64]

There are several points to be made regarding the debate beyond the obvious one that at times local affections could threaten the professional consensus made possible by the civilization thesis. First, it is striking how deeply dependent on secondary historical literature are both sides. Draper and Martin quote different sources, but they both quote them profusely. Said differently, both arguments, while agitated by turbulent rhetoric, flow placidly down the mainstream of historical scholarship. Second, the reader will be struck by how much of the debate depends on the character of civilization present in the mother country at the time of the Atlantic crossing. Both men assume that American customs are simply the development of European transmissions, disagreeing only over which part of Europe planted the seeds. Third, both sides do a fine job of historicizing their opponent's claims: Draper shows conclusively that Massachusetts schools were utterly unlike current common schools, and Martin does the same for New Netherlands. Neither interlocutor, however, was able to extend this contextualist perspective to his own terrain. Thus we are led to the final point to be made, which is that both sides, even well after the debate, assumed that they were on the right hunt when they sought the origins of late-nineteenth-century systems in the colonial past.

The bickering masked an overarching consensus on the legitimacy of the project of tracing the gradual evolution of present institutional systems from their roots in the past. It overshadowed the agreement that all parties had concerning the superiority of present systems and the progressivism implicit in their doctrine of evolutionary civilization. At the turn of the century the schoolmen shared such assumptions as these with the vast majority of their fellow Americans. Only when the doctrine of civilization was overturned by a critical mass did the schoolmen find their historiography at odds with that of noneducationists. Achieving such a coup was the work of unpredicted world events and the later generations that experienced them.

CHAPTER FOUR

Influence and Contextualization in the Twentieth Century

In the view of many historians, the decades surrounding 1900 mark a critical shift in American history. Gentartifice and deference were replaced by masculine aggression and nature-love. Men, having recovered from what John Higham called the "sorrow and weariness left by the Civil War," found renewed pleasure in martial activities, and women joined them in a quest for public voice and participation in vigorous sport. Reticence was repealed as the young practiced a new openness in courtship patterns, journalism traded in restraint for sensationalism, and Comstockery was chipped away by the courts. Victorian assumptions and the culture they bolstered were dismantled and replaced by a hedonistic Freudianism modeled after the bohemian materialism of Greenwich Village, this skillfully marketed by advertisers teaching America to transform itself from a Puritan to a therapeutic orientation, from a culture of production to one of consumption. Although bureaucratic order eroded local and individual self-direction, the inexpensive goods and mass entertainment provided by bureaucracy softened the blow of modernity and led most people to acquiesce to these changes and call them progress.[1]

The most significant result of these shifts for our study is the way in which the new focus on material abundance and prosperity altered notions of progress. Dreams of a profusion of consumer goods made available to an ever expanding market gave "new life to the old ideology of progress" and helped it to "survive the rigors of the twentieth century." With progress redefined as increased material abundance, even the twentieth century's world wars could be seen as progressive, for they did indeed give "added energy to economic development."[2]

The reorientation of the doctrine of progress around material conquests through science and technology rather than moral perfection through gradual evolution led to a profound shift in the way progress was understood by the early twentieth century. Perhaps the best way to get at the new perspective is to recall Lester Frank Ward's distinction between *genetic* and *telic* progress.

For Ward, in contrast to nineteenth-century theorists such as Spencer and John Fiske, there is a crucial difference between biological evolution and social progress. The one is a passive process: "it is the environment that transforms the organism." Biological evolution thus has no directionality to it. Much of human history has likewise been the story of such a passive, reactionary development as humans respond to the changing circumstances of their environment. But the conquest of nature has rendered one species the master of its destiny, has given it the tools to actively manipulate the environment to achieve some desired social telos. It was the conviction of the progressive reformer that "man, by using his intelligence to solve specific problems, could with increasing effectiveness create a future satisfying his developing moral requirements." Progress was no longer the inevitable outcome of a foreordained divine plan or cosmic logic. It depended on "man's will to believe in a certain kind of future and on his willingness to act in scientific, experimental ways to implement his beliefs."[3]

A progress thus redefined could weather the self-doubts of the generation of liberal intellectuals who came of age during World War I and as a result became disenchanted with Americanism. "The supreme horror of the war," Elsie Clews Parsons had said, "lay in its assault on our sense of progress." Lewis Mumford concurred: "Into this world of mechanical progress and human amelioration, the World War came like a baleful meteor from outer space." Although many recent historians have correctly challenged the easy generalization that the war was the cause of all the social change that occurred in the period, it is worth remembering that many who lived through it would never again have easy faith in American progress. This is why the shift in definitions of progress from one focused on intellectual and moral civilization to one based on material prosperity is so important and serves as the first explanation for the continuities between nineteenth- and twentieth-century educational historiography.[4]

The second consideration in working toward an explanation of the tenacity of the principle of progress among twentieth-century educational historians is the internal dynamic of the institutions within which many of them worked. As the century aged, history courses in schools of education continued to be a prominent part of the curriculum, though they came under increasing fire by the 1920s. These courses still needed textbooks that could provide the future teacher with a usable past as a means of self-definition. Textbook accounts therefore were published with increased frequency and with very little change in content. Carl Edward Feigenbaum's exhaustive review of educational history textbooks and monographs for the period 1900–1920 reveals a content substantially the same as that of the late nineteenth century: a linear civilizational progress in which "tradition, authority, and metaphysics" were replaced by "scientific spirit and objectivity." Secular, state-run schools proved the best illustration of this development and so received the lion's share of coverage. This perspective continued to inform textbooks well after 1920. To this day publishers annually recycle the tried-and-true education-as-civilization-building approach for use in courses in educational foundations throughout the country.[5]

But institutional momentum produced more profound continuities than the textbooks reveal, and we need to understand them to properly appreciate the nature of pre–World War II educational historiography. Since Bernard Bailyn wrote, it has been customary to understand the historiography of the schoolmen as (*a*) nearly exclusively focused on schooling rather than the broader cultural educational matrix, and (*b*) disconnected from intellectual currents affecting other historians of the day. In this chapter I will attempt to demonstrate that the first claim needs considerable qualification and explanation, and that the second is simply not true, as the life and work of some of the most important historians of the early twentieth century reveal. To begin investigating these matters we need look nowhere else than to the "wizard of Stanford" himself, Ellwood Patterson Cubberley.[6]

CUBBERLEY AND THE HISTORICAL PROFESSION

A careful contextual appraisal of Cubberley's works will, I believe, reveal just how connected he and the tradition he represents were to the leading historiographical trends of his time. Perhaps the best vantage for surveying these connections is to be found in Cubberley's *Introduction to the Study of Education and to Teaching*, a text he published in 1925 as a student's first introduction to the entire field of education and whose first chapter reproduces in broad strokes the basic story he had earlier chronicled in his famous *Public Education in the United States*. After recounting this story for the introductory student, Cubberley recommends further study in the history of education, and as the burden of justifying such study is upon him, he gives students three reasons why further historical work is worth their while:

> A detailed study of our educational history, as given in a course in the *History of Education in the United States* will reveal to the student a fascinating story. It will also reveal how fully the problems and practices of present-day education are an outgrowth of a long historical development. Still more, the course will interpret to the student the evolution of much of the best in our American life.

Cubberley here provides three justifications for continued study, and taken separately each offers a clue about why the first edition of his *Public Education in the United States*, published in 1920, sold almost eighty thousand copies, and why the 1934 revision sold nearly fifteen thousand.[7]

The task Cubberley set for himself was twofold. First, he had to deal with an educational profession that often wondered aloud at the utility of historical studies and a student population less than eager to embrace them. Lawrence Cremin, in a 1955 article chronicling the development of the history of education as a field of study, detailed the spirited debates over the social utility of educational history to which Cubberley was responding in the preceding quotation. It was clear from a number of student surveys and opinion polls that many educational professionals felt that too much history was being required of education students and that these students themselves found such studies irrelevant to their professional concerns. In response to this situation, some historians of education followed Henry Suzzallo in opting for a history more carefully crafted to meet the contemporary needs of students, while others such as Henry Johnson found such recommendations abominable. Although such commentators as Stephen G. Rich thought Cubberley did not go nearly far enough, it is correct to understand his history as an attempt, as Sol Cohen has explained, to overcome the objections of scientistic colleagues by shifting history of education from a humanistic focus on the theories of European educators to a functionalist emphasis on the development of contemporary institutions.[8]

Second, Cubberley was faced with the challenge of making his department intellectually respectable to denizens of other academic disciplines at Stanford University particularly and in the rest of the country more generally. The passing of the Victorian consensus had brought a thoroughgoing empiricism and positivism into universities, producing a fragmented and undigested mountain of facts, especially in history departments, where belletristic epics had given way to bloodless empirical studies swarming with footnotes but often absent of synthetic perspective. In response, a new generation of historians were calling for a New History, a modern, forward-looking, all-encompassing account that was as empirical as the most rigorous professional history, but infused with progressive values.

Having considered these two audiences, we are now in a position to analyze Cubberley's three justifications as given in the foregoing quotation from *Introduction to the Study of Education and to Teaching*. To reiterate, Cubberley tells us that the history of education is functional because:

1. It is entertaining, revealing to the student "a fascinating story."
2. It explains the present by showcasing "a long historical development."
3. It is edifying in its demonstration of the progress of "much of the best in our American life."

What is striking, however, is that these same three justifications fit perfectly with the major historiographical moves of Cubberley's day, and thus they make an equally persuasive case for his speciality's academic legitimacy. Cubberley can be at one and the same time

1. Entertaining, like the great romantic amateur historians, who were still selling the most books
2. Evolutionary, like the conservative professional historians, who by the turn of the century had assumed control of history departments and dominated the journals and conferences
3. Progressive, like the up-and-coming generation of younger historians from the Midwest

Cubberley's *Public Education* sold so well for so long because it was successful both as a functionalist tract for students of education *and* as a piece of apologetic scholarship sympathetic to the sensibilities of several generations of academics. A survey of the changes in the historical profession during the decades of Cubberley's influence will help us understand just how connected his work was to "major influences and shaping minds of twentieth-century historiography."[9]

The last decade of the nineteenth century saw the momentum of leadership in American history writing shift from the great amateurs to the first generation of university-trained professionals. The amateurs had written glorious narrative history filled with heroic deeds, cliff-hanging plots, evocative and exotic scenery, fine morality, and insight into character. Their aesthetic was essentially romantic, their view of history evolutionary in a mystical sense that owed more to the great romantic poets than to Darwin and Wallace. Their gaze was constantly on the great individual, on personality and its striving in the face of obstacles in nature, other humans, and the sublime. Their nationalism was as religious as it was political, a patriotism of the spirit. Amateur history was popular, selling well among a public that delighted in novelistic devices and craved a usable past for its faith in America's greatness and virtue. The greatest of the romantic amateur historians almost all came from New England and descended from the earliest Puritan stock: Parkman, McMaster, Winsor, Bancroft, Prescott. They were usually men of means and always men of genteel culture. But in the changing world of Gilded Age America, they were quickly going out of fashion. Their reading public dwindled as mass culture replaced more polite forms of leisured consumption, and a new group of German-trained historians emerged who were quite self-conscious in their professionalism.[10]

The professionalization of American history was one aspect of what was explained in the previous chapter as the general trend away from agrarian democratic culture to a managed, urban order grounded in critical realism. Historian John Higham has presciently described the shift from romantic to professional history:

> What we call scientific history involved much more than a critical approach to evidence; it also subordinated romantic values to a scientific spirit. That spirit was impersonal, collaborative, secular, impatient with mystery, and relentlessly concerned with the relation of things to one another instead of their relation to a realm of ultimate meaning.

The new professional historians, in their attempt to escape the explicitly normative, began to substitute for the story of individual moral agency that of the evolution of depersonalized institutions. The evolution that they espoused differed markedly from the Coleridgean sort of their romantic predecessors. The new evolution was thoroughly naturalized, with a "mechanistic and materialistic" process replacing the old transcendentalist one.[11]

Professional politics may have been just as conservative as those of the amateurs, but the methods of arriving at these political conclusions were ostensibly scientific and thus the politics much more difficult to separate from the history. This connection placed a very heavy burden of proof on those who, like the earliest black historians, disagreed with the professional historians' objective political conclusions. Professional technique tended to be less literary, less prone to cast moral approbation or blame, less focused on scenery or drama. The story that was emerging to replace the old dramatic narrative was that of a slow but steady institutional growth from the earliest seeds planted in the past.

Just who planted the seeds could be a matter of controversy. Herbert Baxter Adams, one of the most influential of the early professionals, was convinced of the Teutonic origins of American institutions and made the study of German roots the emphasis of his famous seminar at Columbia University in the 1880s. Adams's seminar, as we have seen, was the point of origin for many of the early nationalistic monographs in the history of higher education put out by the Bureau of Education under Adams's editorship. It was also the breeding ground for the civic view of American history, the view that, as Adams was fond of quoting it, "history is past politics, and politics present history." Adams's Teutonic theory, popular as it was among the many American graduates of German historical schools, was eventually superseded by the "Imperial School" of Herbert Levi Osgood, which saw American democratic institutions not as transported directly from the German forest, but as emerging out of the struggle and eventual triumph of the forces of nationalistic unity over those of particularistic diversity.[12]

But whatever the origin, it was held by all the early professionals that a gradual evolution of American institutions from the earliest seeds planted in the colonial period was more important for understanding our history than were the heroic deeds of great men. John Franklin Jameson, professional history's most tireless worker and chronicler, describes the shift:

Forty years ago, a man might write on the diplomacy of the American Revolution; nowadays, he is much more likely to write on the history of the produce exchange, or government land grants for railways, or education. Monographs in the field of sociological history or on special topics of the history of civilization are the characteristic feature of our present historical literature. . . . This has been spoken of as the most important tendency of the historical writing of American to-day, not because its votaries or its productions are numerically in a majority, for that may very likely not be the case, but because of the belief that it is intrinsically the strongest tendency and has the future with it.[13]

Jameson's prophecy, claiming the future for evolutionary history of institutions (including educational institutions), was published in 1891. In that year, two young men in Indiana were embarking on careers that would lead them at length into the educational profession. Paul Monroe was working the rounds as a principal in Indiana high schools, and Ellwood Cubberley was graduating from Indiana University. At length both made their way to Teachers College, Columbia University, Monroe in 1897 as an instructor in history and Cubberley in 1901 for graduate training. Cubberley's experience with Monroe was formative for his understanding of American educational history, because it was Monroe more than anyone else who transmitted the inherited Whig historiography to the new professional situation, in his own historical publications, through the immense body of work performed by his graduate students, and in his exhaustive *Cyclopedia of Education*.[14]

Monroe's stunning *Cyclopedia*, published between 1911 and 1913, remained the essential comprehensive reference work in education for decades afterward. Every element of the progress-of-civilization thesis in educational history is present therein in dozens of articles tracing the development of modern statist education from antiquity to the present; in biographies of leading educational theorists; in general historical summaries; and in specific entries on places, people, and events. Contributors included such influential historians as James Harvey Robinson, Charles Homer Haskins, Morris R. Cohen, and Arthur O. Lovejoy, as well as notable theorists such as John Dewey, Franz Boas, E. R. A. Seligman, Edward S. Ames, and Franklin H. Giddings. Whatever may be said of the *Cyclopedia*'s editorial perspective, it cannot be accused of developing outside the mainstream of the critical thought of its day. Just as Barnard's *Journal* was the culmination of the original Whig view of educational history, emerging at a time of explosion in encyclopedic projects, so Monroe's *Cyclopedia* was the culmination of the professional appropriation and extension of the Whig interpretation, produced during another frenetic cycle of compilations and encyclopedic projects.[15]

Another such project was the twenty-seven (later extended to twenty-eight) volume American Nation series, the first comprehensive attempt by multiple professional authors to chronicle the entire history of the United States from the earliest voyages to the twentieth century. The complete edition was first published in 1908, only three years before Monroe's *Cyclopedia*, and its approach to historical interpretation is remarkably similar to that of Monroe and his contributors. The nationalist thesis of the books reflected in the series title is abundantly expressed in the subcategories into which the individual volumes are placed:

Group I.   Foundations of the Nation
Group II.   Transformation into a Nation
Group III.   Development of the Nation
Group IV.   Trial of Nationality
Group V.   National Expansion

Taken as a group, the approach is that of the professional scientist: copious notation and citation of authorities and extensive focus on the gradual development of institutions from their seeds in the past. The reader learns that the national ideas of self-government are derived from colonial precedents such as the "Petition of Right of 1628" or the "little legislative assembly" that "convened in Virginia in 1619"; that the seeds of federalism were sown in the "joint expeditions" against Indians, the French, and the Spanish; that from the colonial roots of school law, college, and academy derived the first impulses that led to nineteenth-century "improvements in lower education" and "development of the first American Universities."[16]

Thus the old Whig thesis, professionalized and rendered encyclopedic by Monroe and Cubberley, which found the origins of the American public school in the early legislation of Puritan towns in 1642 and 1647 and in the compulsory attitude that these towns took toward schooling, looks not like a hopeless anachronism out of touch with current historical thought but quite a bit like a trendy history finding the origins of the Constitution in the Mayflower Compact or the source of the bicameral legislature in the Virginia House of Burgesses. If one begins with the assumption, common to nearly all professional historians of the time, that today's institutions must have grown from seeds planted in the past, the Puritan laws and attitudes do seem to be the best contenders available and thus the logical choice.

What is perhaps most striking about Cubberley in this regard, however, is not his professionalism, for one would expect as much of a graduate student studying under Monroe at century's end. What is remarkable is his residual romanticism. Cubberley's mystical faith in civilization's progress leaps from the pages of his history, as it does from this letter he wrote to accept his position in the Department of Education at Stanford on January 17, 1898:

> There are many reasons why I would prefer education to geology, but the rea-
> son that is greater than all other reasons put together is that in geology one
> must specialize with all his power, if he wishes to achieve anything great, and
> to do this would withdraw me from the cultural side of life. . . . But to work in
> education would. . . . plunge me even deeper into those studies that deal with
> the culture and noble ideals of the race, and would make me supremely happy.[17]

Cubberley's strength—and it might have been one of which he was
unaware—was his ability to harmonize trends that in the hands of other
people seemed utter contradictions. Thus at one and the same time we have
Cubberley the geological scientist/historian digging through the strata of the
past to find the historical origins of impersonal institutions and unconscious
mass developments *and* Cubberley the Victorian synthesizer infusing this story
with all the charm and life of the old amateur enthusiast or of faddish universal historians such as H. G. Wells, John Fiske, Herbert Spencer, and
Hendrick Van Loon. We have Cubberley the institutionalist seeking to get
educational historiography beyond its old-fashioned "devotion . . . to the
history of educational theory" by chronicling the development of the American school organization, but casting this institutional history in the familiar
terms of a great intellectual debate. Much of the power in his historical account comes from his masterful use of battle vocabulary to create a thrilling
narrative tension based on the struggle of good scientific, secular, statist
education to triumph over its self-interested opponents. Perhaps the most
famous parts of his text are the fine list of arguments for and against tax-
supported schools and the winsome accounts of, indeed, great men, such as
Horace Mann and Henry Barnard, who sacrificed so selflessly for the sake
of the institution. In Cubberley the impersonal scientific history and the stirring romantic narrative combined to make his text both historiographically
viable and readable to several generations of undergraduates.[18]

But this dichotomy resolved does not exhaust the meaning of his text,
in fact does not even get at its essential dynamic. *Public Education in the
United States* does not really belong to the turn of the century, though developments in the historical profession during those days certainly made their
mark on it. At its heart the book is a product not only of the institutionalistic
professional history but also and especially of the intellectual trends usually
associated with the progressive historians.

At the center of progressive history is the conviction that times change—
a thoroughgoing historicism that would seem to render the term *progressive
historian* something of an oxymoron. For the progressive, no longer would
the naive account of a linear development of institutions from their original
impulses suffice to explain the present, for the present has been severed from
the past by the blows of changing social forces. The task of the progressive

historian was to develop a meaningful interpretation of the American past given the conviction that the present is revealing a set of unprecedented social situations. There seemed to be two options: one could jettison the past entirely and seek to build from scratch a new society on a scientistic basis, or one could harmonize the old evolutionism with the new progressivism by highlighting the gradual development of *progressive* forces. The former option was favored by the emerging discipline of sociology, but the latter was most often chosen by the great progressive historians, and it was chosen by Cubberley. "Modernity" for these scholars "was indeed different, but it was the outgrowth of progressive historical forces." The study of the past was construed as "an instrument to the solution of present problems—to the elimination of contemporary irrationality."[19]

Consider the following examples, both classics of progressive historiography. Charles Beard's 1913 *Economic Interpretation of the Constitution of the United States*, perhaps the most famous of progressive historical works, was frequently cited by intellectuals of the early decades of the twentieth century as one of the "books that changed our minds." The source of its appeal was nothing less than its ahistorical claim that the Constitution emerged out of the clash of competing economic interests, that it was created and ratified not by "the whole people" but "by four groups of personality interests." Beard's thick, descriptive prose is ultimately reduced to an easy generalization that pits a liberal Declaration of Independence against a conservative Constitution.[20]

In the same fashion, Vernon Louis Parrington's 1930 *Main Currents in American Thought* takes two categories of persons, the one democratic and the other antidemocratic, and relegates every significant man of letters from the colonial period through 1920 to one or the other. Period after period is interpreted as a grand battle between these two "main currents": the "Chief Stewards of Theocracy" versus "Independency"; the "Mather Dynasty" versus early Liberals; Jonathan Edwards versus Benjamin Franklin; Tories versus Whigs; English Federalists versus French Democrats. Again, when the details have all been stripped away, the plot is reduced to a fight between reified progressive forces and environmentally conditioned conservative forces. Historian Robert Allen Skotheim explains of Parrington: "Ideas for which he had sympathy were more likely to be depicted with little or no reference to the environment, whereas ideas he disliked were more likely to be related to and 'explained' by the environment from which they came." Liberal ideas are the "currents" and conservative ones are the "reefs," "barriers," and "foundering bark" holding back progress.[21]

Similar in narrative structure to these two extremely influential works, Cubberley's *Public Education in the United States* pitches a battle between the forces of progress and reaction, constantly waged and eventually won by public-spirited men and their far-sighted institutional creations. "In 1825," says Cubberley, "schools were the distant hope of statesmen and reformers." After twenty-five years of "bitter contests" between the "friends of free schools" and the "church and private-school interests," at length justice won out and by 1850 public schools "were becoming an actuality in almost every Northern State." Perhaps no better illustration of Cubberley's tendency to split historical actors into good guys and bad guys can be found than his list of the sorts of persons for and against the schools:

   I. *For public schools.*
      Men considered as:
         1. "Citizens of the Republic"
         2. Philanthropists and humanitarians.
         3. Public Men of large vision.
         4. City residents.
         5. The intelligent workingmen in the cities.
         6. Non-taxpayers.
         7. Calvinists.
         8. "New-England men."
  II. *Lukewarm, or against public schools.*
      Men considered as:
         1. Belonging to the old aristocratic class.
         2. The conservatives of society.
         3. Politicians of small vision.
         4. Residents of rural districts.
         5. The ignorant, narrow-minded, and penurious.
         6. Taxpayers.
         7. Lutherans, Reformed-Church, Mennonites, and Quakers.
         8. Southern men.
         9. Proprietors of private schools.
       10. The non-English-speaking classes.

The list, distasteful as it was to many after World War II, is fully in step with Parrington's characterizations of liberals and conservatives. And in 1928 Parrington won the Pulitzer Prize.[22]

Cubberley's philosophy of history was essentially progressive. All history could be split into two stages, and the present was located precisely at the point of transition between them. The first stage was the "community-centered traditional society" and the second the "modern, differentiated, industrial society." It was the burden of progressive history both to provide an account of how we came to the present moment of transition between the stages and to connect this account to a program for future action. The progressive historian was not content merely to understand the world—he, or increasingly she, wanted to change it. No longer could America rely on its western frontier as a release valve for the tensions and traumas of urban industrial life, for the frontier had closed. The new frontier was a social one, and among the leaders in the movement for social change were the progressive historians. Thus the culmination of Cubberley's historical account is a blueprint for the future:

> Within the past quarter of a century we have come to see, with a clearness of vision not approached before, that education is our Nation's greatest constructive tool, and that the many problems of national welfare which education alone can solve are far greater than the schoolmaster of two or three decades ago dreamed.

The student's careful study of educational history will allow her or him "to view present-day educational problems in the light of their historical evolution," and thus to solve the "problems of the present and near future."[23]

But again, what is striking in Cubberley is his ability to synthesize perspectives usually seen as oppositional. Conservative evolutionists tended to concentrate on "the character of institutions, understood in terms of their origins," whereas progressives "focused on changes in institutions, explained in terms of surrounding environment." Cubberley's genius was to do both these things at the same time, by stressing the progressive propensities of various moments in the history of the schools, thus providing progressive education with a usable past, and by connecting these moments in a narrative of conflict with more traditional ways of doing things, thus demonstrating the essential dynamic of change.[24]

It is certainly not incidental that most of the momentum of progressive historiography was centered at Columbia University. There E. R. A. Seligman, J. H. Robinson, and Charles Beard hammered out their conception of American history as "primarily a conflict between over- and underprivileged classes." There Carl Becker studied, and there bridges were built between these scholars and some of the faculty at Teachers College, most notably on the issue of social studies education and the production of history textbooks with a functional and reformist bent.[25]

Even from his post at Stanford, Cubberley continued to draw intellectual sustenance from Columbia. He sent his best students there for doctoral training and continued for decades an active collaborative agenda with Teachers College faculty. Given these connections, it is not surprising to find Cubberley's romantic yet institutional history suffused with progressive themes. Although his focus is on institutions, it is almost incidentally so, for his real goal is to demonstrate the hallowed progress of civilization, and schools merely prove a convenient mechanism for revealing it. Progress simply means the replacement of the communal, religious, and familial with the centralized, secular, and managerial. The schools demonstrate this sublime progress as little else in our history does, and so a focus on the schools, and especially on their organization, seems entirely appropriate. Seen in this light it makes little sense to criticize Cubberley's near exclusive focus on the schools. He focused on them rather than on the family or the church or the press or other informal modes not so much because he thought education and schooling were the same thing (though he did use the words interchangeably) but because he had his eye trained on that which demonstrates liberal progress, and clearly the quintessentially liberal educational institution is the American public school. Other institutions only needed to be mentioned as they joined or resisted this indomitable advance.

There are many other elements in Cubberley's writings that partake of the progressive ethos not only in its historiographical connection, but also in ways more typical of its social character. Cubberley, for example, is quite explicit in his antiegalitarianism:

> The new period of advance which we now seem to be entering also bids fair to be very paternalistic, perhaps even socialistic. . . . Our city schools will soon be forced to give up the exceedingly democratic idea that all are equal, and that our society is devoid of classes, as a few cities have already in large part done, and to begin a specialization of educational effort along many new lines in an attempt better to adapt the school to the needs of these many classes in the city life.

For Cubberley, as for a number of progressives who were attracted to certain Italian political experiments, democratic progress would have its inevitable casualties, and one such casualty would seem to be the sort of independent autonomy traditionally associated with Jacksonian democracy. In 1927 the consummate progressive Herbert Croly noted that "whatever the dangers of Fascism, it has at any rate substituted movement for stagnation, purposive behavior for drifting, and visions of great future for collective pettiness and discouragement." In the same year that Cubberley's first edition of *Public Education* was published, progressive pundit Harold Stearns was declaring the idea of egalitarian democracy moribund in his *Liberalism in America.* Just two years before Cubberley's second edition, John Chamberlain in *Farewell to Reform* "abandoned the whole democratic dream."[26]

To take another example, Cubberley's anti-immigrationism, with its racist tinge, is justly infamous. What one must remember when assessing progressive views on race and immigration is progressivism itself, for "progress" by definition assumes the superiority of the present to the past. The immigrant therefore is something like a time traveler, a vestige of dying days magically transported through new technologies into the modern industrial state with no advanced preparation. Clearly, if progress is to continue, this backward group must either be quickly upgraded by education or somehow kept from ever reaching these shores in the first place. In a world of strikes and riots, of fragmentation and transformation on all planes, a bit of consolidation, a touch of scientifically grounded social control, seemed just the thing to keep the country on its course, to help overcome its "serious case of racial indigestion." Few were the voices expressing fear of Big Brother in the early twentieth century.[27]

We have now seen how Cubberley's work did not emerge "in almost total isolation from the major influences and shaping minds of twentieth-century historiography" but inhabited precisely the same intellectual space as did that of his contemporaries in political and intellectual history. His anachronism was the spirit of the age, as the popularity of Beard's redactive *Economic Interpretation of the Constitution of the United States* makes clear. His definition of education as schooling was no more provincial than Parrington's equation of thought with literature; his evangelism no more pronounced than progressivist panegyrics such as Robinson's *Mind in the Making* or Harry Barnes's *New History and the Social Studies*. Cubberley may not have cited or even read these and other such works (though he *did* cite Edward Eggleston!), but the same influences that set the stage for the major historiographical movements of the early part of the twentieth century left their mark just as clearly on his thought and work. While his unqualified optimism concerning professionalistic, managerial organization makes him certainly less interesting today than more ambivalent thinkers such as Carl Becker and Henry Adams, and while his assumptions did not shift dramatically when times changed as did Charles Beard's or Walter Lippman's, it could be argued that he is thereby more characteristic of his day than were these more complex figures, and this fact explains in a good measure the criticism that would eventually be heaped upon him. To abandon Cubberley was to abandon progressivism itself, as the anachronistically progressive schoolmen of the 1950s and 1960s recognized all too well when the judgments began to rain down upon them.[28]

Cubberley was less an architect of the future than a popularizer and synthesizer of the present, offering to a huge and captive audience repetitive books that reinforced dogmas already well entrenched in the schools of education. But, as Stuart McAninch has argued, this was his strength. His textbooks reproduced for a popular audience the same encyclopedic perspective ensconced in Monroe's *Cyclopedia* and perpetuated by the internal dynamics of the professional training he helped standardize. If, as Robert Wiebe has argued, "the heart of progressivism was the ambition of the new middle class to fulfill its destiny through bureaucratic means," then Ellwood Cubberley was in sync with the palpitations of his day. As we shall see, by the late 1950s the progressive paradigm had become anathema to many of the younger scholars distrustful of the "organization man" and eager to follow any mores but the ones represented by the "gray flannel suit." Those into whose hands Cubberley's organization had been passed would certainly have to reckon with the criticisms of such people, but Cubberley had by this time passed on. A contextually sensitive appraisal of his historical works such as we have offered here suggests that we ought leave him to rest in peace.[29]

THE FORGOTTEN COLLABORATION BETWEEN HISTORIANS AND SCHOOLMEN

In previous chapters I have demonstrated the continuity of purpose and perspective that exists between writers of educational history and those composing other aspects of American history—indeed, they were often the same people. It has been the unfortunate tendency of educational historians writing since 1960 to think of their predecessors as disconnected from mainstream historical developments. But in fact there has been an abundance of cross-fertilization throughout the twentieth century. Historians operating outside schools of education have turned to schoolmen's historiography whenever their research required it, and the schoolmen themselves have consistently incorporated the results of mainstream scholarship into their own accounts.

Until World War II, the "experiment in modernization" of progressive history was the most influential movement in American historiography, and educational historians were quick to join ranks. That the educationists found progressive historiography amenable is not surprising. What may perhaps surprise the investigator is the depth of their immersion in it. Edgar W. Knight's 1929 *Education in the United States*, for example, relies heavily on the Beards' *Rise of American Civilization*, Becker's *Beginnings of the American People*, Parrington's *Main Currents in American Thought*, and Thomas J. Wertenbaker's *First Americans*, as well as the more traditional, but nevertheless current, professional history of James Truslow Adams, C. M. Andrews, and John S. Bassett. While the development of public schools continues to be the driving force in his narrative, throughout Knight's text the social, political, religious, and economic conditions that accompanied the school's rise are foregrounded. Particularly interesting given its publication date is Knight's emphasis on the economic interpretation of history, bolstered by the studies already mentioned as well as more focused efforts such as Ernest L. Bogart's *Economic History of the United States*, H. U. Faulkner's *American Economic History*, and Carl R. Fish's *Rise of the Common Man*.[30]

Similarly, Stuart G. Noble's 1938 *History of American Education* relies heavily on mainstream history for its context. Like Knight's, his colonial coverage leans heavily on Eggleston's transmission-of-civilization thesis and on what had by then become canonical works in progressive historiography such as Parrington's *Main Currents in American Thought*. In the very year that Noble's book was offered for consumption by student teachers, a young Richard Hofstadter was reading Parrington for the first time and finding his volumes "immensely rewarding." Noble's contextual coverage is similar in scope to Knight's, drawing, in addition to the works mentioned above, on such authorities as Frederick Jackson Turner, Michael Kraus, Tremaine McDowell, Merle Curti, Oscar Cargill, and Allan Nevins. Chapter titles illustrate the effect such studies had on his treatment of schools: "The Heritage of English Culture," "The 'Age of Enlightenment' in Colonial America," "The Romantic Era," and "The Drift into Modern Realism" take their place alongside more predictable chapters on the rise and expansion of public education.[31]

In fact, the tendency among educationists, as among historians more generally, was strongly in the direction of a broad cultural history, and this despite the fact that their critics were challenging them to make their products more functional for the classroom. In 1925, Stephen G. Rich, for example, in the midst of an unflinching indictment of educational histories for their lack of functionality, conceded that there was "an increasing tendency to treat the history of education as a general history rather than as an isolated development." Some commentators, indeed, thought that the schoolmen took their contextualization too seriously. Edgar B. Wesley, for example, chided Freeman Butts and Lawrence Cremin in 1953 for spending so much time situating their story:

> Eight of the sixteen chapters deal with general and cultural history. The other eight chapters are devoted to the history of education. . . . Why? Could they not safely assume that the reader already has had at least a high school course in American history?[32]

Methodologically, educational historians, situated as so many of them were in a social science school, were drawn especially to anthropology and to quantitative methods of data analysis as aids in their historical production. It could even be argued that institutional affiliation in schools of education allowed for technical innovations in historical production that would only become fashionable among other historians during the cliometric movement of the 1970s and the rush by professional historians of that decade to apply the anthropological insights of Clifford Geertz, Victor Turner, and other theorists. Similarly, some educational historians such as Paul Monroe and I. L. Kandel, focused as they were on the development of state systems of education, were led into the domain of comparative history well before the vogue for modernization theory or the innovative work of George Frederickson and other recent historians made the comparative perspective fashionable.[33]

Even as the schoolmen were making good use of other branches of professional history, the professionals were incorporating the research of the schoolmen without objection. In 1964, William Brickman compiled a list of such works that went on for some four pages, including books by such notables as Arthur M. Schlesinger, Sr.; Samuel Eliot Morison; Henry Steele Commager; Alice Felt Tyler; Louis Harlan; Richard Hofstadter and Walter Metzger; and even Richard Storr, the guiding voice of the original 1957 critique of educationist historiography. In every case schoolmen's historiography was relied on for fact and interpretation, and annotations often described such works as "indispensible" or "outstanding."[34]

We might add other titles to Brickman's list. Monica Kiefer's pathbreaking 1948 *American Children through Their Books*, for example, chronicles in rich detail the gradual emergence out of Puritan darkness of a modern, secular, moralistic, tender view of childhood. Along the way we learn that schooling too was "directed by far reaching social forces from religious to secular interests" and that "certain positive forces . . . stimulated an interest in a democratic system of instruction . . . [and] continually centered public attention on the necessity of a free elementary school system." Authorities she cites for such views include Frederick Eby and Charles F. Arrowood, Edgar W. Knight, Stuart G. Noble, and Frank Graves, all educationists. Samuel Eliot Morison, in his *Puritan Pronaos*, relied on William Heard Kilpatrick's figures for his literacy statistics. That doing so would eventually earn him the ire of Kenneth Lockridge does not take away from the noteworthy fact that this respected historian and confirmed critic of progressive education based his own claims on the work of one of progressive education's leading spokesmen.[35]

At the same time a number of historians demonstrated in their professional activities a willingness to collaborate with educationists that belies claims of a growing isolation between the groups. Progressive historians such as James Harvey Robinson, Charles Beard, and Carl Becker were active in the social studies movement of the 1920s and 1930s. As early as 1920, Beard had begun his long collaboration with educationists as he and William C. Bagley produced their series of history textbooks, aiming to replace the dry, pedantic efforts of the past with lively narratives of American and world progress. More than five million copies of these books were sold. Merle Curti and Beard were on the Board of Contributors of the progressive educational journal *The Social Frontier* from 1934–38. Beard and George S. Counts dominated the American Historical Association's Commission on the Social Studies, a group consisting of prominent historians and educators that produced over a period of about ten years a substantial literature on social studies education. Notable historical productions stemming from this group, in addition to a number of books by Beard, include Charles E. Merriam's *Civic Education in the United States*, Henry Johnson's *Introduction to the His-*

tory of the Social Sciences, Howard K. Beale's *History of Freedom of Teaching in American Schools*, and Merle Curti's *Social Ideas of American Educators*. All these titles save Johnson's were written by respected historians who were not professional educators, a fact that should dispel in some degree the lingering assumption that pre-1960 historians had "shamefully neglected" the history of education.[36]

Merle Curti is himself perhaps the best example of the sunnier side of affiliation with educationists. His *Social Ideas of American Educators* was notable for being the first "integrated" piece of professional history (recall its chapter on Booker T. Washington), and, as one commentator described it, for bringing the history of education "into the mainstream of historical writing." And this was in 1935. Collaboration with Counts and admiration for Dewey led him in 1937 to Teachers College, where he taught history until 1942. During this time he was working on what was to become his most enduring work, the encyclopedic *Growth of American Thought*, whose first edition was published in 1943. In it, Curti self-consciously appropriated Dewey's instrumentalism in an attempt to interpret ideas in a functional manner, offering an environmental analysis for the purpose of promoting social reform.[37]

Not surprisingly, *The Growth of American Thought* gave major attention to schools and colleges, offering interpretations that were in complete accord with the dominant strain of educationist historiography. "Although little was done" in the revolutionary period "to improve the conditions of rural common schools," thanks to the influences of Lancaster, the New York Free School Society, and the work of De Witt Clinton, the ground was cleared for "the great educational revival in the later 1820s and 1830s." Although "the battle for the extension of educational opportunities to the children of common men was not entirely won by 1850," "the half-century year marked the triumph of the principle of state-supported and-supervised schools for all children, regardless of rank." We learn that "the Massachusetts Act of 1642 set a new precedent in extending the traditional compulsory principle," that "thanks to such men as Horace Mann, Henry Barnard, Calvin Stowe, Caleb Mills, Calvin Wiley, and others, many of the best features of the well-established state schools of Prussia were grafted onto the American national plant . . . creating public sentiment for better schools . . . organization, supervision, standards, teacher training, and the beginnings of a professional attitude into American public education." In 1944 this book won the Pulitzer Prize.[38]

Advancing the social frontier was not the only benefit Curti derived from his time at Teachers College. There he was exposed to the growing tendency to understand education in social-scientific terms, to apply the methods of scientific research to educational problems. Curti's wife, Margaret Wooster Curti, was in the vanguard of such study, contributing learned articles on the potential cultural bias of intelligence tests and producing a widely used textbook, *Child Psychology*. All these influences combined to make Merle Curti uniquely primed to work with a synthesis of history and social science technique, and thus he was the logical choice to chair the Social Science Research Council's Committee on Historiography.[39]

The social scientific influence ultimately led to one of the miracles of pre-1960 American historiography, Curti's 1959 *The Making of an American Community*. This engaging piece of local history anticipated the community studies movement by nearly a decade, using such novel source material as census records and local court documents to bring to life the entire social situation of Trempleau County, Wisconsin, from settlement patterns and home life to local government and economy, all based on the sophisticated quantification of data prosecuted by Margaret Wooster Curti. Thus a rich context was constructed for situating the history of schooling, to which Curti devoted a full chapter. This study's tremendous impact on such later community historians as Philip Greven, Stephan Thernstrom, Kenneth Lockridge, and John Demos has often been noted, but the fact that Curti's interests derived not from British labor history or the *Annales* school but from his connections to Teachers College and the social science know-how of his educationist wife has not received the attention it deserves.[40]

Given all this evidence, it becomes clear that accusations about the isolation of the discipline of educational history or about the inability of its practitioners to take into consideration a broad cultural context are inaccurate. Unfortunately, focus on these issues has hidden from view more significant developments in educational historiography that were occurring in the twentieth century before World War II. In hindsight, the deeper significance of the period lies not in the dance between professional historians and educators but in the growing diversity of interpretations being offered by an increasingly heterogeneous group of practitioners. Although the Whig interpretation was still dominant, two major trends began to challenge its hegemony.

The first came as different sorts of people began to do educational history. Whereas nineteenth-century historiography had been with rare exception the province of middle-class Anglo-American Protestant males, the twentieth century saw the beginnings of a powerful tradition of African American educational historiography, a marked increase in the production of scholarship by women, and a growing sophistication among the descendents of Catholic and Jewish immigrants. To all these developments was joined the fallout from world wars and economic depression, which led some interpreters to call into question many of the most hallowed assumptions of the Whig view. What emerged by the end of World War II was a field whose practitioners were a far less homogeneous lot and whose narrative core, unchanged at its deepest level since colonial times, was no longer persuasive to a growing number of Americans.

Diversity and Controversy
in the Twentieth Century

The lights of the world went out.
—James Truslow Adams

While most recent observers of educational historiography during the twentieth century have been chasing the red herring of an alleged communication gap between educationists and mainstream historians or an assumed unwillingness on the part of educational historians to take into consideration the broad cultural context within which formal modes of instruction have developed, trends of a more enduring nature have passed by undetected. As more and different sorts of people began to receive training in historical research the field grew ethnically and sexually diverse, shifting the parameters of historical production in fundamental ways. In addition, American involvement in war and the shifting religious alliances of a changing population made their mark on the histories that were written in the twentieth century, sparking controversies that cut to the very core of the hallowed Whig view.

The landscape of American higher education was transformed in the twentieth century as the modern research university replaced conscience-raising clergy with fund-raising laity, community with bureaucracy, and elitism with popular appeal. In 1900 about 4 percent of the population between the ages of eighteen and twenty-one were enrolled in postsecondary education. By the 1940s the figure had risen to 18 percent, and the increase was not limited to the traditional white, male student. In 1870 there were 11,000 women in institutions of higher education. By 1900 there were 85,000, and by 1920 there were 283,000. Over this period, women went from being 21 percent of those enrolled to 37 percent. Although the first generation of "educated women" bemoaned the seeming loss of scholarly dedication they observed in the young female students of the 1920s and 1930s, it was clear that white women had arrived in higher education and were there to stay.[1]

African Americans, however, had a much more difficult time of things. Although colleges and universities had, often with reluctance, admitted other ethnic minorities, in 1900 only eighty-eight African American students, out of a population of some ten million, were awarded degrees from white colleges. In 1917, of the twenty-five hundred black students enrolled in colleges in the south, only twelve attended state institutions. Although there were notable exceptions, among them Atlanta, Howard, Fisk, Wilberforce, and Lincoln universities, higher education for most blacks was extremely limited curricularly even into the 1930s, when 40 percent of all students enrolled in higher education were taking precollegiate instruction. But during the same period, a very small elite had managed to secure the highest of training: by 1939 119 blacks had been awarded doctoral degrees by leading white colleges and universities. It was from these ranks that the first great black educational historians came.[2]

PIONEERS OF BLACK EDUCATIONAL HISTORY

The first black educational historians did not set their own agendas. They were fundamentally apologists who were trying in various ways with different degrees of success to vindicate their people in the face of charges that were the received orthodoxy in mainstream professional history. It was extremely unfortunate for blacks that the professionalization of historical scholarship "happened to coincide with the peaking of racist thought among American intellectuals." This being so, the pathbreaking black historians had to contend with a powerful and sophisticated historiography claiming for itself the authenticity of scientific validity. Fronted by scholars of such high caliber as William A. Dunning and Ulrich Bonnell Phillips, the prosouthern redemptionist historiography emanating from the early professionals challenged black historians with claims of the innate mental weakness and evolutionary backwardness of their race. With such a challenge in mind, the African American educational historians' "great man" approach makes perfect sense: they countered claims of uneducability by providing examples of well-educated blacks of the past. This tendency to vindicate the race by providing examples of historical notables is the chief, though not exclusive, characteristic of the educational histories of the first great black educational historians, W. E. B. Du Bois and Carter G. Woodson. Although contemporary historians often disparage their predecessors' emphasis on great individuals, in the case of the black educational historians such an approach was actually clever strategy, for what was at issue was precisely whether Negro blood was capable of producing greatness.[3]

Carter Woodson is commonly and justly dubbed the founder of Negro history. Although he had forerunners to be sure, most notably George

Washington Williams, it was Woodson who created and sustained the institutions necessary to establish Negro history as a legitimate historical endeavor. It was Woodson's genius to take what little interest there was in Negro history (evidenced by the existence of societies of Negro history in New York by 1911 and Philadelphia as early as 1897) and consolidate it around an agenda of both serious scholarship and vigorous popularization. Having studied at such luminary institutions as the University of Chicago, the Sorbonne, and Harvard University (Ph.D. in 1912), Woodson was uniquely situated to provide a level of academic polish to Negro history that heretofore had not existed. His entrepreneurial spirit enabled him to combine this scholarly disposition with a penchant for marketing that led to the establishment of several major institutions. The Association for the Study of Negro Life and History was established in 1915, with its quarterly, *Journal of Negro History*, commencing publication in 1916. Associated Publishers was incorporated in 1921 to print scholarly works in Negro history that mainstream publishers would not consider. The *Negro History Bulletin* was initiated in 1937 as an outlet for popularizing the idea of a "Negro history week," which Woodson had conceived as early as 1926. The *Bulletin* joined Woodson's textbook *The Negro in Our History* as the major source of information on Negro history used in public schools across the country. Thus in the work of one man we see a unification of two types of Negro history, "the long tradition of writing on the black past on the part of black intellectuals and polemicists, on the one hand, and the professionalization of American historical study and the triumph of 'scientific' history on the other."[4]

But for the purposes of educational historiography, Woodson's most important contribution was his 1919 work, *The Education of the Negro Prior to 1861*. Although originally intending to write a postbellum book, he found the sources and felt the calling to write on the earlier period. The book is suffused with the same sort of inspiration he himself noted in the source material: "the accounts of the successful strivings of Negroes for enlightenment under most adverse circumstances read like beautiful romances of a people in an heroic age." The romantic genre is an appropriate designation for this book, which pulses with the drama of conflict, of noble striving against near insurmountable odds, of the struggle between the forces of light and darkness. In hindsight we are attuned mostly to his treatment of philanthropy, of black and white teachers, of black agency and white oppression, and this is as it should be. But to really appreciate Woodson's book we must remember that it inhabits a period in which the ancient learning of Greece and Rome still spoke to the educated mind, when gentility and poise were still virtues in some quarters, and when the recounting of glorious deeds of old had not quite lost its fashion. In short, though Woodson has successfully appropriated the new professional sensibilities, his story is still suffused with the spirit of the leisured amateurs.[5]

Woodson breaks down the period into two phases:

> The first extends from the time of the introduction of slavery to the climax of the insurrectionary movement about 1835, when the majority of the people in this country answered in the affirmative the question whether or not it was prudent to educate their slaves. Then followed the second period, when the industrial revolution changed slavery from a patriarchal to an economic institution, and when intelligent Negroes, encouraged by abolitionists, made so many attempts to organize servile insurrections that the pendulum began to swing the other way.

Woodson sees the results of the educational shutdown initiated by the slave owners as having had profound and lasting consequences: "Reduced thus to the plane of beasts, where they remained for generations, Negroes developed bad traits which since their emancipation have been removed only with great difficulty."[6]

Even these brief quotations tell us much about Woodson's perspective. He inhabits the broad intellectual mindset often dubbed "racial uplift" and subscribes to the traditional faith among African Americans that schooling, especially literacy, is the key to such uplift. But beyond that, we may discern in Woodson foreshadowings of two often conflicting emphases in African American history as he focuses attention both on the deeds of Negroes themselves that affected their subsequent history *and* on the oppressive nature of white rule, which produced in Negroes certain psychological traits that continue to retard their social progress. Present perspective would likely fault Woodson for focusing as he does to such a great degree on the philosophy of Negro education held by whites (and prominent white males at that), and by the emphasis placed on white societies, church bodies, individual "friends of the race," and such. But we must recall that Woodson's agenda is that of the apologist who is not only presenting to his black readership the fine traditions of education that they may take as their own, but also aiming to persuade a white readership of an equally impressive egalitarian tradition with its roots in the Lockean republicanism and Enlightenment ideals proffered by such luminaries as Franklin, Madison, Jay, and Jefferson.

Thus we are not surprised to find a Beardian strain in Woodson's prose, an attempt to do for Negro education what Parrington tried to do for American letters, to present two contrary historical traditions of white attitudes toward the Negro, the one progressive and enlightened, the other backward and philistine. Woodson seeks to both encourage his white readers with examples of virtue and to convict them with examples of vice, all within the context of a progressive interpretation with which they would be familiar:

Recovering from the social upheaval of the Revolution, caste soon began to claim its own. To discourage the education of the lowest class was natural to the aristocrats who on coming to power established governments based on the representation of interests, representation of suffrage, and the ineligibility of the poor to office.

What Woodson is doing in essence is grafting a particular racial perspective on the emerging progressivist interpretation of history, hoping the two will combine in the historical imagination. Thus there are two social forces that are crucial for understanding the shift from the first to the second phase of Negro educational history in this book, and Woodson wants them both to be considered progressive: "These forces were the industrial revolution and the development of an insurrectionary spirit among slaves, accelerated by the rapid spread of the abolition agitation."[7]

But Woodson is not only an apologist; he is also a Negro historian writing Negro history. In this respect his book deserves more recognition than it has received for its pathbreaking use of sources that would only become standard materials during the heyday of the new social history. Using slave advertisements in newspapers, travel accounts, and missionary logs, Woodson re-creates the range of educational experiences open to slaves. This strain culminates in his treatment of urban education, where Negro agency is vividly evident, more in the South than the North: "In northern cities like Philadelphia and New York, where benevolent organizations provided an adequate number of colored schools, the free blacks did not develop so much of the power to educate themselves."[8]

In the end, however, it is the apologetic strain that provides the take-home lesson of his text:

> Observing closely these conditions one would wonder little that many Negroes became low and degraded. The very institution of slavery itself produced shiftless, undependable beings, seeking relief whenever possible by giving the least and getting the most from their masters. . . . The bad traits of the American Negroes resulted then not from an instinct common to the natives of Africa, but from the institutions of the south and from the actual teaching of the slaves to be low and depraved that they might never develop sufficient strength to become a powerful element in society.

This thesis of external obstacles is what gives unity to Woodson's account, providing the dramatic tension and the setting for the profound accomplishments of notable slaves, reinforcing the "uplift" ideology accepted by educated blacks and whites alike, and explaining why the then current degree of Negro educational accomplishment was at something of a nadir.[9]

Notoriously, Woodson and W. E. B. Du Bois could not get along. But for all their squabbling over turf and funds, the two writers provide historical narratives that are remarkably complementary. Du Bois's historical consciousness had been formed by many of the same forces as had Woodson's: he had been reared in the romantic universal "great man" history of Thomas Carlyle and others, schooled in the latest of German methods under Albert Bushnell Hart at Harvard and then in Germany itself, and aggravated by the racist historiography then ascendant among professional historians. While Woodson's educational history focused on antebellum times, Du Bois's was concerned in the main with the Reconstruction period and its legacy. His historical grasp extended far beyond this period, but his major educational history focused on it for the particular role this era played in his larger revisionist purposes.[10]

Central to those purposes was both a challenge to the great-man tradition of the older romantic history and a challenge to the disengaged professionalism of the new. In 1897, Du Bois declared what would remain the central theme of all his historical writings for half a century: "The history of the world is the history, not of individuals, but of groups, not of nations, but of races, and he who ignores or seeks to override the race idea in human history ignores and overrides the central thought of all history." And this central thought is of the most profound relevance to contemporary concerns: "One cannot study the Negro in freedom and come to general conclusions about his destiny without knowing his history in slavery." With his eye on both the race as a whole and its present situation, Du Bois prosecutes his educational history.[11]

The substance of that history changed remarkably little over a thirty-year period. Du Bois was an astonishingly prolific writer, comfortable in all genres, one of the few truly great "men of letters" our country has produced. It should not surprise us therefore to find repetition of themes in his work. Recent historiography has been much concerned with his 1935 *Black Reconstruction* because of its powerful, defiant articulation of what was then the reverse of professional opinion but is now the orthodox view. While Du Bois's achievement has been justly praised in this regard, it has been too infrequently noticed that in the main his interpretations offered in 1935 with exquisite documentation had been present from his earliest educational history, the 1901 *Negro Common School*.[12]

The Negro Common School is not only a history of Negro education. It is first and foremost a sociological study of then current educational conditions. Although Du Bois had been trained as a historian at Harvard and had written a historical dissertation, sociological methods seemed to him to offer most promise for political and social reform at the turn of the century.

From his post at Atlanta University, he fronted a comprehensive sociological study of all aspects of Negro life, especially the new urban life that was fast replacing traditional farming cultures. *The Philadelphia Negro* (1899) was Du Bois's first attempt; this work is now a classic in the field, still relevant for understanding the issues surrounding the northern urban experience. One of these issues was education, and Du Bois devotes the first part of his chapter on education to a brief history of the rise of the formal segregated school system. The history is largely descriptive, interpretive only to the extent that it embodies what was always the fundamental narrative of his educational history-writing: a narrative of ascent, of systemic growth and gradual progress. But in *The Philadelphia Negro* the picture is rendered powerfully complex by consideration of factors other than just formal schooling. Du Bois is able to conclude that for freedmen "the question of economic survival is the most pressing of all questions." While education is important and blacks have come a long way, it is clear that race prejudice and economic forces play a stronger role in Negro history than had been customarily admitted, that education alone cannot defend a Negro proletariat against management and race prejudice combined.[13]

In 1896, the first annual Atlanta University conference for investigation of city problems was convened, and it continued to be held annually for fourteen years. The results of these conferences, an annual series of publications, became the intellectual raw material that Du Bois was to draw on for much of his life. Of particular interest to the educational historian are numbers 5 and 6, *The College-Bred Negro* and *The Negro Common School*. In both studies the emphasis is on present conditions, but these conditions are explained by their history. *The College-Bred Negro* first puts forth what would soon become a signature Du Bois emphasis, a focus on the "talented tenth" who have been educated at the elite black colleges. The historical emphasis is on the nobility of the efforts to found liberal arts colleges for Negroes and on the leadership that the Negro community has enjoyed from their graduates, as well as from graduates of white colleges. Particularly notable is Du Bois's (characteristic for him) emphasis on women collegians: while at historic women's colleges, "the color prejudice is much stronger and more unyielding"; nevertheless some 250 Negro women had graduated from a college by 1900, and the benefit this group had on morality reinforced DuBois's theme of the "success of higher education under the limitations and difficulties of the past."[14]

With *The Negro Common School*, we come to DuBois's central educational insights and most significant bequeathals to future scholarship. It was here that he first articulated what would become some of the most important evidence for his thesis in *Black Reconstruction*: that common schooling for all races was in the South a gift of the black Reconstruction legislatures:

> Although recent researches have shown in the South some germs of a public school system before the war, there can be no reasonable doubt, but what common school instruction in the South, in the modern sense of the term, was founded by the Freedmen's Bureau and missionary societies, and that the state public school systems were formed mainly by Negro reconstruction governments.

As with the Negro colleges, the history of black common schooling is again a history of ascent, of institution building and positive contributions to society, this time with blacks themselves playing a more active role in the process, assisted by the noble Freedman's Bureau. Funding inequities since the founding of the school systems are documented, along with enrollment increases and other statistical measures. But while the double thesis of a black historical contribution met by funding inequities is present and defended by the data, Du Bois's scholarly, even pedantic format of extensive quotations from documents obscures the message and dilutes its impact. It was the job of later work to clothe these historical insights in more fitting prose.[15]

According to biographer David Levering Lewis, Du Bois always regarded his 1910 move from Atlanta to New York "as the fork in his career leading from science to propaganda." Frustrated over the limited impact of his sociological studies, Du Bois turned to journalism and popular literature as outlets for his message. In 1924 he consolidated in one volume many of the historical threads he had been spinning for three decades, and the public was treated to *The Gift of Black Folk*. The work is a masterful synthesis of Du Bois themes, from the great-man contributions of notable black individuals to the racialist-tinted characterizations of uniquely African contributions to civilization. Included in the melee of folk music, arts, religion, and women's suffrage is the cause of education, and the thesis Du Bois produces is both a recapitulation of *The Negro Common School* and a précis of *Black Reconstruction*. Free public schools are described as one of three gifts given by the Negro to the South during Reconstruction, the others being democratic government and new social legislation. The schoolmarm and the Freedman's Bureau are praised and the contribution of educated blacks is celebrated. The work is thin on research and thick with memorable rhetoric, but the thesis is clear and persuasive to the contemporary reader. It is so, however, largely because of the impact of his historical magnum opus, *Black Reconstruction*.[16]

In *Black Reconstruction*, Du Bois's educational history is richly integrated into his broader account of the period. Permeating the history are two grand themes: class conflict and unstoppable modernization. Southern planters, devoted to a premodern production form, sought to stem the tide of progress and "fell back on a doctrine of racial differences." Formal schooling was thus out of the question in the South, for it was an aspect of the modernization project. The South might have modernized agriculture, but "this would have involved yielding to the demands of modern labor: opportunity for education, legal protection of women and children." But Du Bois is no northern triumphalist. Northern industry "began in 1879 an exploitation which was built on much the same sort of slavery which it helped to overthrow in 1863. It murdered democracy so completely that the world does not recognize its corpse." Yet while the nation was captivated economically by the northern capitalist, emotionally and spiritually it was sustained by the "crusade of the New England schoolmarm."[17]

The schoolmarm and then the Freedman's Bureau were the first shafts of light for southern blacks, and these early luminations slowly gave way to the full day of Reconstruction educational legislation. Education had been denied slaves for so long that "the very feeling of inferiority which slavery forced upon them fathered an intense desire to rise out of their condition by means of education." And given their moment of power during Reconstruction, they did so. Beginning with war refugees and continuing through philanthropic societies, the bureau, and the black initiatives of the various state legislatures, Du Bois chronicles the growth of Negro schooling in the South. Because his focus is on the agency of blacks in the process, his emphasis is less on the experiences of students and teachers during all this than on the politics, a politics conducted largely by black legislatures. In South Carolina, for example, the Reconstruction government replaced laws prohibiting education of blacks with the first ever laws compelling common school education for all children by taxation. Readers familiar with standard progressivist educational history will not be surprised at Du Bois's portrayal of these trends. When Georgia rescinds and dismantles its Reconstruction school system in 1875, for example, Du Bois glosses, "[T]his was in fact a restoration of education to local reactionary control. . . . Alabama felt the result of this narrow policy for many years." Cubberley could have said it no better.[18]

But several forces threatened the gains made in the Negro legislatures. "First, the schools were built upon military force and outside workers, rather than the community itself." Second, resources were always too few to truly construct a comprehensive system. Finally, the return of home rule signaled what could have been the end. But at just that moment salvation was provided by northern philanthropy, "which at the very beginning of the Negro education movement contributed toward the establishment of Negro colleges. . . . Of the history of this astonishing movement to plant the New England college in the South, and to give the Southern black man a leadership based on scholarship and character, almost nothing has been said. And yet this was the salvation of the South and the Negro. . . . Had it not been for the Negro school and college, the Negro would, to all intents and purposes have been driven back into slavery."[19]

Concerned as he was with making a case for the integrity of the Negro race and its claims to political and social equality, Du Bois's focus is more on the positive contributions of blacks to furthering the cause of their own education and even that of all Americans. That there had been a decline in educational accomplishment since Reconstruction he was of course aware, and some of his sociological data provided evidence for it, but it took the diligent scholarship of a third pioneer of African American educational history, Horace Mann Bond, to carefully document and account for the phenomenon and to use it as a political weapon in the battle for Negro civil rights.

Horace Mann Bond inhabited much the same world as Woodson and Du Bois, being one of the very few highly educated blacks of the early twentieth century. But where Woodson brought to the table the skills of the historian and Du Bois was too much the Renaissance man to limit himself to one methodology, Bond brought the questions, concerns, and intellectual equipment of the confirmed social scientist. All three were acquainted with progressivism, inclined to apologetics, interested in race uplift, and attuned to the scholarly discourse of their profession. But where Woodson told a narrative based on literary sources and Du Bois offered either obscure scholarship or rhetorical bombshells, Bond gave a subtle analysis based on quantification and a keen awareness of the ideas current among educational professionals.[20]

Bond was born in 1904 into one of the South's most prominent African American families. After studies at Lincoln University, he received his Ph.D. from the University of Chicago in 1936. His life was marked by an inner tension between the desire to do first-order scholarship and the sense of administrative duty he felt to the black institutions. After serving in numerous teaching and administrative positions, he became the head of Fisk University's department of education in 1937 and eventually rose to become president of Lincoln and finally dean of the school of education at Atlanta University in 1957, a position he held until he left in 1966 to direct the Atlanta University Bureau of Educational and Social Research. Bond's prominent positions in schools of education must be kept in mind to fully appreciate his intentions in his most important work of educational history, *The Education of the Negro in the American Social Order*.[21]

The book was first written during the Depression, in the context of increasing political radicalism and an increased emphasis on the economic interpretation of history. As such it contains a social-forces perspective that very closely resembles the sort of rhetoric one might have read at the time in the progressive journal the *Social Frontier*:

> The intense shock of the change which is taking place has dislocated the entire structure of our life, because invention in labor-saving devices has outrun the

capacity or willingness of men to make changes of corresponding importance in the mechanism of government and social organization.

One wonders whether he might not have had George Counts's tracts on his desk as he wrote, "Strictly speaking, the school has never built a new social order; it has been the product and interpreter of the existing system." As the social frontiersts were wont to do, Bond calls for a cadre of experts who understand the times to lead the way in fashioning a new school that is sensitive to the cardinal principles of our new social world and is prepared to engage in the task of fostering a new type of education appropriate to it.[22]

Thus Bond skillfully maneuvers his way into the mainstream of progressivist educational historiography, where the rise and triumph of the modern bureaucratic public school is gospel truth. But Bond, like Woodson and Du Bois before him, embraces this tradition primarily to include the advance of Negro institutions as another mark of educational progress. From this standpoint he is able to accept the broad consensus view while at the same time praising Reconstruction reform efforts and condemning Redemption reversals. Appropriation leads to subversion as he argues that current inequalities are inconsistent with the goals of public education, that a truly progressive educational system would provide more equitable funding and more humane facilities for its Negro children.[23]

Bond's strategy does lead him into an occasional inconsistency of his own, however, and this must be understood to properly interpret his work. Horace Mann Bond was always by disposition an integrationist, a mild-mannered scholar, and a gentleman. The economic analysis he embraced was an acquired taste for him, employed more as an argumentative strategy than as a foundational premise of history. This point must be understood if we are to appreciate his panegyric to Booker T. Washington, in which, despite an awareness that industrial education "left the Negro farmer and worker largely helpless in the face of technology and agricultural overproduction" he cannot find fault with the man or his labors. Similarly, Bond is quite positive in his appraisal of northern philanthropy, though again the economic analysis occasionally rears its head to check the account. One can almost discern in the book an internal tension between the Bond whose disposition was Washingtonian and the Bond whose intellect was, perhaps regretfully, persuaded by Du Bois's analysis.[24]

In 1933, Carter Woodson published a collection of essays he had been writing over a period of years criticizing Negro higher and professional education titled *The Mis-education of the Negro*. The book is difficult to categorize from our perspective today because of its odd mixture of critiques. In the book Woodson assumes many voices: the elite professional, criticizing the low caliber of work done in the Negro colleges; the Garveyite nationalist, condemning the Eurocentric curriculum and inattention to Africa; and the Bookerite, claiming that the colleges are not nearly so successful as are the industrial schools at preparing black leaders and promoting racial uplift. This confusion is perhaps one reason why Woodson can be read selectively and appropriated for almost any racial agenda one might propound. But for Bond the book was easily interpreted: "The material should never have become a book."[25]

What Bond objected to beyond the factual inaccuracies and logical inconsistencies was the heated rhetoric of the text, the tendency toward polemic, jarring to the refined sensibilities that Bond's own life and work displayed. For Bond it was silly to criticize the educated Negro, for that sort was the only element among Negroes who could demonstrate the potential of Africans for civilization and moral assimilation. This perspective is clearly expressed in the retrospective Bond offered in the 1965 revision of his *Education of the Negro in the American Social Order*:

> An analysis of the background of distinguished Negroes is astonishing in revealing the substantial number who, largely by chance, were extracted from their original culture-slave or "free"—and reared in the disciplined regimen of a standard, or above-standard, American cultural family pattern. . . . The process of acculturation is accelerated by formal, systematic education. As this book indicated thirty years ago, any efforts to acculturate the African, who became the American Negro, were limited up to the time of emancipation to sporadic and exceptional labors with the small free portions of this population, and to individuals.

Whatever we may make of these opinions today, Bond must be understood as one of the finest expositors and representatives of the integrationist ideal in black life and thought. This is how we ought to read his *Education of the Negro in the American Social Order*, with its steady flow of irrefutable evidence concerning the "savage inequalities" in funding between black and white schools. Bond, in good liberal fashion, is appealing to the conscience of white America, forcing it to observe the decline in schooling opportunities for black Americans in the hopes that something may be done. After reading Bond, educators would think twice before resorting to comfortable clichés or easy biological explanations of inferior performance.[26]

Although by 1960 most mainstream historians had not come to terms with the evidence and arguments of African American educational historians, subsequent generations of historians would. Methodologically and ideologically, the trailblazers of black educational historiography have had an influence on contemporary historians that outweighs Cubberleyan institutionalism and rivals Bailynesque culturalism. Good institutional histories are of course still produced and fine culturalist texts are commonplace, but much of the dynamic work of recent years has been dominated by concerns of race, concerns that were first addressed in the largely educational history of Woodson, Du Bois, and Bond. From Louis Harlan's Bond-inspired *Separate and Unequal* to James D. Anderson's Duboisian *Education of Blacks in the South* to Vanessa Siddle Walker's Woodsonesque use of sources and celebration of black achievement in *Their Highest Potential*, much of the best educational history of the past forty years has realized the agenda of these men who were largely ignored in their own day.[27]

THE FLOWERING OF WOMEN'S EDUCATIONAL HISTORIOGRAPHY

In 1960 only the most prescient could have forecast the flood of work that was to come in African American educational history, but that same year saw the death of the unquestioned master of the already well established field of women's educational history, Thomas Woody. By that time, in notable contrast to the output of the black pioneers, Woody's magnificent *History of Women's Education in the United States* had become a classic work, cited as the essential authority on its subject and the only complete treatment in existence. As late as 1989, Maxine Schwartz Seller could say that Woody's project "remains the authoritative, indeed the only, comprehensive survey of the history of women's education in the United States."[28]

Woody's work was in one sense both behind and ahead of its time. Winifred Wandersee's study of women's attitudes toward work between the world wars has shown that the feminist movement of this time failed to appeal to women who refused to sacrifice family concerns to their own autonomy. That women worked in greater and greater numbers during these decades was more the result of their wish for an increased standard of living for their families than of any desire for personal fulfillment in an expanded sphere. Particularly after the Depression, most women embraced the domestic sphere and tended to resist academicist training. In a survey from the latter half of the 1940s, Margaret Mead found that among student teachers, "most of the expressed wishes are for . . . practice in home-making, in child care, in public speaking, in teaching live children rather than merely learning the history of education out of a book." Woody's volumes, in contrast, breathe the spirit of bookishness and of early feminism as they celebrate with intense documentation the emancipation of women from their traditional roles as wives and mothers through the agency of education. Thus he is the most capable spokesperson for what we will call the *liberationist* perspective in women's educational historiography.[29]

But though Woody's book is the most complete account, it was not without predecessors. One historian whose work was similar to Woody's both in thesis and in tone was Willystine Goodsell. Goodsell was an archetypal Teachers College progressive: all her postsecondary education was obtained there; her dissertation, "The Conflict of Naturalism and Humanism," was written under John Dewey; and she herself taught at Teachers College for thirty-one years. Yet despite her many celebrated works, at her retirement in 1936 her rank remained that of associate professor. In addition to engaging in her educational work Goodsell was active in other progressive causes: she was a member of the American Civil Liberties Union and the Foreign Policy Association and director of the American Eugenics Society and the Euthanasia Society of America. In 1915 she published her magnum opus, *A History of the Family as a Social and Educational Institution*, in which she chronicled her subject from the earliest "primitive family" through its "patriarchal" incarnation among the Hebrews, Greeks, and Romans and, taking account of medieval developments, culminated with the modern West, particularly the English family of the seventeenth and eighteenth centuries. All 340 pages of this global history, however, were mere prolegomena for her treatment of the American family, and it was in the context of Western civilization's family history that she presented the same basic outline of women's educational history that Woody was to canonize fifteen years later.[30]

Goodsell made three basic points in her history, each of which became the standard view in successive feminist educational histories. The first was that "the improvement in the status of women . . . has been synchronous with their higher education." Woman's educational progress made possible her political and social advances. The second was that the Revolutionary War marked a great divide between the bleak outlook for women during the colonial period and the brighter day when "public opinion began to change." The third described the path that progress took, from the shallow finishing school, through the intermediate female seminary, to—ultimately, after the criticisms and labors of Emma Willard, Catharine Beecher, and Mary Lyon— normal schools and colleges. Throughout this development runs the theme of gradual emancipation from a narrow domestic sphere to increased autonomy. "No longer confined, with almost religious strictness, to the confines of home, church and neighborhood," women at last were able to take "an active part in movements for social betterment."[31]

In her 1923 work, *The Education of Women*, Goodsell repeated and augmented her claims. We read again of the growth from the "spineless" finishing schools, turning out their "deplorably deficient" products, to the "new liberal education for woman which should make them not only more intelligent wives and mothers but more skillful teachers in the rapidly growing schools." We learn of the careers of Willard, Beecher, and Lyon, who laid the foundations on which "other far sighted women" such as Alice Freeman Palmer and Ellen Richards built quality higher education for women.

The growth of coeducation and women's colleges after the Civil War provides evidence of just "how far modern nations have advanced beyond the age when women's realm was everywhere believed to lie solely in the domestic circle."[32]

As a final contribution, Goodsell edited and introduced some of the most important writings of Willard, Beecher, and Lyon in *Pioneers of Women's Education in the United States*, a title that reflected her view of these three women. In this, as in the other works, her stress was on the progress attained in the movement away from either the complete neglect or the misdirection of female education through the "showy accomplishments" and "lamentable lack of sound instruction" of the finishing school toward the more rigorous, scientific higher education of the modern woman freed from her narrow domestic sphere.[33]

Thus the general contours of an interpretation had been laid, and Thomas Woody followed them precisely. Woody's biographer, Thomas Francis McHugh, has documented his extensive correspondence with Goodsell from his project's inception to its final publication, and Goodsell's spirit infuses its pages. "If we were not such literalists," asserted Woody of his book's title, "it might be called a history of women's emancipation in the United States." And so it was. In two volumes of rich research and capable organization, Woody demonstrates progress from "the extremely narrow spirit," "the harsh theology that quickly disposed of childhood," and "the decidedly unfavorable" attitude of the Puritans toward women's intellectual training to the sunny "New Concept of women's education" that rose in cities where instructors, "free from the hampering restraint of the church, the town 'prudentials' and the heavy hand of tradition" began to offer to women an education that went beyond the finishing school. A great cloud of witnesses, including such luminaries as Benjamin Rush, DeWitt Clinton, Willard, Beecher, Lyon, and Thomas Gallaudet are called on to demonstrate the triumph of the "New Concept" theory, while hundreds of pages are devoted to its institutional embodiment in the female academies and seminaries, which paved the way for the greater accomplishments of normal schools, women's colleges and professional schools, and most especially, the coeducation of public schools and universities. Thus was canonized Goodsell's basic account, and all subsequent historians who bothered to treat the subject at all, schoolmen or not, followed it.[34]

Throughout his text, Woody is at pains to demonstrate how critical was the role of education in the political gains that women had made by the 1920s. "Though political emancipation is the great symbol of women's victory," he wrote, "their intellectual emancipation, because of its priority and fundamental character, was of vaster significance." This thesis of intellectual emancipation is the unifying theme of his work, providing the plot line that makes sense of the astonishing array of institutions, personalities, theories, and arguments he presents. It also provides us with an explanation of why the old Whig view of the rise and triumph of the public school has had such staying power in the twentieth century: if Woody was right to connect political advancement with the extension of schooling to women and especially to their role as teachers, then a negative appraisal of the rise of schools necessarily condemns the political advances women have made. Feminist and educationist history thus united must rise or fall together.[35]

The tone Woody set and the thesis he developed have to this day remained orthodox. Like authors of much subsequent feminist historiography, Woody did not shy from valuative statements. As he wended his way through the developments of three hundred years of history, he was quick to point out which trends were "causing a negative" and which "a positive acceleration." As social developments since the 1930s have largely popularized his convictions, few have been the voices to rise up and censure him for taking history from the domain of description to that of judgment. Although elements of his account have been challenged, his skillful equation of education with liberation has had remarkable staying power, and it is the chief attribute that unites both his sort of educational history and that of a group of female historians who in other ways were so unlike him.[36]

Goodsell and Woody wrote educational history in the style of the professional educator: richly grounded in a rise-of-Western-civilization context, heavily dependent on mountains of primary source documentation, predictable in its plotline, and logically organized and clearly written but without style or humor. The first half of the twentieth century saw the flowering of another sort of educational history, one that is remarkable not so much for its content—for it largely kept to the liberationist interpretive position articulated by Goodsell and developed by Woody—as for its style, which was reminiscent of the literary feminism of the Victorian era. Whereas Woodsell and Woody were modern professionals, these authors maintained a rather feminine style.

In 1946, Viola Klein summarized the traits that the twentieth century seemed to ascribe to feminine character: "[P]assivity, emotionality, lack of abstract interests, greater intensity of personal relationships, and an instinctive tenderness for babies." The "feminine" style, then, is sentimental. It is concerned less with ideas and institutions than with people's lives, especially their emotional lives. In the first half of the twentieth century, several women writers joined the rush to produce textbooks for the thousands of captive readers in history of education courses around the nation. To distinguish their works from the many others available, they appealed to the reader's sentiment. No short quotations can do full justice to the engaging reading that such an approach provides, especially when it is contrasted with the dry prose of so many of these writers' competitors, but a few examples may at least offer a hint of what these women were about.[37]

Luella Cole was concerned that most textbook histories of education "lack liveliness and reality." The typical textbook, she complained, "is not primarily about people; it is about ideas, trends, movements." Seeking to correct this misplaced emphasis, she produced a book that "undergraduates can read and will want to read." Rather than chronicle the growth of school systems or the development of progressive philosophy, Cole tells the life stories of "twenty-two men and one woman," subtly weaving the facts of educational history into the narrative as a mother might sneak medicine into corn syrup. Here is just a sample of her technique, from her treatment of the life of Friedrich Froebel:

> Froebel worked tirelessly, in a glow of almost fanatic enthusiasm about his new undertaking. . . . Even the death of his wife, although a great blow to him, did not prevent him from developing his first little group of children into a school of some fifty preschool youngsters who ranged in age from one to seven. He now felt himself ready to advertise his new type of school, but he wanted a really good name for it. Up to this point he had used the descriptive but clumsy title, *Kleinkinderbeschäftigungsanstalt*—literally, an institution where small children are occupied—but this name was apparently too much even for a German. One day as he was taking a walk with Middendorf, the right word came to him. "Eureka," he cried, "I have found it! KINDERGARTEN it shall be called."[38]

Agnes Benedict's *Progress toward Freedom* is another example of a work in this genre. Her prose is popular, more like that of the historical fiction of the day than of the textbooks of the schoolmen. But the content is all Whiggery. The old colonial schools are bleak prisons for the few children rich enough to pay for them. The colonial master is of course a sadist, as this excerpt illustrates:

> Suddenly there is a shrill titter. The Master unfolds his long form and strides across the floor. Like a fury he descends on the boys and comes back dragging small William by the ear. In the other hand is a heavy, wicked-looking rawhide whip. For several minutes there is no sound but raining blows, the Master's quick breathing, and a low whimper. Holding his shoulder, his face contorted, William goes slowly back to his seat. The room is very still now. The Master, his face red, resumes his seat.

But after three hundred years of educational progress, the scene has changed dramatically:

> Johnny's eyes are shining; he is whistling softly, his walk is quick and purposeful. . . . he grins a hasty "good morning" to Miss Baily before he pulls off his

sweater and drags his chair over to the corner where the others have brought theirs. In the center of the group, on a larger chair, smiling down at the eager faces, sits Miss Baily. Teacher? Smocked and short-haired, it is hard to tell Miss Baily's age. Johnny calls her, outside of school, a "good guy." He says, "You know she'll be fair." Her eyes, like the children's are bright and eager. She is an adventurer with them.[39]

Historian Ann Douglas classically argued that in the nineteenth century, Calvinism was defeated in America not by a vigorous Romanticism but by an "anti-intellectual sentimentalism" whose spirit lives on in twentieth-century mass culture:

> The triumph of the "feminizing," sentimental forces that would generate mass culture redefined and perhaps limited the possibilities for change in American society. Sentimentalism, with its tendency to obfuscate the visible dynamics of development, heralded the cultural sprawl that has increasingly characterized post-Victorian life.

If Douglas is right, then our feminine authors present us with a profound irony. Most of them were avid followers of the philosopher John Dewey. As Agnes Benedict proclaimed, "It is because of John Dewey that this book has been written. He has made the story of American education one of progress toward freedom." The irony is that the style itself, by turning the student's attention from the structural "foundations" of education to the sentimental lives of educational reformers, may have defanged the very progressivism that these authors celebrated.[40]

Sentimental textbooks aside, women produced a number of more scholarly contributions to the profession. Most of them took approaches that had not been previously considered by male historians. Eleanor Wolf Thompson examined antebellum women's magazines for evidence regarding popular attitudes toward female education. Vera M. Butler did the same for early New England newspapers. Monica Kiefer studied colonial children's books to get at social attitudes toward children and their education. Angie Burt Bowden searched through scrapbooks and talked to old-timers to provide a county-by-county history titled *Early Schools of Washington Territory*. Marion M. Thompson Wright, the first African American woman to complete doctoral training in educational history, produced a detailed community study, *Education of Negroes in New Jersey*. Lillian G. Dabney, a second black Ph.D., did the same in her *Negroes in the District of Columbia*. And Jeanne Noble produced a laudable synthesis of these and other studies on African American women titled *The Negro Woman's College Education*. What is of interest in these books is not so much the conclusions reached in the research, for it was typically that of the reigning progressive orthodoxy of the day. What is of note is the fact that women in this period began to write sophisticated historical monographs evidencing tedious work in previously untapped sources, and that their presence and products tended to shift attention from institutional and intellectual history to social history. Usually they did not use their material to challenge received opinion, but rather to enrich it by integrating into standard accounts the experiences of women and children.[41]

THE WHIG INTERPRETATION UNDER FIRE

The contributions of African American men and of women scholars, black and white, to educational historiography in the first half of the twentieth century were rich and influential. But because of the association both groups made between schooling and the advancement of their cause, their work tended to reinforce the prevailing Whig interpretation of history that had long dominated the profession. The only evil in the rise and triumph of formal public education was that vast sectors of the population had been excluded from its bounties. The struggle of these groups for access into the white man's systems could only be written as a narrative of ascent, and that narrative, as backdrop, assumed the Whig view of the institutions themselves.

But there were other forces abroad adding to the diversity of interpretations, and this diversity often reflected controversies of the times. Educational historiography was not unaffected by challenges in the wake of war to Germanic tendencies in American institutional life. Nor was it spared in the challenge to public schooling's hegemony by an increasingly competent and self-confident parochial system. In both cases the historiography of American education was for the first time given an alternative interpretation that told a tale not of linear "progress to freedom" but of a betrayal of cherished American ideals by sympathizers of Prussian statism.

At first blush, Charles Hubbard Judd seems a strange candidate to spearhead an assault on the Prussianization of American schooling by historical argumentation. He was an empiricist's empiricist, having studied with Wilhelm Wundt at Leipzig and pioneered experimentation in educational psychology. When he succeeded John Dewey as the dean of the School of Education at the University of Chicago in 1909, one of his first activities was to abolish the introductory history of education class and replace it with a topical course quite similar to the course in educational foundations later worked out at Teachers College. His tenure at Chicago is best remembered as the transition from Dewey's style—encouraging highly permeable boundaries and collaboration between teachers and researchers—to his own highly professional style of pure research and specialization. Historian Ellen Lagemann describes the change: "Whereas communication among the members of the Dewey circle had resonated with overlapping and shared professional and personal interests, communication between Judd and his colleagues bespoke a cool, impersonal, sleek, efficient organization." During and after World War I, Judd was a leading practitioner and champion of the measurement-and-survey movement in educational research, and he clearly evidenced in his publications and administrative decisions an antipathy toward the professional advancement of women as well as certain "hereditarian and racial determinist attitudes."[42]

But Judd was no Prussophile. Although he was an orthodox Wundtian and strong advocate of the research model of higher education, in many ways he despised the German character. His experience in Leipzig was one of loneliness and insecurity, and he blamed German aristocracy:

> I never became adjusted to German life or to the Germans. . . . The formality of the intercourse between German students was something against which my democratic training in America made me recoil most violently, and the snobbish attitude of most of the people whom I met seemed to me intolerable.

While at Leipzig, Judd took his second minor in the history of pedagogy under Johannes Immanuel Volkelt, largely because of the unspoken "privilege of taking one easy minor." Later, as a young professor of psychology and pedagogy at the University of Cincinnati, Judd regretted having cribbed the course and prepared for his lectures in the history of education with "two months of arduous labor. . . . I read the history of education all day for two months and learned much that was entirely new to me."[43]

Judd traced the German snobbery he so despised to the dual system of German education, where the common people attended the *Volksschule* and the aristocrats the *Gymnasium*. The evil of this scheme is a persistent theme in his works, from his 1914 essay in *School Review* to his 1940 book, *The American Educational System*. Judd was also, like many of his day, itching for reform of the elementary school by shortening its duration from eight to six years and by creating an institution that would smooth transition to the high school. By 1918 he had found a way of putting these two preoccupations together, and the war with Germany provided a public forum for his remarkable idea.[44]

In April 1918, Judd published in the progressive, widely read *New Republic* a fascinating historical argument for the necessity of creating junior high schools. In the process he produced one of the first accounts ever to challenge the Whig view of educational history, which had dominated the field since Carter, Burton, and Barnard. In just three pages he presents the outlines of a comprehensive interpretation of American educational history that shakes the Whig view to its core.

In the seventeenth century, claims Judd, the colonists imported from Europe a dual system of education created for an aristocratic society: there were free common schools for the poor to teach them rudimentary things and fine grammar schools to teach the well-to-do the higher branches they would need at the colleges. But gloriously, with the Revolution came a democratic spirit that altered America's educational landscape to give us "that unique creation of democratic enthusiasm for the spread of learning—the American academy," which "taught all . . . subjects to the sons and daughters of the humblest homes. Popular education was under way on a scale never attempted in Europe. The district school did what it could and the academy took up the task wherever the district school laid it down."[45]

All was going well and a democratic evolution was under way when a group of reformers, understandably concerned with the rather desultory and haphazard education that resulted from such a decentralized system, unfortunately looked to Prussia for solutions. These men imported into our free land the German *Volksschule*:

> It is one of the curious ironies of history that American educational leaders in the middle of the last century were so intent upon getting something for the common people that they borrowed one of the most potent devices of aristocracy for the suppression of the common people.

Although the reformers were successful in implementing the oppressive elementary school with its eight-year program of rudimentary learning designed to keep common people in their place, thankfully, "the district school and the academy had so firmly established the principle that a common boy and girl can go on with higher training that the *Volksschule* did not succeed in forcing on this country a dual school system." The academy became in time the high school, and all that is needed now to overcome our sad inheritance is to "get rid of an eight-year, rudimentary, vernacular school. . . . In this way we shall get what the district school and the academy started to give us before we were allured from the path of democracy by the enticements of Prussian organization."[46]

The year 1918 was a prolific one for Charles Judd. In addition to the April *New Republic* article, he produced in June a number of the *University of Chicago War Papers* called "Democracy and American Schools" which repeats exactly the argument that elements of undemocratic education such as the eight-year elementary school are "remnants of European influence," imported "during the decade between 1840 and 1850, when . . . American educational leaders were greatly influenced by the Prussian *Volksschule*." Before the June article appeared, his book-length treatment of these themes was published as *Evolution of a Democratic School System*, the fullest expression of Judd's revisionism:

> The prospects of advance toward a strictly democratic educational system were bright as a result of the growth, in the early years of the nineteenth century, of the American academy and of the district school. But in the midst of this advance, in the middle of the last century our leaders carried us back toward medievalism by borrowing from the least democratic nation in Europe one of its fundamental institutions. They brought to America the Prussian common school.

In this volume, resurrecting Carter's declension thesis, Judd allows that since after the Revolution schools "sank to a lower ebb than ever before," something needed to be done. The reformers should have "worked out an American institution" rather than "accept the European model." But to our great fortune, the legacy of the academy lives on in the public high school. If we can simply implement a "new institution," which he here calls the junior high school, we can "cure the breach between elementary schools and high schools." A final 1918 publication, Judd's textbook *Introduction to the Scientific Study of Education*, again rehearsed this argument in the small section it devoted to historical matters.[47]

It was a glorious campaign. Capitalizing on nativist sentiment that was at fever pitch because of the war effort, Judd was able to connect his desired reform to democratic anti-Germanism. Having long before learned the lesson that "a manuscript must be prepared for readers, not for the satisfaction of the author," Judd successfully offered his message to a broad, influential middlebrow audience in the *New Republic*, to patriots eager for academic support in the *War Papers*, and to the captive audience of future teachers in his textbooks. The reader would likely forget the particulars of the historical argument but come away with the distinct impression that to be for the junior high was to be for American democracy. Subsequent events proved Judd and his allies successful as various incarnations of the junior high were adopted in state after state.

But there was one sort of reader who would not forget the historical particulars; and for the professional educational historians who had made a career declaiming on the glories of Horace Mann and his reforms, this new account came as a shock and an affront that must be rebutted. No less a figure than Paul Monroe rose to the challenge, and his refutation was published in June of 1918 in *School and Society* just as Judd's third front was advancing via the *War Papers*. It should be noted that Judd and Monroe shared many traits common to an early twentieth century educationist, though they were institutionally affiliated with rival schools. Both were religiously committed to empirical methods, honoring facts as reverently as their parents had honored Bible verses. Both were convinced of the necessity of reforming the elementary school along lines suggested by advocates of the junior high. Both had pursued advanced study at German universities and were committed to professionalism through the development of academic disciplines and the prosecution of original research. That they shared so much makes their debate a fascinating example of the human passions that empiricism can often only thinly veil.

Monroe begins his attack by aiming straight for the jugular of scientific method:

> There are many reformers who will seek aid to their reform from the conditions brought about by the Great War, but no assistance of permanent value can be achieved by a distortion of the facts or by arousing prejudice based on misinformation. . . . A refutation is needed both to protect a desirable educational reform from the charge that it is founded on prejudice, which is without basis in fact, and to vindicate the claims of early American democracy to one of its finest products, a universal public school system.

From there he makes the long familiar case that the "great educational movement" of the nineteenth century was not the fruit of Prussian autocracy but was "the first genuine expression of American democracy in education." He shows from many of the same sources cited by Judd that the common school reformers appropriated only select elements of the Prussian system—teacher training, age-based grading, small class size—rather than Judd's pernicious eight-year program, which Monroe claims was a later development. And as for the academy, it would be "far easier to show" that it "was really an imitation of an institution previously existing in aristocratic European societies. . . . It was the popular demand for an institution responsive to the public needs, under public control, and open to all because supported by public funds, that led to the replacing of the academy by the high school." In a final flourish, Monroe agrees with Judd about the propriety of a reform, adding that one argument for doing so is that the step has already been taken "by the leading European countries, including Germany."[48]

In just two weeks, Judd was back with a response to what he considered Monroe's "quite dogmatic" "caustic statements" and "paragraphs of invective." His evidence does little to counter Monroe's rehabilitation of the reformers, as he is evidently content that to merely establish an association with Prussia is to prove culpability. But regarding the academy, he scores a serious blow, quoting from Monroe's own *Cyclopedia* a clear description of the democratic nature of the early American academy. To this response Monroe offered a final volley in which he takes his own personal swipes at Judd as well as reaffirms his position, closing powerfully:

> I do quite disagree with Dr. Judd by holding that the early nineteenth century German influence on American education was good and not evil, and submit that to substantiate his general position he will have to prove that the training

of teachers, the systematizing and psychologizing of school method, the compulsory attendance of pupils, the supervision of instruction, government support through taxation, the abolition of corporal punishment, and the enrichment of the curriculum are evils.[49]

Judd evidently felt no compulsion to respond, and thus the controversy ended without resolution. Monroe continued for decades to publish detailed histories of American education in the Whig tradition and Judd continued to recapitulate his own position in a number of introductory textbooks intended for the course he initiated as a replacement for the History of Education course at Chicago. One might be tempted to think that, given the lack of change in the accounts that leading educational historians presented, Judd's revision had had little impact and Monroe's rebuttals had won the day, but this is not the case. Judd's position may or may not have been scientifically tenable, but he had done the better job marketing his view than Monroe had done of his. While the professional educator would probably have followed the Judd-Monroe controversy to its conclusion, the informed layperson would have stopped at the *New Republic* article and never read Monroe's rebuttal, tucked away in an educationist journal. As we shall see, Judd's interpretation was to find fertile ground when a second world war made the Germanic origins of state education increasingly suspicious and when a maturing immigrant population began to flex its intellectual muscle by taking on one of America's most hallowed institutions. Judd himself, racialist that he was, would doubtless have been surprised to hear his own side of the debate taken up by a bevy of Catholics and Jews, but so it was.

In the twentieth century, public debates over the role of church and state in schools loomed large. In the 1920s, the United States Supreme Court began a trajectory that culminated in the 1947 *Everson v. Board of Education* decision, which held that the Fourteenth Amendment to the Constitution extended the First Amendment's establishment clause to the state and local levels of government. Thus the Court took upon itself responsibility for adjudicating local church-state conflicts in schools, and their guiding principle was a strict separationism that required absolute neutrality on the part of the state, thus in theory prohibiting not only preferential support of religion but nondiscriminatory support as well. Yet the specific judgments often seemed to contradict the broad principles enunciated, confounding commentators, confusing the public, and generally causing much analytical ink to be spilled. The 1948 *McCollum v. Board of Education* and 1952 *Zorach v. Clauson* decisions, taken together, allowed release-time religious instruction as long as it was given off of school property. The *Everson* decision itself upheld the common practice of offering state aid for textbooks and transportation to parochial schools. Particularly in the *Everson* and

McCollum cases, the Court's opinions hinged on historical arguments that were, at the very least, highly debatable.[50]

At the same time, it was becoming clear that the civic sphere was warming to religious influences. Efforts such as those in Michigan and Oregon to require all children to attend public schools were squelched by the Supreme Court's verdict in *Pierce v. Society of Sisters* in 1925. By 1939, the growing concern over fascist and communist totalitarianisms led many to call for a return to the religious values undergirding Western civilization. Participants in the White House Conference on Children in a Democracy, for example, were adamant that something had to be done to foster religious life in the schools:

> Practical steps should be taken to make available to children and youth through education the resources of religion as an important factor in the democratic way of life and in the development of personal and social integrity. To this end the Conference recommends that a critical and comprehensive study be made of the various experiences both of the churches and of the schools in dealing with the problem of religion in relation to public education. The purpose of such a study would be to discover how these phases of education may best be provided for in the total program of education, without in any way violating the principle of the separation of church and state.[51]

Thus was spawned a daunting body of literature analyzing the issues of church and state in schools and arguing particular positions. Authors of many of these works included historical accounts to bolster their arguments, and the profound differences between these histories provide a fascinating study of the social uses to which history is put as well as the most extensive example before the 1960s of conflict in educational historiography. In addition, current events such as these made their mark on young scholars of the day, precipitating an impressive outpouring of serious academic monographs both by Catholics and non-Catholics on the history of religious education in the United States.

The production in the 1920s and 1930s of a significant body of monographic literature on the history of religious education has not been acknowledged by previous accounts of educational historiography during this period, and the oversight has fed into tendencies to view post-1920 historiography as representing a period of stagnation and decline. While it is true that new studies declined at Teachers College as the glory days under Monroe came to an end, a number of historians at Catholic schools and public universities were drawn to educational and religious topics in response to the debates swirling around them. One such study characteristically explained how the choice of subject derived from the recent attempts to make unconstitutional private schools, which are mainly religious ones, in Michigan and Oregon; from the question raised in Tennessee as to the right of a state to prohibit teaching of scientific theories contrary to the religious tenets of the majority; from the court decision in Mt. Vernon, New York, prohibiting the teaching of religion in private religious education schools on school time for school credit; and from recurring attempts in various states to make daily Bible reading compulsory in public schools.[52]

Historical studies were thus made of the relationship between religion and education in various parts of the country and during various time periods. Uniting these seemingly disparate studies is the recurring thesis that the gradual secularization of American public schooling was the result not, as one declared, of "hostility toward religion" generally, but rather of "the prevention of discrimination between denominations." Another concurred: "Since the Mann period the chief problems have concerned the separation of the state from religious education of any type, due to the mutual jealousies of Protestants, Catholics, and Jews." Sadie Bell, in one of the most compelling of these efforts, found that denominational distrust explained the failure of legislation to add religious components to Virginia schools, but the very religiosity of the people had produced a condition whereby education was pervaded "with a strong religious tone" despite the fact that there was no "recognition of that fact in law." What emerges, then, from these works, is a picture of American education that is anything but the steady march toward secularism proclaimed by some and bewailed by others.[53]

But it was not the writers of doctoral dissertations who carried on with Judd's revisionism. A number of popular writers in the 1940s and 1950s, from distinguished clergy and respected religious educators to journalists and laypeople, passionately expressed their concerns about the implications of recent court decisions and offered their own views on the issues. Many of these authors sought in one way or another to connect the current situation to the past, and oftentimes the connection they hit upon was very similar to Judd's perspective. The Georgia Catholic Laymen's Association, for example, created to counter Tom Watson's crusade in Georgia against Catholic schools, knew just where public education came from:

> The State-school idea is not American. It did not originate in our country, but in Prussia, and although greatly modified in its adaptation, nothing can erase the Prussian stamp of its origin.

Liberty Magazine concurred as it spoke out in opposition to the Towner-Sterling Bill, designed to place all schools under a federal department:

It is Prussianism of the old type because before the great war the Prussian Kaiser compelled all children to attend the public schools in the grammar grades, and no denominational elementary schools were permitted in the German empire.

Although not developed into full-blown accounts, these assertions, one from a Catholic and one from a nativist publication, tell us something about shifting popular attitudes regarding the role of the federal government in American life, particularly in the schools.[54]

A number of writers developed this basic orientation into a more sophisticated history of education, and herein lay the controversy. In the wake of a war for the soul of Western civilization there was also a historiographical battle for the soul of America. All parties believed there to be a discernible and worthy American tradition of religious education, but the particulars of that tradition were intensely debated. On one side were Catholic and a few other writers who tended to focus on long-standing religious traditions in schooling and who held to a narrow interpretation of the First Amendment as originally intending to prohibit only the establishment of a particular national church, not indiscriminate aid to religion generally. On the other side were many Protestants and professional educators who held to an expansive interpretation of the First Amendment and saw the history of religion and education as one of gradual progress toward complete separation. Both groups claimed for their perspective the hallowed title of "the American tradition." But they differed sharply over just what that tradition was, and this difference led to profound disagreement over the origins of secular public education. Were public schools a logical development from colonial seeds, as Whig historiography had long asserted, or were they some sort of historical aberration by foreign importation?

The Catholic/libertarian side of the debate was revisionist to the core. "There is no trace," proclaimed John F. Noll, "of the public school in our American foundations. It is not mentioned in our national constitution. . . . It did not exist in the colonies. It did not exist in the States for more than fifty years after the formation of the union." The American tradition has thus always been, in the words of leading Catholic public intellectual John Courtney Murray, one of "accommodation—or, if you will . . . cooperation between church and state." Union Theological Seminary professor Henry P. Van Dusen concurred, sharply spelling out the critical difference between the rival conceptions:

The theory of "a wall of separation between church and state" as currently propounded, far from being a perpetuation of the national tradition, represents a novel innovation in direct contradiction to the conviction of our forebears and the established habits of the nation.[55]

Perhaps the greatest articulation of this version of "the American tradition" came from the pen of Marxist-turned-Conservative-Jew Will Herberg.
For Herberg, America's educational history is the tale of a conflict between
two rival traditions of thought. The first, the Anglo-American tradition, is
premised on subsidiarity—parents and other local agents in the past delegated
to the state what had become too big a job for them to do by themselves,
and hence they retain "their original *prior* right to educate their children."
The second, the Continental tradition, assumes that education is an "intrin-
sic activity of the state, designed primarily to inculcate a common doctrine
and create a uniform mentality." The origins of our school system were Anglo-
American, but in periods of heavy immigration the Continental tradition has
flowered, because "the public school was expected to make Americans out
of the children of immigrants." The most egregious example of this came when
certain states sought to abolish private religious education altogether. "Inspired by the Continental idea of the teaching state," these well-intentioned
but totalitarian movements "were trying to remake American public education in its image." The *Pierce* decision, however, put a stop to this and reas-
serted the American tradition:

> The old American doctrine that the "rearing and education" of children is the
> prerogative of the parents, who have a prior right as against the state. . . . This
> is the American philosophy of public education.[56]

The obvious policy implication for this view is a gradual move toward
a pluralization of the sort of schooling considered public through the extension of funding to parochial schools, and some variation on this theme usually
followed the historical introduction in these writers. Clearly, those interested
in bucking up the existing system of monopolistic, secular state schooling
would have to come up with an American tradition of their own.

As might be expected, the public school had its share of defenders, most
of them grounded on the bedrock premise that, in the words of religious
historian Conrad Henry Moehlman, "public education has become the greatest achievement of the United States, and has always remained true to the
American tradition." The American tradition, for these people, is best found
not in the religious traditions of the early settlers or the masses, but in the
"radicalism of the first amendment." R. Freeman Butts of Teachers College
fleshed out this tradition, which begins not in the colonies, but at the nation's
founding:

> The historic principle of separation of church and state as defined in 175 years
> of American history is a desirable tradition to maintain in American educa-
> tion. . . . Far from being a perversion of the original meaning of separation,
> the principle enunciated in the Everson case is the logical culmination of the

authentic historical tradition of the principle of separation of church and state as it has developed from 1776 to the present time.[57]

There were two basic lines of defense that had to be taken by friends of the public school. The first concerned the claim of Prussianization. Whereas critics seeking to make a historical case for government aid of religious instruction stressed the novelty of the experiment with public education and its genesis in a nondemocratic political context, these defenders maintained a continuity thesis. Vivian T. Thayer, for example, rehearsed the familiar Whig view that "[i]n the past two hundred years the American people have evolved a unique institution expressive of the best in American life. This institution is the American public school." For her, the common school movement was no foreign import, but the culmination of a natural evolution from the "meager beginnings" of colonial religious instruction through the expanding civic and economic impulses that gave rise to academies and on to the nonsectarian Protestant schools that flowered into the secular public education of the present time. Throughout this "evolution of moral education from sectarianism into non-sectarianism and from non-sectarianism into secularism" there was no "loss of interest in the moral training of the young" and hence we need not return to an explicitly religious form of schooling.[58]

The second line of defense concerned origins. Critics such as Herberg and Noll had held that the church and the family were first in the field, that they had delegated to the state a role in schooling and hence maintained a prior right to the training of the young. Freeman Butts countered by appealing to the old New England school laws:

> From the very beginning of the American colonies education was one of the powers and rights of political sovereignty. . . . Teachers were given licenses by governors, legislatures, and town governments. . . . parents were *not* free to let their children go uneducated and . . . government had the right to set up schools or exert its authority to provide the education that would protect the state from mischief. . . . Private schools as we think of them today in America, controlled by private corporations or by religious bodies, were *not* first in the field, but generally appeared about 100 years after town schools and governmentally licensed teachers were in the field.

It is therefore Herberg's "Continental" tradition that turns out to be the real American tradition for defenders such as Butts and Thayer. The state has the prior right to education, and the nation's founding documents require an absolute separation between church and state in schooling. In this view, any and all forms of state aid to religions instruction are unconstitutional and a threat to the American tradition.[59]

So for the first time in the history of American educational historiography, two incommensurable accounts of the origins and trajectory of American public education were developed, and those whose task it was to adjudicate for a broad audience between the two rival interpretations had a difficult time of it. A fascinating example of waffling between the two views occurs in Lewis Paul Todd and Merle Curti's successful textbook, *The Rise of the American Nation*. In the edition that was marketed to public schools, we find this passage:

> The town schools of colonial New England have been rightly regarded as one of America's greatest contributions to modern civilization—public responsibility for education of all the people. And free public education, paid for through government, has been—and is—one of the strongest roots of democracy.

Yet in the John Carroll edition of this text, intended for use in Catholic schools, the final sentence of the passage reads thus: "And education, public or private, however paid for, has been and remains essential to our society and one of democracy's strongest roots." It was not clear by 1960 whether a secular, state-sponsored public system or an entrepreneurial, pluralistic private system was the authentic American way, and with the epochal 1962 *Engel v. Vitale* and 1963 *Abington v. Schempp* decisions, banning, respectively, school prayer and Bible readings from the public schools, the debate would only grow more intense.[60]

This controversy, unlike the more full-blown revisionist debate that was to take the discipline by storm in the late 1960s and 1970s, was largely one between professional educators and their critics from outside who, in the words of William Clayton Bower, recognized that "changes in the past half-century . . . require that the problem shall be re-examined in the light of both the contemporary American and the international situation." What Bower and others outside the professional school of education realized, and what educationist defenders failed to understand, was that the intellectual climate of post–World War II America was far different from the one that had nurtured public education in the past. In a world that had witnessed atomic destruction and death camps, it was increasingly difficult to proclaim a cheery faith in progress through scientific method and pragmatism. The spat over the development of secular education was merely the first volley of what would eventually become a full-scale war against the Whig interpretation of educational history.[61]

Why Bailyn Was Right
Despite Being Wrong

Once we knew that it was possible for a people to destroy the enemy, themselves, and all bystanders, the world itself was changed. And no sentence written with that knowledge of man's new capacity could be meshed into any sentence written the week before.

—Margaret Mead

In 1956, Archibald Anderson worried that just as in the past "the History of Education" had "lost its once dominant position in the teacher-training program by being smug and non-progressive," so today "it may do so again." This statement, so out of touch with the intellectual currents of the day, expresses in microcosm why the assault by professional historians on the historiography represented by writers such as Anderson was successful. Bernard Bailyn's indictment spoke to the young historians of the time not because it described the history of the discipline he was chronicling with accuracy but because it provided a critique of the progressive approach to history, which, as he put it, relates "the struggle between two essentially unchanging elements, the one destined to fail, the other to triumph." Younger historians were tired of triumphalist history that gloried in a present they found disturbing and trumpeted a future they found frightening. Bailyn's success derived from his application to educational historiography of general intellectual trends that had been developing in the United States since World War II. In this chapter, we will begin by pointing out some of Bailyn's interpretive mistakes and close by showing from the context of Bailyn's project why these mistakes did not really matter to most of his readers.[1]

EGGLESTON, DAVIDSON, AND THE SEARCH FOR
AN ALTERNATIVE TO WHIGGISM

Bernard Bailyn begins his famous *Education in the Forming of American Society* with a review of educational historiography. His strategy is to set up two possible traditions, one represented by Edward Eggleston's *Transit of Civilization* and the other by Thomas Davidson's *History of Education*, both published in 1900. The concupiscence that gave birth to what Bailyn considers to have been sixty years of anachronistic, provincial, evangelistic educationist issue was that historians of education follow Davidson rather than Eggleston. Eggleston, in Bailyn's view, represents a richly contextualist approach to education, conceived broadly as the method by which a society transmits its civilization to the next generation. Davidson, by contrast, stands for all the educationists who see in the history of their discipline the legitimization of their own professionalizing project and so equate a narrow history of schools with the evolution of all the best in human civilization. It is a powerful formulation, not least because of its elegant simplicity. But it is also false.[2]

There are certainly aspects of Eggleston's perspective that would appeal to a writer such as Bailyn. Eggleston was a constant champion of deep contextualization: "The little world as seen by the man of the seventeenth century must be understood." And this man was not of the elite classes but an average person. Eggleston, in a sense, was one of the first American historians to seek to get at the mentalities of ordinary people in the past, and he did so, not incidentally for Bailyn, with a felicitous literary style capable of winning a popular audience.[3]

But this is only one side of Edward Eggleston, and it is not the dominant one. Although his impulse to analyze the popular mind is Bailynesque, his own conclusions and interpretations are doctrinaire modernism. Where Bailyn argues for understanding the past on its own terms, Eggleston "saw ideas mainly as an index of how 'progressive' and 'modern' life was in the past." A brief look at Eggleston's life story, ironically similar to that of Ellwood Cubberley and many another of that generation's educationists, will explain why his interpretation of American educational history, far from being a possible point of departure, was in fact orthodox Whiggery.[4]

Edward Eggleston, like Cubberley, Monroe, and Thomas Woody, was born to pious parents in rural Indiana. His early life was marked by both an intense Methodist spirituality and a strong inclination toward intellectual polymathy. Reflecting back on his formative years, he was inclined to see these two impulses as contradictory, and he was happy to relate that the enthusiasms of his youth were gradually dispelled as the light of learning purged him of superstition and sectarian zeal. Whereas he had at one time lingered over the mystical simplicity of Thomas à Kempis, in his maturity he placed that work on the top shelf, preferring to "walk in wide fields with Charles Darwin." His life demonstrates a "steady progress toward virtual agnosticism," from Methodist circuit-riding minster to popular novelist to social gospeler to, finally, scientific historian. "When Eggleston lost religion," says historian Charles Hirschfeld, "he found science."[5]

Like many another convert, Eggleston looked back on his past with a mixture of good-natured sentimentality and contempt, and his entire historical oeuvre was marked by this combination. Eggleston could move effortlessly from a quaint, congenial discussion of the folkways of the past to a strong denunciation of that same past's intolerance and bigotry. Unlike many of his day, he thought the customs and ideas of the past worth investigation, but like most others, he was glad to be beyond them. "Any history written in the modern spirit," he told students in his extremely popular textbook *History of the United States*, "is the story of the progress of civilization." The final paragraph of his 1900 presidential address to the American Historical Association rang out with these words:

> History is the great prophylactic against pessimism. There never was a bad, in the five progressive centuries, that was not preceded by a worse. . . . Never was the race better situated than in this nineteenth century—this twentieth century on the verge of which we stand.[6]

This progressivism born of a conversion from religion to science had a profound effect on Eggleston's historical writings, as many commentators from his own day to ours have noticed. Barrett Wendell, in his original review of Eggleston's *Transit of Civilization* for the *American Historical Review*, was quick to point out just "how remote Dr. Eggleston is from imaginative sympathy with the past which he tries to revive." Eggelston's investigation into such novel historical realms as medicine, property, astronomy, and education was in the words of a more recent commentator, "part of a general desire to write the history of the past in terms of what Eggleston hoped would be the future." Given his evolutionary assumptions about the nature of human progress, one would hardly expect anything else. Repeatedly Eggleston stressed how "American institutions were all historical developments from colonial germs," and he saw it as the historian's task to "trace with simplicity our present institutions from their springs downward." We are not surprised to find, then, that his investigation of the history of America education, far from being novel or suggestive of an alternative approach, is nothing more or less than the classic Whig view.[7]

Eggleston's most extensive treatment of education occurs in chapter 5 of his *Transit of Civilization*, and it is just as much, if not more, of a rollicking gallop through the history of civilization as any contemporaneous educationist work. Beginning with the "skimmed-milk asceticism" of the early monastic schools that taught "the doctrine of the damnation of infants un-baptized, and much other lore now at last happily obsolete" in a "barba-rous mediæval Latin, often grotesquely macaronied with the vulgar speech," Eggleston passes to the revival of the Latin school in England under John Colet and others. It was this school that the first colonists imported, but stu-dents were not ready for such training and so dame schools emerged to deal with rudimentary matters. We learn of hornbooks, primers, and Latin gram-mars, of grammar schools and writing schools, of Henrico, Harvard, and William and Mary, and especially of the 1647 Massachusetts school law:

> By this curious law of 1647 the Puritan government of Massachusetts rendered probably its greatest service to the future. The act was not modern in aim, and for a long time it was inefficient, but from that quaint act there has been slowly evolved the school system that now obtains in the United States.[8]

Eggleston sides with Draper in finding the inspiration of the idea of state-directed compulsory schooling not in England but in Holland, which itself had got it from John Knox in Scotland. He chimes in with Carter regarding the declension thesis: "[T]he educational decline in all the colonies was in-evitable and it was universal." But, gloriously, hindsight shows us that the golden thread of the idea of tax-supported state education remained unbro-ken, to reemerge in the 1830s and 1840s, "Through all this period of dark-ness and decline the colonies . . . preserved in form and something more that which has proved an invaluable legacy for the future—a system of schools sustained in part by enforced local taxation." The writing is lively and the anecdotes memorable, to be sure, but this much touted study that "should have been a seminal work," that "should have led to a highly imaginative treatment of the theme of education in American history . . . [but] did not" in fact is simply a précis of the Whig view, surrounded by a contextualization as full of anachronisms and chronological snobbery as any educationist tome.[9]

Just as Edward Eggleston was not really a missed opportunity, so Tho-mas Davidson was not really the architect of all that came after him. Harry Hutton and Philip Kalisch have decisively shown that far from being "semi-nal" (to use Bailyn's term), Davidson's book was more often ignored or even scorned as so much mystical metaphysic. A careful reading of Davidson's significant body of educational history reveals a fascinating potpourri of Darwinian science, Victorian anthropology, Aristotelian metaphysics, and Christian theism that is intellectually fascinating to be sure but utterly with-out parallel in the literature. Davidson's immense reading in the philoso-phy of all periods jostles about on the pages to produce in his works an overabundance of mesmerizing historical generalizations that at first strike the reader as profound and synthetically brilliant, but quickly pass from the mind as the hypnotic prose continues on to further and yet higher levels of abstraction.[10]

Taken together, Davidson's many books are so complex that it is difficult to pull from them what we might call a unified point of view. Those who have tried to do so have often been unsuccessful. This was certainly the case with Bailyn, who honed in on one section of Davidson's preface in his *History of Education* to interpret him as an apologist for the educational establishment, which of course he was not. Davidson was if anything a peripatetic freelancer, a homeless world citizen who was as comfortable teaching among New York workingmen as he was in William T. Harris's study. Likewise, J. J. Chambliss was somehow able to convince himself that Davidson "refuses to hold forth an optimistic view of progress or to promise the ultimate triumph of reason," despite the fact that the defining concept of his *History of Education* is that

> HISTORY, as at present understood, is a record of evolution. . . . EDUCATION is conscious or voluntary evolution. Hence, HISTORY OF EDUCATION is a record of such evolution, and begins at the point where man takes himself into his own hand, so to speak, and seeks to guide his life toward an ever more definite, coherent heterogeneity.[11]

One thing that we can say about Davidson is that he, more than anyone else, realized the potential of the advance-of-civilization thesis for producing broadly contextual accounts of educational history. His books chronicle the development of race consciousness, political attitudes, ethical norms, and aesthetic and literary tastes and only rarely address formal pedagogy or school organizations. Many other nineteenth-century writers, as we have seen, officially held this broad view of educational history, though few of them had the intellectual apparatus to pull it off. Davidson, however, was able to do so in a manner that still makes for exciting reading. But in this regard he was rather the last and greatest in a long line of men of letters than the founder of a professional discourse. As there is very little of formal pedagogic theory or institutional development in his pages, they were usually dismissed by those who came after him.

If it is the case, then, that neither Davidson nor Eggleston exemplifies the options that Bailyn associates with their names, the question arises of whether there might have been some other example, some alternative to which Bailyn might have pointed as inspiration for a renewed history of education that could get the profession beyond the tired clichés of an overanthologized Whig history. While there really was nothing in the historical literature paralleling in substance what Bailyn wanted, no historicist rendering that would seek to recover the strangeness of the past on its own terms rather than seeing it as a prologue to the present, there were moments when Bailyn's tone at least was anticipated.

Bailyn's style in *Education in the Forming of American Society*, to the chagrin of many established professional educators and to the delight of many of his younger readers, was thick with the smirk and sneer of satire. It was this attitude, this pose, that did so much to make his book both engaging reading and fodder for heated discussion. But Bailyn was not the first critic to lampoon the products of educational historiography. One thinks, for example, of Welland Hendrick's 1912 *Joysome History of Education*, a carnivalesque spoof of all other histories of education, full of snappy one-liners, not a little spleen, and memorable, humorous caricatures of the great educators of the past. Here is only one example of the sort of thing with which his pages are stocked:

> The first settlers of Virginia, having forgotten to bring their children with them, were prone to vent their educative efforts upon the untutored children of the forest. It cannot be denied that reference is here made to the Indians. Recognizing the fact from Smith's psychology that the end of education is to make people good and that the only good Indian is the dead Indian, they proceeded at the psychological moment to make good. Not being able to reach all the objects of their solicitation, in this way, owing to the short range of their primitive methods, they introduced among their pagan pupils the civilizing influence of whiskey and consumption, in this way instituting what may be viewed in the light of a finishing school.[12]

Hendrick may have anticipated the drollery, but his goal was more the good punch line than any radical revision of the historiographical tradition. Bailyn was anticipated in a more profound manner by another author writing at the turn of the century, the then popular but now obscure Scottish clergyman-turned-essayist/lecturer Kenneth Sylvan Guthrie. Guthrie's *Values of History of Education* is the first example I have been able to find of a thoroughgoing critique of the entire Whig tradition of educational history.

In this short work Guthrie attacks two tendencies in the historiography, both of which would be recapitulated in Bailyn's work six decades later. First, he criticizes the proclivity among educational historians to write their stories without a thorough understanding of the socioeconomic context within which the events they chronicle unfolded. For example, when discussing the historiography of the struggle between the classics and modern subjects, Guthrie observes, with memorable imagery:

> To read the books, one would think that for six centuries two dragons, the Latin and the Vernacular, had been waging a rather useless war in the brain or heart of school teachers. But the fact underlying this pedagogical problem was

the social actuality of the continued use of Latin; so that the choice of Latin or Vernacular was not a matter of fancy, but of decision into which class of society the pupil should go, what professions should be open to him, what friends he should make.

Second, and more profound, Guthrie challenges the bedrock assumption underlying educational historiography from the colonial period. He rejects the notion of progress itself, specifically in its Hegelian incarnation. For this he gives four reasons:

1. *Human psychology does not change.* "There can be no Hegelian development of human nature."
2. *To conclude progress while assuming it is a circular argument.* "While indeed it is very illuminating to read of the detailed causes that led from one successive educational system to another, may there not be a danger of looking on them as efficient causes, rather than formal causes—that is, really, results?"
3. *Regress is a historical reality.* "Instead of progress, high achievements in certain lines have been followed, for millenniums, by crudity and rudimentariness."
4. *A statist, consolidated future may not be rosy.* "Perhaps personal liberty is greater under chaotic and hence not omniscient government than it might be if the government became too scientific. Perhaps the government might be benevolent; and then again, it might be a convenient method of extermination."[13]

Guthrie's contentions here, especially the fourth, are in hindsight quite startling, even chilling. Written at the height of American optimism regarding the future, when Edward Bellamy's *Looking Backward* was still respected by millions of readers, Guthrie's fears of the totalitarian state seem strangely out of place. But by the time Bernard Bailyn wrote, public imagination had all but forgotten Bellamy's cheery vision of the year 2000 and was haunted instead by George Orwell's *1984*. To understand this shift is in large measure to understand why Bailyn's criticisms were so well received by his contemporaries despite their negligible value as a guide to the historiography he was canvassing.[14]

THE DEATH OF PROGRESS AND THE END OF EDUCATIONAL HISTORY

On August 20, 1945, only six days after peace with Japan had been declared, *Time* magazine was already aware of the momentous shift in human consciousness precipitated by the dropping of two atomic bombs:

The greatest and most terrible of wars was ending, this week, in the echoes of an enormous event—an event so much more enormous that, relative to it, the war itself shrank to minor significance. The knowledge of victory was as charged with sorrow and doubt as with joy and gratitude. . . . With the controlled splitting of the atom, humanity, already profoundly perplexed and disunified, was brought inescapably into a new age in which all thoughts and things are split—and far from controlled.

But the bomb was only the latest in a litany of horrors that had followed one after another with little time for intellectual assimilation. *Politics* editor Dwight McDonald, reflecting back on the forces with which his generation had had to contend, provides as good a list as any of the troubles: "the depression, the rise of Nazism, the Spanish Civil War, the Moscow Trials, the Nazi-Stalin Pact, the war itself, forced-labor camps, Truman's atomic bombings." And after the war, the rumored systematic genocide practiced in the German death camps was confirmed, giving rise to the age's most potent image of the lie of human progress. Bruno Bettleheim, in his "Individual and Mass Behavior in Extreme Situations," first articulated the concept of infantile regression at the hand of the totalizing brutality that was the camps; the extension of Bettleheim's thesis to phenomena as disparate as antebellum Negro slavery or, astonishingly, twentieth-century middle-class housewifery, is evidence of just how powerfully the image engaged the American imagination.[15]

For many who lived through it, the war and its aftermath signaled the end of an age of progress, of scientific advance toward human happiness, and the beginning of what historian William Graebner has called the "age of doubt." "Never before," he writes, "had progress seemed so fragile, history so harmful or irrelevant, science so lethal." Whereas the 1933 World's Fair had celebrated the "Century of Progress" and the 1939 fair had showcased science as "Building the World of Tomorrow," the decade of the 1940s had no fair. Richard Hofstadter, accounting in 1968 for the demise of progressive history, noted that "the war, the bomb, the death camps wrote finis to an era in human sensibility, and many writers of the recent past were immolated in the ashes."[16]

The shift from faith in science's ability to advance civilization to a pervasive fear that civilization had met its demise is behind much of the intellectual activity of the 1940s and 1950s. From Malcolm Cowley's rehabilitation of William Faulkner's nonlinear narrative style to Benjamin Spock's bestselling glorification of primitive methods of child rearing, from Rachel Carson's dark exposé of humanity's destruction in *The Sea around Us* to Sidney B. Fay's 1946 American Historical Association presidential address calling the concept of progress "logically meaningless" and suggesting that "it ought perhaps therefore to be shunned by the historian," literary America was suffused with discontent over the modern world we had created.[17]

The contingencies of the age suggested to many the need for increased control, for a more thoroughgoing rationalization of all life into manageable and comfortable segments, and for a common cultural vision. Billy Graham's revivals; Richard Hofstadter's consensus-building classic, *The American Political Tradition*; Gunnar Myrdal's assimilationist manifesto, *An American Dilemma*; and the public prominence of deracinated, cosmopolitan, Jewish intellectuals in New York City all point in their own way to an America seeking salvation in organized political and cultural unity.[18]

Not the least significant organizing force after the war was higher education. In 1940, there had been 146,929 faculty members serving in the nation's postsecondary institutions. By 1950 that number had grown by nearly one hundred thousand, and by 1960 it was at 380,554. Whereas in 1940 only 9.1 percent of eighteen- to twenty-four-year-olds were residents in an institution of higher education, by 1950 the figure was 16.5 percent and by 1960 it was 20.5 percent, a total increase in just twenty years of nearly two million students. The growth itself says much about postwar ambitions and consolidationism, but it also calls to mind the enormous organizational problems facing the managers of these systems. Their bureaucratic response, praiseworthy or blameworthy as it may be, well illustrates the postwar tendency to construct coherence from chaos by organization and rationalization.[19]

This tendency was observable among the professorate as well, flooded as it was with new recruits whose research tremendously increased the volume of knowledge being produced, mandating a relentless specialization on all fronts. Educational historians, like many other specialists, desired for their discipline increased organization, and so a convention was called in Atlantic City in February 1948 by R. Freeman Butts of Teachers College and Claude Eggertsen of the University of Michigan. Approximately eighty persons attended, and a proposal was drawn up to create a continuing History of Education section within the National Society of College Teachers of Education (NSCTE). This proposal was accepted by the society's executive committee, and on April 3, 1948, the first professional organization for educational historians was born.[20]

Within months, membership had grown to 102, a journal proposed, and a study of the present status of history of education in teacher training programs initiated. The first issue of the *History of Education Journal* was released in the fall of 1949 under the general editorship of Claude Eggertsen, with associate editor Archibald Anderson of the University of Illinois and board members Butts, H. G. Good of Ohio State, William F. Drake of the University of Missouri, and Arthur H. Moehlman of the University of Iowa. It was clear from the tenor of the first volume that the focus of the new organization and its publications would be on the application of educational history to teacher training, on working out a more functional history that could, as Butts put it in the first number, "contribute to the improvement of teacher education" by weeding out the "stale and the useless" and replacing it with "scholarship on matters that make a difference," such as "current controversies that beset the making of educational and public policy."[21]

Even in the first issue it is apparent that not all the denizens of the newly created society have kept faith with their Whig past. The internal debate that has received the most attention from commentators is that which occurred between the "functionalist" group centered around the Committee on Historical Foundations, and a more amorphous "liberal" group of historians such as Newton Edwards and Stuart Noble who advocated a more disciplinary and intellectualist approach to the history of education. This debate indeed seemed the major issue at the time. But the makings of a more profound disagreement was presaged even in 1949 by Flaud C. Wooten, whose review of grand old man Thomas Woody's *Life and Education in Early Societies* reflects a change in sensibilities that would in time be the death knell of the education-as-civilization synthesis, which had guided the profession since its inception.[22]

Wooten, for perhaps the first time in a major educationist publication, rejects the doctrine of the progress of civilization, demoting it to the status of an ideology:

> Ideologically, [Woody's book] is based on the abandoned views of Herbert Spencer and E. B. Tylor. Certain references drawn on by Professor Woody are no longer relied on by cultural anthropologists. . . . one looks in vain for any reference to Malinowski and his satellites, Firth and Raum, to Ruth Benedict, Margaret Mead, or Hortense Powdermaker, or to Kluckholm [*sic*], Herskovitis [*sic*], or Opler. . . . Over 50 percent of the references are dated before 1920.[23]

The reference to cultural anthropology is significant, for it was the anthropologists who had first called into question the assumptions of Victorian race-science. Beginning with German émigré Franz Boas, whose environmentalist anthropology had flourished in Berlin in the 1880s until it was "overwhelmed by an intellectual mood that was nationalist, imperialist, and racialist," American anthropologists had gradually worked out a relativistic, pluralistic, historicist definition of culture that was having a tremendous impact on other academic disciplines during the late 1940s and 1950s. "The concept of a plurality of historically conditioned cultures" first articulated by Boas and popularized by his students, many of whom Wooten mentions in his critique, gradually replaced the venerable notion of culture as "a single sequence of evolutionary stages."[24]

Woody's response to such criticism is recorded in the journal's following issue, and it perhaps best illustrates just how distanced writers of his sort were from the emerging postwar intellectual temper. Too many thinkers, according to Woody, "seem to cringe" before the future "as something fearful, rather than something fraught with hope,"

> and, looking backward to some idealized past, they write a story of man's degeneration and the debasement of society. Civilization is on the way out, they say. On the contrary, the Golden Age, a better civilization than any yet known, may lie ahead.

In defense of the antique anthropology required to sustain his view, Woody cautions against accepting so-called new insights, reminding readers that logician Peter Ramus was by many declared superior to Aristotle at the height of Protestant scholasticism. This example is a significant clue to Woody's perspective, for of course the reader would know that Ramus was the father of strict deductionism, the antithesis of inductive science and its progressive technological products. Despite the instantaneous death of one hundred thousand civilians at the dropping of a bomb and the systematic murder of nearly six million Jews by one of the most sophisticated cultures in the world, history remains for Woody a series of progressive scientific revolutions causing a rise from "local primitive enclaves" to "the highest civilizations" of the modern West.[25]

As the years passed, the older progress-of-civilization adherents grew increasingly defensive and the young critics of modernity became frisky and daring. George E. Arnstein in 1954 had the gall to incriminate no less a figure than Ellwood Cubberley, showing that "a good deal" of Cubberley's work was "obsolete thanks to intervening research, that most of his books should not remain in use today." What Arnstein particularly questioned was Cubberley's underlying assumptions about the nature of history:

> What is "world progress"? What does "improvability of the race" mean? Is his history of "real service"? What is the "proper setting" of the history of education? What is "progress"? What is included in "education"?

As the 1950s progressed, it was becoming increasingly clear that a massive rift in sensibilities was emerging between those who continued to celebrate "America's rich educational heritage which is one of her more important contributions to man's march toward civilization," as one writer put it in 1955, and another, mostly younger group of historians who were aching for something new. Bernard Mehl spoke for them when he cut through the hype promoting the spate of recent textbooks that had so successfully integrated the story of educational institutions into the broader context of American social history. Acknowledging their success in this regard, he nevertheless pointed out the need for a deeper sort of revisionism:

> The major fault of the new writings is that the New History of Education has nothing new to say. It itself is in the process of becoming inert. It utilizes the same catchwords and the same labels. We know who are the villains and who are the heroes. There is no doubt that all four texts are competently written, but one misses a fresh point of view in any of them. . . . The story they all tell is the same. And the story is now old stuff.[26]

So even among educationists there was a growing dissatisfaction with the received view, newly contextualized though it be, and a hunger for something new. But what? Was there no alternative to the dreary litany of progressive achievement, of the slow human ascension up the ladder of civilization? In fact there was an alternative tradition, the tradition to which Bernard Bailyn was heir. Although he never seemed to recognize it himself, the truly authentic alternative for which Bailyn was looking was not to be found in the moralizing Whiggery of Edward Eggleston's historical potluck but in the perspective hammered out by his own predecessors at Harvard University. At the same time, members of the postwar historical profession, like the educationists, were deeply interested in rationalizing the profession's scholarship and consolidating its organizations. In due time this organizational impulse met up with the Harvard interpretive slant, and the product, Bailyn's *Education and the Forming of American Society*, was just the sort of thing for which eager educational historians had been searching.

BAILYN IN CONTEXT

In an important sense, Bernard Bailyn's challenge to the Whig view of educational history had its origins in one of the more reactionary moments of modern historiography. In the early twentieth century, American historians, like many other Americans, had been in a debunking mood. As we have seen in the case of Edward Eggleston, the Puritans especially were rarely treated with anything approaching sympathy. Not a few professionals would have concurred with H. L. Mencken's scorn of the Puritan's "utter lack of aesthetic sense, his distrust of all romantic emotion, his unmatchable intolerance of opposition, his unbreakable belief in his own bleak and narrow views." Charles Francis Adams had dubbed the time between 1640 and 1740 in New England the "glacial period," and few were the dissenting voices among early professionals.[27]

Into this hostile environment a group of Harvard professors entered, with the aim of rehabilitating the Puritans. Kenneth Murdock's sensitive biography of Increase Mather signaled the tone the revisionists would take, and Samuel Eliot Morison's immense output systematically worked out the revision on all levels of Puritan society. His 1930 *Builders of the Bay Colony* repristinated the early years of the colonies by richly detailing their European context and by vividly describing the howling wilderness. His 1936 *Puritan Pronaos* carried the story forward through the second and third generations. The Puritans who emerge from Morison's pages are not gloomy fanatics consumed with "the haunting fear that someone, somewhere, might be happy" but turn out to be rather normal people: cheerful, interested in matrimonial bliss and child rearing, inclined to temperate but convivial dining and drink, passionately devoted to education.[28]

Most important for our purposes are not so much Morison's particular conclusions as his methodology and the general tenor of his thought. Morison was a great admirer of the romantic style of historical writing, possessing "an almost flawless ear for natural and effective prose rhythms." Indeed, Bernard Bailyn thought Morison "the greatest American narrative historian since Francis Parkman." Although his professional activity spanned nearly all the historical fads of the twentieth century, he never lost his commitment to popular narrative. "Morison's career," writes Gregory M. Pfitzer, "was characterized from beginning to end by a single, persistent theme—the struggle to reconcile a 'professional' identity with the need to reach a larger, nonprofessional audience." The tone set at Harvard by Samuel Eliot Morison was one of keen interest in making history lively for and relevant to the American people.[29]

As the Romantics had done, Morison used a method of bringing the past to life for his wide readership, in which he devoted significant energies to re-creating the setting of his historical dramas to build a convincing context that made the past an exotic and mysterious place. While his historical peers and immediate predecessors ignored the Puritans or scorned them outright, Morison sought to make them agreeable to modern readers not by painting them as moderns (though he did fall into this on occasion) but by re-creating the complexity of their cultural situation in a way that would breed understanding. This could best be accomplished not by looking back on the past using our own modern categories but by re-creating the historical world of the New England Puritans themselves, largely by comparing their civilization to that of the English mainland whence it sprung. Seen in this light, the seventeenth-century Puritans turn out to look like not conservatives fruitlessly trying to suppress change but innovators in their own right. This is especially the case in education, as Morison explains:

> If secularization be progress, the New Englanders took an important step in advance by placing their schools under the control of the communities and commonwealths, and by insisting that the school teachers be laymen. If diffusion of education be progress, New England again deserves credit for making her education in many places free as well as public.[30]

What is particularly fascinating about Morison's approach is the extent to which a vastly different sensibility has led him to embrace the same interpretations offered by professional educators in their own historical works. Morison himself was confused on this point, convinced that his work was opposed to that of the educators. "It seems to be an axiom with Professor Knight," he said, referring to Edgar W. Knight's textbook *Education in the United States*, "as with many other professional educators of today, that schools inspired by the spirit of religion, or conducted by ecclesiastics, are worthless." In another place he discloses more fully his bias against the education profession:

> In contrast to Jefferson's ideas of education, creating from bright young people of every social class a cultivated elite to govern the country, the Jacksonian ideal was education on a dead level, and out of the Jacksonian egg was hatched the ugly duckling of John Deweyism, which continues to befoul American education to this day.

Given such proclivities, it is scarcely surprising that Morison thought his own work antithetical to that of the educationists. But both were interested in presenting the Puritans in a positive light: the educationists because Puritans were the ostensible founders of the glorious American system of compulsory schooling, Morison because he was a faithful son of New England. While Morison's thick contextualism and narrative skills provided a more charming presentation of the educational endeavors of the Puritans than they often received from the schoolmen, the final product was not in essence different from orthodox schoolman historiography, save in one crucial way.[31]

The one crucial difference was that Morison saw Puritan education as only one ingredient in the broader recipe of Puritan intellectual life. His *Puritan Pronaos* covers in orthodox fashion the Puritan schools, Harvard, the early legislation, primers, hornbooks, and all the rest, but it also includes chapters on printing and bookselling, on libraries, theology as revealed in sermons, historical and political literature, poetry, and scientific efforts. What emerges is not a narrow focus on schooling, nor even a more sophisticated contextual effort that situates the history of schooling in its sociocultural setting, but one that sees schools as only one manifestation of a broader intellectual program.

Herein lie many of the origins of Bailyn's historical impulses. Morison bequeathed to Harvard both a narrative style with popular appeal and a romantic penchant for contextual detail that resulted in a powerful reconception of Puritan education as only one aspect of a larger intellectual world. His students and heirs would challenge many of his own findings, would free themselves from his apologetic imperative, and would develop historical approaches that would take the story far beyond what could be conveyed by exclusive reliance on literary sources, but Morison's basic orientation was continued in the work of Harvard students such as Clifford Shipton and, especially, Perry Miller.

Perry Miller received his doctorate from the University of Chicago; he subsequently spent 1930 studying with Murdoch and Morison at Harvard and never left, teaching there until his death in 1963. Like Morison, he was a World War II veteran, a self-styled anachronistic "lone wolf," an independent mind in the age of machines. He joined with a number of the intellectuals of his day in connecting scholarship to contemporary concerns by writing in public media accessible to an audience beyond the ivory tower. Unlike Morison, however, he had a deeper sensitivity to the intellectual underpinnings of society. His mind inclined more toward synthetic interpretation than narrative exposition. He was one of a number of public intellectuals who, "addressing a wide audience after World War II, . . . brought to their work an awareness of the complexity of and tragedy in human nature." It was this sense of tragedy that set his work apart from that of most prewar history and, especially, the embarrassingly optimistic educational history that remained the characteristic product of the postwar schoolmen.[32]

Miller's bedrock assumption was that "the mind of man is the basic factor in human history." He saw it as his calling (the term is appropriate) to preach the meaning of America "to the twentieth century." To do this, he would have to articulate the intellectual assumptions of America's first settlers and account for the changes that later generations would make to this original stock of ideas. The meaning of the twentieth century must be traced to its beginnings, and so Miller's most extensive and influential work was in the intellectual history of the Puritans. Taking seriously sources and ideas that most historians felt inconsequential and vacuous, Miller was able to recreate with stunning insight and creativity the mental world of the early Massachusetts divines from their heretofore neglected sermons.[33]

The most significant contribution of Miller's profound work *The New England Mind* to our story is its archaeology of a vanished culture's mental state and its probing investigation of why and how that culture changed. "The history of ideas," maintained Miller, "demands of the historian not only a fluency in the concepts themselves but in the ability to get underneath them." In volume 1, *The Seventeenth Century*, he attempts to do just this for the mental world of the Puritans, and in volume 2, *From Colony to Province*, he seeks to explain the changes to the original fund of ideas made by a people responding to new circumstances. In these and other works the focus was on the agonies of thought that early Americans endured as they wrestled with their medieval inheritance on the one hand and the emerging modern world on the other. It was the moment of transition, the critical shift, that was always the climax of Miller's investigation and the goal of his interpretation.

Whether his attention was tuned to Jonathan Edwards's anguished bout with modernity, to the fate of apocalypticism in the wake of Newtonian mechanical laws, or to the connections between Puritan and revolutionary ideas, Miller was always concerned with understanding the past as uniquely and qualitatively different but somehow related to the familiar present. It was the historian's task to make the connections with clarity and fidelity.[34]

Thus Miller's major contributions to the Harvard historical milieu into which Bailyn was baptized was his profound concern with ideas and their adaptation to changing environments, and with the connection of these ideas to major historical questions. But he contributed lesser qualities as well. Like Morison, Miller was a rather cantankerous critic of professional education. Although more subtle than Morison, Miller was nevertheless not above the occasional swipe at "the stranglehold—of the schools of education" on teacher training. This spirit too he bequeathed to Bernard Bailyn.[35]

Concerned as he was with ideas rather than institutions, his history rarely came into direct contact with educationist historiography, but in a difficult essay composed in 1949, Miller did offer a critique of the standard account of educational history and a suggestion for an alternative. Specifically, he thinks that the school's role as agent of an "ever-triumphant diffusion" of knowledge has been overplayed by self-interested and single-minded historians. A possible alternative approach to educational history would be an investigation into the way schools have been responsible for "domesticating the disreputable." For example, when Emerson first came on the scene, he scandalized the nation and was exiled from Cambridge. Now he is read in any high school literature course. Educational history would do well to take into consideration the social uses of schooling, in this case the tendency to defang potentially offensive and subversive ideas by incorporating them into the curriculum. What needs to be noted in this essay is not so much Miller's own historical account, interesting though it is, but two important, more atmospheric qualities. The first is his persistent jabs at professional educators, whose textbooks—"where the obvious is never left unaccounted for"—are their own best satire. The second is his instinct, like Morison's, to ask not how society has influenced the schools but how schools have influenced society.[36]

Into such a context Bernard Bailyn entered, after serving, as had Morison and Miller, in World War II. He received his M.A. from Harvard in 1947 and his Ph.D. in 1953. Bailyn's early work clearly marks him as heir to the tradition of colonial studies prosecuted by Morison and Miller, but with an emphasis on social history that he acquired largely from his mentor Oscar Handlin. In fact, his work taken as a whole is something of a synthesis of the approaches of these three eminent Harvard historians. Bailyn harmonized Handlin's focus on social developments with Miller's interest in the fragmentation of ideas by composing a Morisonesque narrative whose barest outlines go something like this: The European colonists came to the New World attempting to transmit their medieval social systems. But the wilderness environment posed unanticipated challenges that weakened traditional centers of authority and gradually produced a fragmented social world challenging all inherited ways. This new state of affairs precipitated two major historical movements. The first was the intentional, deliberate creation of new institutions to fill the authority gap left by the passing of old folkways, and the second was the rationalizing of the new social reality by intellectuals during the Revolution. The real social revolution had already occurred by 1776, but at the founding, ideas finally caught up with reality.[37]

Much of Bailyn's early work is best viewed as an outgrowth of, through direct challenge to, Perry Miller's approach to history. Whereas Miller had devoted exclusive attention to the preachings of Puritan divines, Bailyn, in his dissertation, published in 1955 as *The New England Merchants in the Seventeenth Century*, sought to shift attention to the broader forces at work in the decline of Puritanism's hold on the commonwealth. When criticized for the book's lack of empirical grounding, Bailyn responded with a methodologically pioneering study, coauthored with his wife, Lotte, *Massachusetts Shipping*. In this study the Bailyns used computer data analysis of shipping records to demonstrate the magnitude of commercial growth in the colonies, connecting this immense commercial change to the intellectual world Miller had uncovered.[38]

But Bailyn's most enduring scholarly contribution was his work on American Revolutionary pamphlets. Just as Miller had been the first to take seriously the horde of Puritan sermons neglected by generations of historians, so Bailyn for the first time paid serious and detailed attention to the enormous body of Revolutionary publications, seeking out the meanings behind key words as he reconstructed a lost historical world from these literary remains. In the same way that Miller's students Nathan Huggins and Ann Douglas would apply his method to the literature of the Harlem Renaissance or the intellectuals of 1920s New York, so Bailyn extended Miller's careful textual analysis into the Revolutionary period to describe the lost mentality of civic republicanism.[39]

What Bailyn most admired in Miller's approach was his "capacity to conceive of a hitherto unglimpsed world," his "profoundly romantic" capacity, not to focus on "merely one problem or one issue or one theme," but to think in wholes and to imagine, as the great novelists do, an entire world. Crucial to this capacity is the ability to contextualize, and Bailyn's understanding of the benefits of contextualization are most clearly spelled out in an essay he composed to explain the greatness of four historians he admired, the first of whom was Perry Miller:

All four of our historians are contextualists. That is, they sought to understand the past in its own terms: to relocate events, the meaning of documents, the motivations of historical actors in their original historical sockets. Their greatest suspicions and vigilance were directed at anachronism. They are forever doubting that words meant then what they mean now, that motivations are always the same, that circumstances repeat themselves significantly. What seem to them most revealing are the differences between past and present, not the similarities; it is the differences that excite their imagination, that suggest the lines of discovery to them. And they were therefore keyed to surprises: it is the capacity for surprise rather than for the satisfaction of familiar recognition that made their work possible.[40]

Here was to be found a new perspective that educationists such as Bernard Mehl and George Arnstein, tired of the familiar story and aching to be surprised, might eagerly embrace. But scholars of Bailyn's capacities were usually drawn to such emerging fields as the history of the family or to the exalted realm of intellectual history. It would require some sort of outside force to cause a student with tendencies like Bailyn's to approach such a mundane affair as the history of educational institutions. That force appeared in the combined efforts of the Fund for the Advancement of Education's campaign for the study of the role of education in American history, and the Institute of Early American History and Culture's "Needs and Opportunities for Study" conference, on early American education.

In 1943 the College of William and Mary joined with Colonial Williamsburg, Incorporated to establish an organization that would foster research and publication in American history "from its beginnings to the close of the Jeffersonian era." The founding purpose of the Institute for Early American History and Culture was to broaden study of this period to include more than military and political history. To further this end, the institute sponsored several conferences in 1952–53 in the fields of early American science, early American law, and Indian relations prior to 1830. A standard procedure was followed:

> At each conference a distinguished authority presented a written survey, which was discussed freely and critically by the other participants, and the writer was then invited to submit a revision of his paper for publication, together with a bibliographical supplement especially designed for those desiring to work further in the given field.[41]

This was not a new idea. Professional historians had been holding collaborative conferences and publishing bibliographies for decades. In the early 1930s the American Historical Association's Committee on the Planning of Research had called a series of conferences on the status of historical scholarship that led to conclusions quite similar in spirit to the aims of the Institute for Early American History and Culture. In its report, significantly titled *Historical Scholarship in America: Needs and Opportunities*, the call had been made for, among other things, studies of the "social conditions and forces as reflected and affected by education." It was declared that "the historian is better qualified to investigate many of these problems than are the specialists to whom they have been too exclusively relegated. They belong in any large synthesis of social-cultural history." Even before the war, then, general historians were calling for a broad, cultural approach to educational history prosecuted not by educationists but by themselves.[42]

That call was amplified after World War II by two groups, whose collaboration made Bailyn's book possible. By the late 1950s, the Institute for Early American History and Culture had moved on from science, law, and Indian relations to an interest in education and religion. Plans were thus initiated for a conference on early American education. But whereas earlier conferences had been specialized affairs, interesting only to a small subset of the historical profession and producing helpful but hardly groundbreaking work, the Conference on Early American Education was to be of an entirely different order, for the institute had successfully positioned itself to benefit from the largesse of the most generous source of private support for educational history that had yet appeared in the United States.

In April 1951, the Ford Foundation, responding to the mounting criticism of what was derisively termed "progressive education," created the Fund for the Advancement of Education, largely through the ministrations of Robert M. Hutchins. In its first decade, the fund distributed fifty million dollars in grants to support approximately five hundred experimental programs at leading colleges and universities, mostly to improve the quality of teacher training. Methodologically, the fund was open to all sorts of perspectives and efforts, but it was explicit in its aims:

> Liberal education is the first essential in the education of every American, and particularly of every teacher.
> It is in no way undemocratic to seek out and nurture superior talent.
> American schools, if they are to produce any significant number of intellectual superior human beings, must re-establish the priority of the intellect.

The fund's president, Clarence H. Faust, sounded the keynote of its agenda when he expressed encouragement over what seemed to be "a new appreciation of the central importance of general and liberal education as preparation for the wise execution of the responsibilities of citizens in a democratic society." Throughout the 1950s under Faust's leadership, the Fund for the

Advancement of Education was a leading enabler of education reform advocating academic excellence.[43]

One of Faust's goals was to get teacher training out of the hands of the professional educator and back into mainstream academia. A 1957 publication by the fund clarified and gave historical grounding for this ideal:

> We have two distinct traditions of teacher education in the United States. The older tradition, which long controlled the education of secondary teachers, and which still controls the education of college teachers, provides the basis for what may be called the academic or liberal arts view of teacher education. The second tradition—which is newer although it now has a history of well over one hundred years—is that of the professional educator. . . . The two traditions represent totally different concepts of the nature of man, of the learning process, and of the proper role and limitations of free public schools. . . . The older one holds that *formal* education is properly centered in the world of knowledge and is concerned with the development of the mind. The newer traditions prefer to place stress on the "whole child."

Given this conception, it is unsurprising that the fund gave its most generous support to colleges and universities seeking to academicize teacher training by sponsoring courses taught by liberal arts faculty in schools of education and by creating fifth-year master's degree programs that would qualify liberal arts graduates to teach in the nation's public schools with only minimal teacher preparation. In 1952 and 1953, both sorts of programs were instituted at Harvard University. Noted philosopher Israel Scheffler began what was to become a career-long association with the School of Education by teaching courses in educational philosophy, and the school's history of education course was taken on by a promising young historian named Bernard Bailyn. By 1957, some $535,600 in fund monies had been devoted to Harvard programs, and Bailyn was often connected to the grants. On August 13, 1955, for example, Bailyn was on the roster of a seminar on educational reporting in the local community sponsored by the fund. But his most direct and significant involvement with the fund concerned President Faust's interest in exploring "the possibility of a fuller investigation of the role of education in American history."[44]

In 1954, Faust and executive associate Lester W. Nelson called together an impressive group of historians to begin discussing the contributions that educational history might offer to an attempt to understand American society. Their goal was to take this history beyond the characteristic institutional focus on schools "as effects or outgrowths of our society" and instead analyze "the effects of education on our development as a people." On December 11 and 12, the fund assembled Paul H. Buck, Bernard Bailyn, Merle Curti,

Ralph H. Gabriel, Richard Hofstadter, Francis Keppel, E. C. Kirkland, Walter Metzger, Arthur M. Schlesinger, Ralph W. Tyler, and O. Meredith Wilson to discuss the matter. After the conference, Richard J. Storr was added to the group and given the responsibility of producing a draft of tentative conclusions. This document was circulated among the group and a second conference, this one at Harvard on May 12, 1956, led to the formation of the Committee on the Role of Education in American History, consisting of Buck, Faust, Hofstadter, Schlesinger, and Storr. This group issued a report published by the fund in 1957, titled *The Role of Education in American History*. Its authors asserted that the role of education in American history was obscured as a result of shameful neglect by American historians and called for proposals that would remedy this situation by bringing educational work into the mainstream of American history. Fifteen thousand copies were printed, most of which were sent gratis to the entire membership of the American Historical Association. It did not take long for proposals to come in.[45]

Between May 1957, when the committee's document was first circulated, and October 16–17, 1959, when the Institute for Early American History and Culture held its conference at Williamsburg, Virginia, the Fund for the Advancement of Education bequeathed a total of $108,336 to support the study of the role of education in American history. In addition to the $11,712 grant for the committee's budget itself, proposals from a number of institutions were accepted for various amounts:

University of California, Berkeley	$15,000
University of Chicago	8,600
Columbia University	5,000
Harvard University	14,600
Indiana University	8,114
Kentucky Research Foundation	13,310
State Historical Society of Wisconsin	25,000
College of William and Mary	7,000[46]

The last-listed grant, for seven thousand dollars to the College of William and Mary, was in support of the Conference on Early American Education, organized by the Institute for Early American History and Culture. These additional funds allowed the institute to procure a much more extensive and distinguished panel of historians than it had obtained for previous conferences, and the keynote speaker for this installment was to be Bernard Bailyn. As we have seen, Bailyn had been present at the initial planning sessions sponsored by the Fund for the Advancement of Education, and in the late 1950s, his star was rising in the historical firmament. With Bailyn the fund was guaranteed a stimulating presentation that would reflect its own convictions regarding the field of study under investigation: the Institute for Early American History and Culture was guaranteed a presentation by a historical prodigy who would surely speak to the needs and opportunities for study in the domain of education. And as readers of *Education in the Forming of American Society* know, the speaker did not disappoint.

Bailyn's address had both critical and constructive components. The critique was essentially an application to the domain of educational historiography of contemporaneous academic criticisms of professional education that were currently winning a wide hearing in the popular press. Perhaps the most successful of the critics was the historian Arthur Bestor. Bestor had revealed how "departments of education or pedagogy" kept a "stranglehold upon teacher training" because neglectful academics had left "a vacuum into which the professional educationist moved." He saw this phenomenon operating in educational historiography as well:

> Torn from its context of general historical change, the history of school systems becomes a chronicle almost devoid of meaning. Worse than that, it may easily become the kind of distorted history which presents the past as a mournful catalogue of errors, redeemed by some few feeble gropings toward that perfection of wisdom which the present generation (and the instructor in particular) alone possess.

In the same way, with remarkably similar language and tone, Bailyn bewailed the separation of educational historiography "from the main stream of historical research, writing, and teaching" and bemoaned the educationists' dreary litany of inert facts, forming "no significant pattern." Just as Bestor had asserted that academics must "bring these isolated fragments of the basic disciplines back into the departments where they belong," so Bailyn urged that educational history be liberated from the entanglements of the educationists and returned to the general historian, who is its rightful keeper.[47]

Bailyn's immensely influential historiographical critique, then, turns out to be simply a commonplace of Sputnik-era educationist bashing. We have seen that its substantive elements, from the Eggleston/Davidson dichotomy to the Cubberley mystique, from the charge of historiographical isolation to that of an inability to contextualize, do violence to the historical record. But none of this mattered in the end, for Bailyn's message was ripe for its time. A profession imprisoned in its own past, unable to escape the smothering perspective of world progress through the expansion of formal educational systems, was desperate for anything that would provide relief from the burden of optimism rendered odious by a postwar intellectual context. Bailyn's attack included much that was mistaken, but his fundamental instinct to highlight history's otherness rather than its similarity to the present provided those sickened by their discipline's sanguinity a most welcome opportunity for penance. But Bailyn was not only the prophet convicting a profession of its sins. He was also the catechist, offering direction to chastened novices along paths of righteousness.

In Bailyn's constructive component, he applied the synthesis he was formulating in other domains of early American history to the subject of education. Read in conjunction with his other work during these years, this "essay in hypothetical history" is not surprising. In his famous and oft-anthologized 1959 essay, "Politics and Social Structure in Virginia," for example, Bailyn showed how notions of the state were originally "woven into the texture of everyday life" and "indistinguishable from a more general social authority." But the wilderness experience fragmented this inherited and inarticulate understanding, compelling Virginian statesmen to devote formal attention to the creation of political institutions to control their splintering society. This same thesis had also driven his studies of New England merchants, who at first needed no formal economic theory or explicit discussion of their goals, for their commercial world was the natural result of a complex network of kinship patterns and personal relationships. Only when these patterns began to break down in the New World did the need for deliberative economic policy emerge. Thus it is with education, yet another example of "the rapid breakdown of traditional European society in its wilderness setting."[48]

For Bailyn, the original education of the colonists was a "direct inheritance from the medieval past." It occurred within the complex network of family, church, and community in a manner that was "largely instinctive and traditional, little articulated and little formalized." But the "strange and forbidding" wilderness presented problems that fragmented these inherited institutions and made requisite a more deliberative, intentional educational response. To restore a sense of order, the colonists began to pass school laws and to create all sorts of formal educational institutions that took the place of the lost educative authority of the family. Henceforth, education would be an individual affair, related not to the automatic acquisition of familial traditions but to "a self-conscious quest for appropriate forms of behavior." Religious pluralism only increased the differentiation and hurried along the shift from an education "whose origins lay in the half-instinctive workings of a homogeneous, integrated society" into that of "the jarring multiplicity, the raw economy, and the barren environment of America," where education became "controversial, conscious, constructed: a matter of decision, will, and effort."[49]

It was a command performance. The fund got its money's worth in a powerful formulation whose final pages shifted attention from society's impact on educational systems to these systems' impact on society, and in a spirited condemnation of yet another aspect of the ed school menace. The institute's goal of stimulating new research in neglected areas of early American history was successful beyond its most optimistic expectations. For his part, Bailyn's association with the fund's committee had placed him, as a very young scholar, among the cream of the historical profession, and the immense impact of this one perfectly timed publication would give him near legendary stature among educational historians for generations to come, especially as his subsequent works proved him to be perhaps the greatest American historian of the later twentieth century.

A SURPRISINGLY LIMITED LEGACY

For all the stimulus that Bailyn's brilliant, creative synthetic sketch gave to subsequent historians, there remain ironies in his legacy that have seldom been noticed by his heirs, and we are all his heirs. We have seen in this study how the tradition of professional educationist historiography—that historiography that since Bailyn's work has fallen under such severe disrepute—had been able to provide its readers and practitioners with a coherent, integrated picture of the whole of educational history thanks to its assumptions concerning the role that education has played in the progress of civilization. Since Bailyn cast this tradition aside, no formulation, not even one from so committed a synthesist as Bailyn himself, has been able to re-arrange the facts of history into a meaningful pattern to which all practitioners can consent.

Bailyn's own work, itself so keen on establishing the transatlantic context of early American education, was ironically a major contributor to the increasing provincialism that has overtaken American history in general and educational history in particular. In 1991 Maxine Seller, in her presidential address before the History of Education Society, complained that "we treat the nation as though its boundaries were impenetrable walls." No one could have said that of any major educationist historian from Henry Barnard to Thomas Woody. Just as the collapse of Latin as the universal language of scholarship in the sixteenth and seventeenth centuries contributed to the demise of a transnational community of learning, so the rejection of Victorian assumptions that found a reciprocal relationship between the evolution of school systems and the evolution of civilization has bequeathed to the present a historical world drowning in unassimilated detail, methodological pluralism, and interpretive anarchy, a condition that historian Peter Novick compares to the period of the Judges in Jewish history, to those days when "there was no king in Israel." Bailyn himself has lived to regret and criticize strongly contemporary tendencies toward historical fragmentation. But in the field of educational historiography, no work so liberated practitioners from the guiding hand of a coherent interpretative tradition than *Education and the Forming of American Society*.[50]

A second irony is related. Although many scholars did in fact respond to the specific needs and opportunities for study that Bailyn articulated, hindsight suggests that the most influential social use of Bailyn's book occurred not among historians of early America but among nineteenth-century revisionists. Bailyn's original critique of established interpretations turned out to be merely the first skirmish of a full-scale war, the cloud that would in time become the deluge. These developments were of course unforeseen by Bailyn, nor would he have countenanced much of the revisionist agenda, freighted as it was with anachronistic readings informed by contemporary political goals. But the fact remains that his book has been appropriated innumerable times by the historiographical mythology that introduces articles or situates book reviews as the event that started it all. A generation that had only heard stories of World War II but saw in vivid Technicolor what American arms could and could not do to the Vietcong would take Bailyn by the hand and lead him to places to which he had not dreamed he would be going.

The result has been often and accurately described as an explosion of historical study, both quantitatively and qualitatively. Monographs and articles have multiplied, new methodologies appropriated, professional standards raised, graduate programs and learned societies placed on firm footing. Bailyn's little book is nearly always cited by those inclined to retrospection as the seminal moment in educational historiography's rebirth as a legitimate academic pursuit. As Jennings Wagoner put it, "Bernard Bailyn's *Education in the Forming of American Society*, published in 1960, set the stage for a revitalization of the history of education." But if my analysis is correct, it would be more accurate to view Bailyn's book as the close rather than the beginning of an era. We have seen in this study the limitations of Bailyn's account of the history of educational historiography. It could be argued, moreover, that Bailyn's positive program for creating a new educational historiography conducted by historians seeking to understand American culture has met with little success.[51]

A case in point is the reception of Lawrence Cremin's work. Cremin, perhaps mistakenly, understood his three-volume trilogy, *American Education*, to be the fulfillment of Bailyn's call for a new historiography of education broadly conceived. Twenty-three years in the making, Cremin's *American Education* remains the most ambitious synthesis of American educational history ever produced. Yet today it is scarcely consulted. Even in its own day it received nothing approaching universal acclaim. Reviewers tended to fault its definition for being so broad as to render the designation *educational history* meaningless. With every volume, the cry intensified that Cremin, in his rush to embrace a broad cultural history, had forgotten the history of the schools. More profound, by the time *The Metropolitan Experience* saw print, it was becoming clear among general historians that there was no longer any such thing as an interpretive mainstream. The very project of writing the history of education into a general account of American development seemed irresponsible, when there no longer remained among scholars any consensus about the main lines of American history.[52]

Just as Bailyn's synthetic ideal and the specific recommendations for achieving it have proved illusory, so his goal of liberating educational historiography from its service to public education has failed. Ironically, this has especially been the case with the work of many of Bailyn's own students. With every successive book, leading educational historian and Bailyn student David Tyack's work grows more narrowly focused on educational policy issues, using educational history to get leverage on current discussions. In *Tinkering toward Utopia*, for example, he and coauthor Larry Cuban say:

> We hope that this book, which takes a century as its time span, will contribute to the broader conversation about educational reform today, for improving public schools is everybody's business.

Similarly, Maris Vinovskis's recent work *History and Educational Policymaking* is an extended argument by example against the sort of pure academicist history his Harvard professor advocated, ending with these words:

> Persuading policymakers to utilize more information about the past and historians to make such studies more readily available will neither be easy nor popular. But it is a worthwhile and necessary goal if government is to provide the type and quality of services that can truly help those most disadvantaged in our society today.

A particularly striking example of the return of presentist historiography, or history-as-prolegomena-to-policy-recommendations, is Ellen Lagemann's *An Elusive Science*. Although dedicated to the memory of her mentor, Lawrence Cremin, Lagemann's book "is an argument from history about current problems associated with educational scholarship." She hopes that her account can "perhaps become an instrument of reform."[53]

Many other recent works likewise explicitly draw out lessons from the past for schools today. Bailyn student Jürgen Herbst's *Once and Future School* canvasses, as his subtitle states, 350 years of American secondary education, all for the sake of outlining a concrete plan for revitalizing American secondary education in the twenty-first century. The genre has flourished in recent years, as witnessed by such titles as David Labaree's *How to Succeed in School without Really Learning: The Credentials Race in American Edu-*

cation; David L. Angus and Jeffrey E. Mirel's *The Failed Promise of the American High School, 1890–1995*; and Diane Ravitch's controversial *Left Back: A Century of Failed School Reforms.*[54]

As these and most other recent productions attest, despite the rhetoric of historiographical mainstreaming, today just as in the 1950s the great bulk of books and articles written by educational historians are about school, often with an eye on issues of contemporary relevance. The methodology is diverse, and works range from traditional institutional histories to biographies of notables to studies of student and teacher populations, politics, philosophy, policy, architecture, curriculum, and extracurriculum. But the history of education still means for most educational historians the history of school. And as hyperspecialization and certain theoretical developments have made the synthetic project practically unfeasible and philosophically suspect among the wider community of historians, there no longer exists any general account of American development into which the findings of educational historians could be incorporated even if there was a desire to do so.

With the historical profession thus situated, it is not at all surprising that educational historians are returning to their institutional home—the professional school of education—and applying the tools of their trade to its concerns. If these trends toward increased focus on present problems associated with schooling continue among educational historians, it may some years hence appear that Bailyn's critique, rather than opening up a new era in educational historiography, in fact initiated a small blip in an otherwise unbroken chain of professional educational historiography functioning as a servant discipline to the wider field of educational research and policy. Although the particular interpretations of the early educational professionals are no longer current, it may be that today's topics and concerns are closer to theirs than to those of Bernard Bailyn. It no longer seems so wonderful, but in many ways Cubberley's world is still our own.

Notes

INTRODUCTION

The opening quote is from Thomas Woody, "Fields That Are White," *History of Education Journal* 2 (Autumn 1950): 17.

1. Raymond E. Callahan, "Leonard Ayres and the Educational Balance Sheet," *History of Education Quarterly* 1 (March 1961): 12.

2. Woody, "Fields That Are White," 9, 3.

3. Bernard Bailyn, *Education in the Forming of American Society* (Chapel Hill: University of North Carolina Press, 1960), 4.

4. Bailyn, *Education*, 9, 11.

5. J. Merton England, book review, *American Historical Review* 68 (October 1962): 236; Morman B. Wilkinson, book review, *Pennsylvania Magazine of History and Biography* 86 (January 1962): 112.

6. Lawrence A. Cremin, *The Wonderful World of Ellwood Patterson Cubberley: An Essay on the Historiography of American Education* (New York: Teachers College Bureau of Publications, 1965).

7. Maris A. Vinovskis, *The Origins of Public High Schools: A Reexamination of the Beverley High School Controversy* (Madison: University of Wisconsin Press, 1985), 9; Sterling Fishman, book review, *History of Education Quarterly* 29 (Spring 1989): 109; Jürgen Herbst, "Beyond the Debate over Revisionism: Three Educational Pasts Writ Large," *History of Education Quarterly* 20 (Summer 1980): 131; Lawrence Veysey, book review, *History of Education Quarterly* 28 (Winter 1988): 701; Thomas Bender, Paul Mattingly, and Peter Dobkin Hall, "Institutionalization and Education in the Nineteenth and Twentieth Centuries," *History of Education Quarterly* 20 (Winter 1980): 452, 459, 457. Doubtless one reason for the endurance of Bailyn's legacy is that so many standout educational historians of recent times were his students. The roster of historians whose dissertations were directed by Bailyn includes Jürgen Herbst, S. Alexander Rippa, David Tyack, Theodore Sizer, Mary A. Connolly, Jonathan Messerli, Craig Hanyan, Philip Greven, David Potts, Carl Kaestle, John M. Hoffman, and Maris Vinovskis. For a complete list, see James A Henretta, et al., eds., *The Transformation of Early American History: Society, Authority, and Ideology* (New York: Knopf, 1991), 263–66.

8. Several of Bailyn's early reviewers, Merle Curti, Arthur Henry Moehlman, and Frederick D. Kershner, Jr., noted that much of the educational history in the decades immediately preceding Bailyn had already moved in the direction he advocated. See Merle Curti, book review, *Historian* 23 (May 1961): 366; Arthur Henry Moehlman, *New England Quarterly* 34 (September 1961): 428; and Frederick D. Kershner, book review, *William and Mary Quarterly* 18 (October 1961): 580.

9. Herbert Butterfield, *The Whig Interpretation of History* (London: G. Bell, 1950).

10. Bailyn, *Education*, 4.

11. Victoria-María MacDonald's excellent study "Hispanic, Latino, Chicano, or 'Other'?: Deconstructing the Relationship between Historians and Hispanic-American Educational History," *History of Education Quarterly* 41 (Fall 2001): 365–413 unfortunately appeared too late to be incorporated into this work. It goes some distance in closing the immense gap in our knowledge of the historiography of Latin Americans.

12. *Nation* 5 (January 18, 1877): 178.

CHAPTER ONE

The opening quote is from Edmund Burke, *Reflections on the Revolution in France* (London: J. M. Dent and Sons, 1960), 137.

1. On Foxe, see William Haller, *Foxe's Book of Martyrs and the Elect Nation* (London: J. Cape, 1963); and on the English Puritans generally, see Margo Todd, *Christian Humanism and the Puritan Social Order* (New York: Cambridge University Press, 1987).

2. Haller, *Foxe's Book of Martyrs*, 142; Peter Gay, *A Loss of Mastery: Puritan Historians in Colonial America* (Berkeley and Los Angeles: University of California Press, 1966), 16.

3. Todd, *Christian Humanism*, 20–21.

4. On the history and transmission of the recapitulation theory of child development, see Charles E. Strickland and Charles Burgess, *Health, Growth, and Heredity: G. Stanley Hall on Natural Education* (New York: Teachers College Press, 1965), especially 6–11.

5. N. H. Keeble, "The Way and the Ways of Puritan Story: Biblical Patterns in Bunyan and His Contemporaries," *English* 33 (Autumn 1984): 224. Most of Bunyan's critics in the 1960s and 1970s assumed that *progress* meant for Bunyan what moderns mean by it, but Philip Edwards challenged this view by contextualizing the term such that it became simply a synonym for traveling. I have followed Keeble in this regard.

6. Edward Johnson, *Wonder-Working Providence of Sions Savior in New England* (Scholars' Facsimiles and Reprints, 1974) 27; Stephen Carl Arch, *Authorizing the Past: The Rhetoric of History in Seventeenth-Century New England* (DeKalb: Northern Illinois University Press, 1994), 77.

7. Johnson, *Wonder-Working Providence*, 133.

8. Johnson, *Wonder-Working Providence*, 216.

9. Arch, *Authorizing the Past*, 90. On the jeremiad as a literary genre, see Sacvan Bercovitch, *The American Jeremiad* (Madison: University of Wisconsin Press, 1978) and the criticism of Bercovitch in David Harlan, "A People Blinded from Birth: American History According to Sacvan Bercovitch," *Journal of American History* 78 (December 1991): 949–71.

10. Arch. *Authorizing the Past*, 147–48, 185.

11. John Franklin Jameson, *History of Historical Writing in America* (Boston: Houghton, Mifflin, 1891), 61.

12. Cotton Mather, *Magnalia Christi Americana; or, the Ecclesiastical History of New-England from its First Planting, in the year 1620, unto the Year of our Lord, 1698, in Seven Books*, vol. 1 (New York: Russell and Russell, 1967), 237.

13. Mather, *Magnalia Christi Americana*, 1: 550–51.

14. Mather, *Magnalia Christi Americana*, 2: 7; 1: 237; 2: 655; emphasis in original.

15. Robert Beverley, *The History and Present State of Virginia, a Selection* (Indianapolis: Bobbs-Merrill, 1971), 3.

16. Alden T. Vaughan, "The Evolution of Virginia's History: Early Historians of the First Colony," in A. T. Vaughan and G. A. Billias, eds., *Perspectives on Early American History* (New York: Harper and Row, 1973), 38.

17. Beverley, *History and Present State of Virginia*, 53.

18. Henry Hartwell, James Blair, and Edward Chilton, *The Present State of Virginia, and the College* (Williamsburg, Va.: Colonial Williamsburg, 1940), 72.

19. For such a quotation, see Thomas Hutchinson, Esq., *History of Massachusetts, from the First Settlement thereof in 1628 until the year 1750* (Salem: Thomas C. Cushing, 1795–1828), 221–22.

20. Herbert Butterfield, *The Whig Interpretation of History* (London: G. Bell, 1950). On the historical philosophy and products of the American Whig Party, see Jean V. Matthews, "'Whig History': The New England Whigs and a Usable Past," *New England Quarterly* 51 (June 1978): 193–208; and Daniel Walker Howe, "The Whig Interpretation of History," *The Political Culture of the American Whigs* (Chicago: University of Chicago Press, 1979), 69–95.

21. Jonathan Edwards, *The Works of Jonathan Edwards*, vol. 4 (New Haven: Yale University Press, 1972), 353.

22. Nathan Hatch, *The Sacred Cause Of Liberty: Republican Thought and the Millennium in Revolutionary New England* (New Haven: Yale University Press, 1977), 39, 41. My discussion draws heavily on this work.

23. Quoted in Stow Persons, "The Cyclical Theory of History in Eighteenth Century America," *American Quarterly* 6 (Summer 1954): 152–53.

24. Frederick Rudolph, ed., *Essays on Education in the Early Republic* (Cambridge: Harvard University Press, 1965), 43–44, 68.

25. J. G. A. Pocock, *The Machiavellian Moment: Florentine Political Thought and the Atlantic Republican Tradition* (Princeton: Princeton University Press, 1975), 513.

26. See Henry F. May, *The Enlightenment in America* (New York: Oxford University Press, 1976).

27. Arthur H. Shaffer, *The Politics of History: Writing the History of the American Revolution, 1783–1815* (Chicago: Precedent, 1975), 2.

28. Louis Masur, ed., *The Autobiography of Benjamin Franklin* (Boston: St. Martin's Press, 1993), 120; Lester J. Cappon, ed., *The Adams-Jefferson Letters* (Chapel Hill: University of North Carolina Press, 1959), 391.

29. Gordon Wood, *The Creation of the American Republic, 1776–1787* (New York: Norton, 1969), 7–8.

30. Mercy Otis Warren, *History of the Rise, Progress, and Termination of the American Revolution Interspersed with Biographical, Political, and Moral Observations* vol. 3 (New York: AMS Press, 1970), 424, 426, 429, 435, 436.

31. David Ramsay, *History of the American Revolution* (London: John Stockdale, 1793), 2: 322–23; Timothy Pitkin, *Political and Civil History of the United States of America from the Year 1763 to the Close of the Administration of President Washington, in March, 1797*, vol. 1 (New Haven, Conn.: Hezekiah Howe, 1828), 152. On the Revolutionary historians, see Arthur H. Shaffer, *The Politics of History: Writing the History of The American Revolution, 1783–1815* (Chicago: Precedent, 1975).

32. J. F. Jameson, *History of Historical Writing in America* (New York: Antiquarian Press, 1961), 84–85; David Van Tassel, *Recording America's Past: An Interpretation of the Development of Historical Studies in America, 1607–1884* (Chicago: University of Chicago Press, 1960), 59–60. On state historical societies and state histories, see H. G. Jones, ed., *Historical Consciousness in the Early Republic: The Origins of State Historical Societies, Museums, and Collections, 1791–1861* (Chapel Hill: North Carolina Society, 1995); and George H. Callcott, *History in the United States, 1800–1860: Its Practice and Purpose* (Baltimore: Johns Hopkins Press, 1970).

33. Jeremy Belknap, *The History of New Hampshire* (New York: Johnson Reprint, 1970), 341–42.

34. Belknap, *History of New Hampshire*, title page, 217, 218.

35. Belknap, *History of New Hampshire*, 220, 221, 222.

36. John Marshall, *The Life of George Washington*, vol. 2 (Philadelphia: C. Wayne, 1804), 2. On the history of George Washington's representation in America, see Barry Schwartz, *George Washington: The Making of an American Symbol* (New York: Free Press, 1987); and Michael Kammen, *A Season of Youth: The American Revolution and the Historical Imagination* (New York: Alfred A. Knopf, 1978).

37. Calcott, *History in the United States*, 101.

38. Marcus Cunliffe, ed., *The Life of Washington, by Mason L. Weems* (Cambridge: Harvard University Press, Belknap Press, 1962), 199; emphasis in original.

39. Callcott, *History in the United States*, 11, 22, 35. The emergence of a romantic American sensibility is connected to novelistic fiction in Cathy N. Davidson, *Revolution and the Word: The Rise of the Novel in America* (New York: Oxford University Press, 1986); and to the language of feeling that dominated post-Revolutionary America until Jackson in Andrew Burstein, *Sentimental Democracy: The Evolution of America's Romantic Self-Image* (New York: Hill and Wang, 1999).

40. On Irving, see Martin Roth, *Comedy and America: The Lost World of Washington Irving* (Port Washington, New York: Kennikat Press, 1976).

41. Washington Irving, *The Sketch Book of Geoffrey Crayon, Gent.*, edited by Haskell Springer (Boston: Twayne, 1978), 48–49, 150–51.

42. Washington Irving, *A History of New York*, edited by Michael L. Black and Nancy B. Black (Boston: Twayne, 1984), 3, title page.

43. Irving, *Sketch Book*, 226–27, 233. Peter Laslett, *The World We Have Lost* (London: Methuen, 1971).

44. Irving, *Sketch Book*, 274, 275.

45. Irving, *Sketch Book*, 211–12.

46. Jack Stillinger, ed., *John Keats: Complete Poems* (Cambridge: Harvard University Press, Belknap Press, 1982), 261.

47. On Miller, see Gilbert Chinard, "Progress and Perfectibility in Samuel Miller's Intellectual History," in Johns Hopkins History of Ideas Club, *Studies in Intellectual History* (Baltimore: Johns Hopkins Press, 1953), 94–122.

48. Samuel Miller, *Brief Retrospect on the Eighteenth Century* (New York: T. and J. Sword, 1803), 30–31, 28–29.

49. Miller, *Brief Retrospect*, 295; emphasis in original.

50. Miller, *Brief Retrospect*, 301, 337.

51. Miller, *Brief Retrospect*, 383, 389. On the extent of literacy in pre–common school New England, see William J. Gilmore, *Reading Becomes a Necessity of Life: Material and Cultural Life in Rural New England, 1780–1835* (Knoxville: University of Tennessee Press, 1989); Lee Soltow and Edward Stevens, *The Rise of Literacy and the Common School in the United States* (Chicago: University of Chicago Press, 1981); and Kenneth Lockridge, *Literacy in Colonial New England* (New York: Norton, 1974). On the vibrancy of academic education before the common schools, see William J. Reese, *The Origins of the American High School* (New Haven: Yale University Press, 1995); Carl Kaestle, *Pillars of the Republic: Common Schools and American Society, 1780–1860* (New York: Hill and Wang, 1983); and Albert Fishlow's pathbreaking essay "The American Common School Revival: Fact or Fancy?" in Henry Rosovsky, ed., *Industrialization in Two Systems: Essays in Honor of Alexander Gerschenkron* (New York: Wiley, 1966).

CHAPTER TWO

The opening quote is from Ralph Waldo Emerson, "Nature," in *The Collected Works of Ralph Waldo Emerson* (Cambridge: Harvard University Press, Belknap Press, 1971), vol. 1, *Nature, Addresses, and Lectures*, 7.

1. Cited in Donald R. Hickey, *The War of 1812: A Forgotten Conflict* (Urbana: University of Illinois Press, 1989), 300, 309. On this conflict, see also Wesley B. Turner, *War of 1812: The War That Both Sides Won* (Toronto: Dundurn Press, 1990).

2. Charles Sellers, *The Market Revolution: Jacksonian America, 1815–1846* (New York: Oxford University Press, 1991).

3. Horace Greeley, *Why I Am a Whig* (New York, 1851), 6, cited in Daniel Walker Howe, *The Political Culture of the American Whigs* (Chicago: University

of Chicago Press, 1979), 21. On private property and democracy, see Sellers, *Market Revolution*, 9–10; and Carl F. Kaestle, *Pillars of the Republic* (New York: Hill and Wang, 1983), 89–92. On Manifest Destiny, see Anders Stephanson, *Manifest Destiny: American Expansionism and the Empire of Right* (New York: Hill and Wang, 1995).

4. One can find in the nineteenth century the occasional pamphlet pointing in the direction of a more pessimistic assessment of common school reform, but these were always marginal contributions, known locally if at all, usually composed by disgruntled college professors pining for the good old days. See, for example, B. A. Hinsdale's *Our Common School Education: With a Digression on the College Course* (Cleveland: Robison, Savage, 1877) and his reformulations in response to the Whiggish critique of his interlocutor, significantly named Andrew Jackson Rickoff, in B. A. Hinsdale, *Our Common Schools: A Fuller Statement of the Views Set Forth in the Pamphlet Entitled "Our Common-School Education," with Special Reference to the Reply of Superintendent A. J. Rickoff* (Cleveland: Cobb, Andrews, 1878).

5. Mark A. Noll, *A History of Christianity in the United States and Canada* (Grand Rapids, Mich.: Eerdmans, 1992), 173, 178. Charles I. Foster, *An Errand of Mercy: The Evangelical United Front, 1790–1837* (Chapel Hill: University of North Carolina Press, 1960).

6. Rush Welter, *Popular Education and Democratic Thought in America* (New York: Columbia University Press, 1962), 103. His treatment of the anti-Catholic united front is at 105–9. Compare Ira Katznelson and Margaret Weir, *Schooling for All* (New York: Basic Books, 1985), 29: "With the singular exception of the animosity of Catholic clergy to the early primary schools it is simply impossible to find opposition to state schooling at the primary level by political and social elites or by working-class organizations." Catholic responses to the Evangelical front are well covered by Lloyd Jorgenson, in *The State and the Non-Public School, 1825–1925* (Columbia: University of Missouri Press, 1987). The escalating war for public school funds leading coalitions of Whigs and Democrats to oppose Catholics is covered in several states by Michael F. Holt, in *The Rise and Fall of the American Whig Party: Jacksonian Politics and the Onset of the Civil War* (New York: Oxford University Press, 1999), 155, 362, 779–80, 845–47, 880–81.

7. On Carter, see K. B. Hutchinson, "James Gordon Carter, Education Reformer," *New England Quarterly* 16 (September 1943): 376–96; Jonathan Messerli, "James G. Carter's Liabilities as a Common School Reformer," *History of Education Quarterly* 5 (March 1965): 14–25; Jonathan Messerli, *Horace Mann: A Biography* (New York: Alfred A. Knopf, 1972), 238–42, 259; and William Reese, *The Origins of the American High School* (New Haven: Yale University Press, 1995), 22–28, 126.

8. James G. Carter, *Letters to the Hon. William Prescott, LL.D. on the Free Schools of New England, with Remarks upon the Principles of Instruction* (Boston: Cummings, Hilliard, 1824); and James G. Carter, *Essays upon Popular Education Containing a Particular Examination of the Schools of Massachusetts and an Outline of an Institution for the Education of Teachers* (Boston: Bowles and Dearborn, 1826).

9. On the origins of self-conscious historiography in the Renaissance, see Donald R. Kelly, "*Historia Integra*: Francois Baudouin and His Conception of History," *Journal of the History of Ideas* 25 (Fall 1964): 35–57.

10. Carter, *Letters on the Free Schools*, 1–2, 11.

11. Carter, *Letters on the Free Schools*, 17, 27. On the declension myth, see Reese, *Origins*, 16–33.

12. Carter, *Essays upon Popular Education*, iii.

13. Carter, *Letters on the Free Schools*, 34, 47.

14. Carter, *Essays upon Popular Education*, 24, 25.

15. On Carter's anachronism, see Reese, *Origins*, 22–28, and the literature cited in chap. 2, n. 33.

16. Jonathan Messerli, *Horace Mann: A Biography* (New York: Knopf, 1972), 241; David Wilder, *History of Leominster; or, the Northern Half of the Lancaster New or Additional Grant* (Fitchburg, Mass.: Reveille Office, 1853), 85.

17. Carter, *Letters on the Free Schools*, iv.

18. On Burton, see Whitney Wood Buck, Jr., "Warren Burton: Classmate of Emerson and Kindly Reformer-at-Large" (Ph.D. diss., University of Michigan, 1964).

19. Warren Burton, *The District School as It Was, Scenery-Showing, and Other Writings* (Boston: T. R. Marvin, 1852), 17, 54, 40.

20. Burton, *District School*, 15, 3.

21. Burton, *District School*, 3; Henry Barnard, *American Journal of Education*, vol. 16 (Hartford, Conn.: F. C. Brownell, 1867): 430; 4: 277.

22. Emerson, "Nature," 7; Horace Mann, *Common School Journal* 1 (November 1838): 2–3.

23. Mann, *Common School Journal*, 14–15.

24. On Mann's many controversies, see Jonathan Messerli, *Horace Mann: A Biography* (New York: Knopf, 1972), 328–48, 412–24; and Lawrence Cremin, *The American Common School: A Historic Conception* (New York: Teachers College Press, 1951), 143–51.

25. On the Civil War and the leviathan state, see Jeffrey R. Hummel, *Emancipating Slaves, Enslaving Free Men: A History of the American Civil War* (Chicago: Open Court, 1996); and Wilfred M. McClay, *The Masterless: Self and Society in Modern America* (Chapel Hill: University of North Carolina Press, 1994), 9–148.

26. *Remarks on the Seventh Annual Report of the Hon. Horace Mann, Secretary of the Massachusetts Board of Education* (Boston: Little and Brown, 1844), 6; emphasis in original.

27. Horace Mann to William B. Fowle, April 17, 1848, cited in Messerli, *Horace Mann*, 422–23; Michael B. Katz, *Class, Bureaucracy, and Schools: The Illusion of Educational Change in America* (New York: Praeger, 1971), 5. It was not until 1877 that the first thesis supporting the rehabilitation of the New England Academy was published: Charles Hammond's obscure and seldom cited *New England Academies and Classical Schools* (Boston: Wright and Potter, 1877).

28. David D. Van Tassel, *Recording America's Past: An Interpretation of the Development of Historical Studies in America, 1607–1884* (Chicago: University of Chicago Press, 1960), 57. On John Gorham Palfrey's educational work, see Frank Otto Gatell, *John Gorham Palfrey and the New England Conscience* (Cambridge:

Harvard University Press, 1963), 92–103. On Jared Sparks, see Bert James Loewen-
berg, *American History in American Thought* (New York: Simon and Schuster,
1972), 232–33.

29. J. F. Jameson, *The History of Historical Writing in America* (Boston:
Houghton, Mifflin, 1891), 107. On Bancroft, see Russel B. Nye, *George Bancroft:
Brahmin Rebel* (New York: Knopf, 1944); and Lillian Handlin's less sanguine *George
Bancroft: The Intellectual as Democrat* (New York: Harper and Row, 1984).

30. George Bancroft, *History of the United States of America, from the Discovery of the Continent*, vol. 1 (New York: D. Appleton, 1898), 322, 315, 316.

31. George Bancroft, *Literary and Historical Miscellanies* (New York: Harper
and Brothers, 1855), 493, 509.

32. Sheldon Rothblatt, *Tradition and Change in English Liberal Education:
An Essay in History and Culture* (London: Faber and Faber, 1976), 206. My conception of tradition derives largely from the work of Alasdair MacIntyre, especially
his *Whose Justice? Which Rationality?* (Notre Dame: University of Notre Dame Press,
1988); and *Three Rival Versions of Moral Enquiry: Encyclopedia, Genealogy, and
Tradition* (Notre Dame: University of Notre Dame Press, 1990).

33. Henry Barnard, *The American Journal of Education* (Hartford, Conn.: F. C.
Brownell, 1867) 4: 657. On Barnard, see Edith Nye MacMullen's *In the Cause of
True Education: Henry Barnard and Nineteenth-Century School Reform* (New Haven:
Yale University Press, 1991). For the purposes of historiography, MacMullen's book
ought to be assisted by Richard Emmons Thursfield's more specialized study, *Henry
Barnard's American Journal of Education* (Baltimore: Johns Hopkins Press, 1945).

34. Barnard, *American Journal*, 1: 302.

35. David D. Van Tassel, *Recording America's Past: An Interpretation of the
Development of Historical Studies in America, 1607–1884* (Chicago: University of
Chicago Press, 1960), 121.

36. Linus P. Brockett, *History and Progress of Education* (New York: A. S.
Barnes and Burr, 1860), 17.

37. Barnard, *American Journal of Education*, 11: 3; 3: 563.

38. Barnard, *American Journal of Education*, 1: 301.

39. Cited in Thursfield, *Henry Barnard's Journal*, 92.

CHAPTER THREE

The opening quote is from Max Weber, *The Protestant Ethic and the Spirit of
Capitalism* (Los Angeles: Roxbury, 1998), 182.

1. On the economic consequences of the Civil War, see Glenn Porter, *The Rise
of Big Business, 1860–1920* (Arlington Heights, Ill.: Harlan Davidson, 1992). On
the politics and social consequences of emancipation, see Eric Foner, *Reconstruction:
America's Unfinished Revolution, 1863–1877* (New York: Harper and Row, 1988).
On the war's impact on women, see Catherine Clinton and Nina Silber, eds., *Di-
vided Houses: Gender and the Civil War* (New York: Oxford University Press, 1992).
On the immigrant war experience, see William L. Burton, *Melting Pot Soldiers: The*

Union's Ethnic Regiments (Ames, Iowa: Iowa State University Press, 1988). On increasing governmental centralization, see Jeffrey R. Hummel, *Emancipating Slaves, Enslaving Free Men: A History of the American Civil War* (Chicago: Open Court, 1996); and Stephen Skowronek, *Building a New American State: The Expansion of National Administrative Capacities, 1877–1920* (Cambridge: Cambridge University Press, 1982). On migration to cities, see Raymond A. Mohl, *The New City: Urban America in the Industrial Age, 1860–1920* (Arlington Heights, Ill.: Harlan Davidson, 1985).

2. Mark A. Noll, *A History of Christianity in the United States and Canada* (Grand Rapids, Mich.: Eerdmans, 1992), 329, 330.

3. Daniel Bell, *The End of Ideology: On the Exhaustion of Political Ideas in the Fifties* (Cambridge: Harvard University Press, 1988), 449; Robert Wiebe, *The Search for Order, 1877–1920* (New York: Hill and Wang, 1967), xiii, 12. On postwar class warfare emerging from industrialism, see Nell Irvin Painter, *Standing at Armageddon: The United States, 1877–1919* (New York: Norton, 1987). On business consolidation and resulting conflicts, see Maury Klein, *The Flowering of the Third America: The Making of an Organizational Society, 1850–1920* (Chicago: Ivan R. Dee, 1993). On the northern origins of legal segregation, see C. Vann Woodward, *The Strange Career of Jim Crow* (New York: Oxford University Press, 1966); and on post-Reconstruction southern developments, see Joel Williamson, *A Rage for Order: Black-White Relations in the American South since Emancipation* (New York: Oxford University Press, 1986). On the connections between industrialism, moral reform, and the changing ideas about woman's place, see Rosalind Rosenberg, *Beyond Separate Spheres: The Intellectual Roots of Modern Feminism* (New Haven: Yale University Press, 1982).

4. The "two crisis" view of the collapse of Protestant intellectual dominance is proffered in George Marsden's influential *Fundamentalism and American Culture: The Shaping of Twentieth-Century Evangelicalism, 1870–1925* (New York: Oxford University Press, 1980). For the secularization of colleges and universities after the war, see Marsden, *The Soul of the American University: From Protestant Establishment to Established Nonbelief* (New York: Oxford University Press, 1994); and James Tunstead Burtchaell, *The Dying of the Light: The Disengagement of Colleges and Universities from Their Christian Churches* (Grand Rapids, Mich.: Erdmans, 1998).

5. Lori D. Ginzberg, *Women and the Work of Benevolence: Morality, Politics, and Class in the Nineteenth-Century United States* (New Haven: Yale University Press, 1990), 173. On the Sanitary Commission, see George Frederickson, *The Inner Civil War: Northern Intellectuals and the Crisis of the Union* (New York: Harper and Row, 1965), 98–112.

6. On Sherman's Grand Review in Washington, see Wilfred M. McClay, *The Masterless: Self and Society in Modern America* (Chapel Hill: University of North Carolina Press, 1994), 9–39.

7. Figures from Lewis Perry, *Intellectual Life in America: A History* (Chicago: University of Chicago Press, 1989), 283; James R. Robarts, "The Quest for a Science of Education in the Nineteenth Century," *History of Education Quarterly* 8 (1968): 431–46.

8. On the struggle for control of teacher credentialing between normal schools and state universities, see Christine Ogren, "Education for Women in the United States: The State Normal School Experience, 1870–1920" (Ph.D. diss., University of Wisconsin–Madison, 1996).

9. Bruce Kimball, *The "True Professional Ideal" in America: A History* (Cambridge, Mass.: Blackwell, 1992).

10. H. I. Smith, *Education* (New York: Harper and Brothers, 1842), iii, vi. Information on his professional affiliation from Paul Monroe, "History of Education," in *Cyclopedia of Education*, vol. 3 (New York: Macmillan, 1912), 296.

11. Smith, *Education*, 168–69; 166.

12. W. N. Hailmann, *Twelve Lectures on the History of Pedagogy* (Cincinnati: Wilson, Hinkle, 1874), 52.

13. Karl Weintraub, *Visions of Culture* (Chicago: University of Chicago Press, 1966), 66.

14. Gail Bederman, *Manliness and Civilization: A Cultural History of Gender and Race in the United States, 1880–1917* (Chicago: University of Chicago Press, 1995), 26; Spencer quoted in Cynthia Eagle Russett, *Sexual Science: The Victorian Construction of Womanhood* (Cambridge: Harvard University Press, 1989), 148.

15. E. Anthony Rotundo, *American Manhood: Transformations in Masculinity from the Revolution to the Modern Era* (New York: Basic Books, 1993), 253; Beth L. Bailey, *From Front Porch to Back Seat: Courtship in Twentieth-Century America* (Baltimore: Johns Hopkins University Press, 1988).

16. Philip R. Moran, ed., *Ulysses S. Grant, 1822–1885: Chronology, Documents, Bibliographical Aids* (New York: Oceana, 1968), 92.

17. Lawrence A. Cremin, *The Wonderful World of Ellwood Patterson Cubberley* (New York: Teachers College, 1965), 12. N. H. R. Dawson, Letter dated February 27, 1889, *U. S. Bureau of Education Circular of Information* 1 (1891), 6; N. H. R. Dawson, Letter dated February 19, 1889, *Circular of Information* 1 (1890), 4. On Dawson and the Bureau of Education, see Donald R. Warren, *To Enforce Education: A History of the Founding Years of the United States Office of Education* (Detroit: Wayne State University Press, 1974).

18. Harris, Letter dated October 1, 1891, *Circular of Information* 6 (1891), 3.

19. It should be noted that Harris was the leading architect of both the narrow institutionalist professional histories composed for his bureau and the broad philosophical histories composed for his textbook series.

20. Charles De Garmo, *Herbart and the Herbartians* (New York: Charles Scribner's Sons, 1896), 269; Levi Seeley, *History of Education* (New York: American Book, 1899), 4. For data on increased production, see Milton Gaither, "Progress, Civilization, and American Educational Historiography, 1690–1960" (Ph.D. diss., Indiana University, 2000), 273–88.

21. E. L. Kemp, *History of Education* (Philadelphia: Lippincott, 1901), vi–vii.

22. Charles De Garmo, *Herbart and the Herbartians*, 112; John Dewey, "The Evolutionary Method as Applied to Morality," *The Philosophical Review* 11 (March 1902): 113, 117.

23. Thorstein Veblen, "Why Is Economics Not an Evolutionary Science?" in

The Place of Science in Modern Civilisation (New York: B. W. Huebsch, 1919), 58, 76, 77.

24. Seeley, *History of Education*, 15. For the development of the history of education courses, see William Brickman, "Early Development of Research and Writing of Educational History in the United States," *Paedagogican Historica* 19 (June 1979): 41–76; and J. J. Chambliss, "The Origins of History of Education in the United States: A Study of Its Nature and Purpose, 1842–1900," *Paedagogican Historica* 19 (June 1979): 94–131. Both authors cite studies that reveal a gradual rise in history offerings, until by 1903 students are found to spend more time in history courses than in any other sort. For twentieth-century developments documenting the decline in popularity of history of education courses, see Lawrence Cremin, "The Recent Development of the History of Education as a Field of Study in the United States," *History of Education Journal* 7 (Fall 1955): 1–35.

25. Seeley, *History of Education*, 4; Hailmann, *Twelve Lectures*, 11.

26. Linus Brockett, *History and Progress of Education from the Earliest Times to the Present, Intended as a Manual for Teachers and Students* (New York: A. S. Barnes and Burr, 1860). For later examples of Brockett's works that stress great men of the Civil War, see *The Life and Times of Abraham Lincoln* (1865); *Our Great Captains* (1865); *Men of Our Day* (1868); and *Grant and Colfax* (1868). For examples of his interest in women's history, see *Woman: Her Rights, Wrongs, Privileges, and Responsibilities* (1862); and, with Mary C. Vaughan, *Woman's Work in the Civil War* (1867).

27. Peter J. Bowler, *The Invention of Progress: The Victorians and the Past* (Oxford: Basil Blackwell, 1989), 7.

28. "And I will shake all nations, and the desire of all nations shall come: and I will fill this house with glory, saith the LORD of hosts" (Haggai 2:7 [KJV]); Brockett, *History and Progress*, 184, 241.

29. Brockett, *History and Progress*, 223.

30. Brockett, *History and Progress*, 227, 282; Barnard, *American Journal of Education*, 4 (1860): 277.

31. Mary Peabody Mann, *Life of Horace Mann* (Boston: Walker, Fuller, 1865), 63, 65; B. A. Hinsdale, *Horace Mann and the Common School Revival in the United States* (New York: Charles Scribner's Sons, 1898), 75; E. I. F. Williams, *Horace Mann: Educational Statesman* (New York: Macmillan, 1937), ix–x; George H. Martin, *The Evolution of the Massachusetts Public School System: A Historic Sketch* (New York: D. Appleton, 1894), 158.

32. S. S. Laurie, *Historical Survey of Pre-Christian Education* (New York: Longmans, Green, 1895), 1; F. V. N. Painter, *A History of Education* (New York: D. Appleton, 1886), 6; Gabriel Compayre, *History of Pedagogy*, trans. William Harold Payne (Boston: Heath, 1885), ix; W. T. Harris, "Education," in Nathaniel Southgate Shaler, ed., *The United States of America: A Study of the American Commonwealth, Its Natural Resources, People, Industries, Manufactures, Commerce, and Its Work in Literature, Science, Education, and Self-Government* (New York: Appelton, 1894), 311–12; W. T. Harris, preface to Thomas Davidson, *The Education of the Greek People and Its Influence on Education* (New York: D. Appleton, 1894), v.

33. Richard G. Boone, *Education in the United States: Its History from the Earliest Settlements* (New York: Appleton, 1889), 1, 2, 3.

34. Daniel Coit Gilman, quoting Francis Lieber, "Education in America, 1776–1876," *North American Review* 22 (January 1876): 196; Elsie W. Clews [Parsons], *Educational Legislation and Administration of the Colonial Governments* (New York: Macmillan, 1899), v.

35. Clews, *Educational Legislation*, v.

36. Painter, *History of Education*, 8, 5–6, 87; Laurie, *Historical Survey of Pre-Christian Education*, 1, 2. George W. Stocking, Jr., in *Victorian Anthropology* (New York: Free Press, 1987), describes the battles between monogenetic and polygenetic explanations of race origins in Great Britain.

37. Frederick Jackson Turner, *The Frontier in American History* (New York: Henry Holt, 1920), 38. The source that most of these authors rely on for their formulation of a westward-moving, culture-epoch theory of civilization's progress is Karl Schmidt's *Geschichte der Pädagogik: Dargestellt in Weltgeschichtlichen Entwicklung und im Organischen Zusammenhang mit dem Kulturleben der Volker*, 4 vols. (Köthen, Germany: P. Schettler, 1876–90).

38. Skilton cited in Ernst A. Breisach, *American Progressive History: An Experiment in Modernization* (Chicago: University of Chicago Press, 1993), 11.

39. Turner, *Frontier*, 30, 285; David B. Tyack, *The One Best System: A History of American Urban Education* (Cambridge: Harvard University Press, 1974); Kemp, *History of Education*, vi.

40. On the origins of transpacific expansionism in the 1840s, see Charles Vevier, "American Continentalism: An Idea of Expansion, 1845–1910," *American Historical Review* 65 (January 1960): 323–35. Thomas Hietala, in *Manifest Design: Anxious Aggrandizement in Late Jacksonian America* (Ithaca: Cornell University Press, 1985), examines the connections between Jacksonian land-based expansion and later movements into the Caribbean and the Pacific.

41. Painter, *History of Education*, 289; Hailmann, *Twelve Lectures*, 16, 17; Brockett, *History and Progress*, 291.

42. For the hegemonic view, see Alun Munslow's Gramsci-inspired *Discourse and Culture: The Creation of America, 1870–1920* (New York: Routledge, 1992).

43. George Santayana, *Winds of Doctrine: Studies in Contemporary Opinion* (New York: Charles Scribner's Sons, 1913), 188; Henry Adams, *The Education of Henry Adams, an Autobiography* (Boston: Houghton Mifflin Co., 1918), 343; Robert Muccigrosso, *Celebrating the New World: Chicago's Columbian Exposition of 1893* (Chicago: Ivan R. Dee, 1993), 94; Clarence A. Buskirk in *Chicago Daily Inter Ocean*, April 26, 1893, cited in Robert W. Rydell, *All the World's a Fair: Visions of Empire at American International Expositions, 1876–1916* (Chicago: University of Chicago Press, 1984), 19. For a critical appraisal of the fair, see Gail Bederman, "Civilization, the Decline of Middle-Class Manliness, and Ida B. Wells's Anti-Lynching Campaign (1892–94)," in Barbara Melosh, ed., *Gender and American History since 1890* (New York: Routledge, 1993), esp. 213–17.

44. Cited in Bederman, "Civilization," 214.

45. Cited in Bederman, "Civilization," 214. *Barbarous* and *Savage* were technical terms employed to specify particular stages in the evolution toward civilization.

46. Bederman, "Civilization," 215. My interpretation of the placement of the Woman's Building differs from that of Bederman, who sees it as a slight to the female sex, an example of Victorian attitudes regarding the evolutionary inferiority of women.

47. *The Booker T. Washington Papers*, edited by Louis R. Harlan and Raymond W. Smock, vol. 5 (Urbana: University of Illinois Press, 1976), 697; W. E. B. Du Bois, "The Conservation of Races," in *The American Negro Academy Occasional Papers* (Washington, D. C.: American Negro Academy, 1897), 7.

48. Walter Crosby Eells in "American Doctoral Dissertations on Education Written by Women in the Nineteenth Century," *Educational Horizons* 35 (Winter 1956): 53–56, also lists historical dissertations by Gertrude Marguerite Edmund and Lizzie Eliza Rector.

49. See Shirley Glubok, ed., *Home and Child Life in Colonial Days* (New York: Macmillan, 1969). Leopold von Ranke was the famous German historian whose name was invoked ceaselessly by American historians who misunderstood his romantic conservatism for naturalistic objectivity and used his authority to bolster their project of employing strict dispassionate fidelity toward sources so as to get at the past "as it really was." See Peter Novick, *That Noble Dream: The "Objectivity Question" and the American Historical Profession* (New York: Cambridge University Press, 1988), 26–31.

50. On Earle, see Susan Reynolds Williams, "In the Garden of New England: Alice Morse Earle and the History of Domestic Life" (Ph.D. diss.: University of Delaware, 1992).

51. Michael Kammen, *Mystic Chords of Memory: the Transformation of Tradition in American Culture* (New York: Knopf, 1991), 148; Miles Orvell, *The Real Thing: Imitation and Authenticity in American Culture, 1880–1940* (Chapel Hill: University of North Carolina Press, 1989). On the colonial revival, see Alan Axelrod, ed., *The Colonial Revival in America* (New York: Norton, 1985).

52. Alice Morse Earle, *Child Life in Colonial Days* (New York: Macmillan, 1899); *Customs and Fashions in Old New England* (New York: C. Scribner's Sons, 1894); *Home Life in Colonial Days* (New York: Macmillan, 1898); *Diary of Anna Green Winslow, a Boston School Girl of 1771* (Boston: Houghton, Mifflin, 1894); "Schools and Education in the American Colonies," *Chautauquan: Organ of the Chautauqua Literary and Scientific Circle* 26 (January 1898): 362–66.

53. Earle, *Customs and Fashions*, title page; Earle, *Child Life*, ix, 63.

54. Earle, *Customs and Fashions*, 4; Williams, "In the Garden of New England," 1; Earle, *Customs and Fashions*, 35.

55. Williams, "Garden of New England," 4. On Clews, see Desley Deacon, *Elsie Clews Parsons: Inventing Modern Life* (Chicago: University of Chicago Press, 1997).

56. Peter H. Hare, *A Woman's Quest For Science: Portrait of Anthropologist Elsie Clews Parsons* (Buffalo: Prometheus Books, 1985), 38; Deacon, *Elsie Clews Parsons*, 32–34, 46.

57. John Romeyn Brodhead, *History of the State of New York*, vol. 1 (New York: Harper and Brothers, 1853), 642–643; George H. Martin "Public School Pioneering: A Reply," *Educational Review* 4 (June 1892): 36; cited in Andrew S.

Draper, "Public School Pioneering in New York and Massachusetts," *Educational Review* 3 (April, 1892): 313.

58. Draper, "Pioneering," 314, 321; emphasis in original. On Draper, see Ronald Maberry Johnson, "Captain of Education: An Intellectual Biography of Andrew S. Draper, 1848–1913" (Ph.D. Diss., University of Illinois, Urbana-Champaign, 1970) and Winton Solberg, *The University of Illinois, 1894–1904: The Shaping of a University* (Urbana: University of Illinois Press, 2000).

59. Martin, "Public School Pioneering: Reply," 34, 39, 41, 45; emphasis in original.

60. Nicholas Murray Butler, introduction to Andrew S. Draper, *American Education* (Boston: Houghton Mifflin, 1909), x; Andrew S. Draper, "Public School Pioneering: A Reply to a Reply" in *Educational Review* 4 (October 1892): 250, 252. On Draper, see Ronald Maberry Johnson, "Captain of Education."

61. George H. Martin, "Public School Pioneering: Final Statement of the Massachusetts Claim," *Educational Review* 5 (March 1893): 239; Andrew S. Draper, "Public School Pioneering in New York and Massachusetts: A Final Reply," *Educational Review* 5 (April 1893): 357.

62. See Cremin, *Wonderful World*, 13–14; C. W. Bardeen, *The History of Educational Journalism in the State of New York* (Syracuse, N.Y.: Bardeen, 1893), 3; Seth Low, Introduction to A. Emerson Palmer, *The New York Public School: Being A History of Free Education in the City of New York* (New York: Macmillan, 1905).

63. George Leroy Jackson, *The Development of School Support in Colonial Massachusetts* (New York: Teachers College Press, 1909), 91–92; Edwin Grant Dexter, *A History of Education in the United States* (New York: Macmillan, 1904), 14, 24.

64. William Heard Kilpatrick, "The Date of the First School in New Netherland," *Educational Review* 38 (November 1909): 380–92; Robert Francis Seybolt, *The Public Schools of Colonial Boston, 1635–1775* (Cambridge: Harvard University Press, 1935), 66, 76; Paul Monroe, *Founding of the American Public School System: A History of Education in the United States, from the Early Settlements to the Close of the Civil War Period* (New York: Macmillan, 1940), 7.

CHAPTER FOUR

1. John Higham, *Writing American History* (Bloomington: Indiana University Press, 1970), 83. Works reflected in the wording of this paragraph include John Higham, "Reorientation of American Culture in the 1890's," in his *Writing American History* (Bloomington: Indiana University Press, 1970), 73–102; Susan K. Cahn, *Coming on Strong: Gender and Sexuality in Twentieth-Century Women's Sport* (New York: Free Press, 1994); Rochelle Gurstein, *The Repeal of Reticence: A History of America's Cultural and Legal Struggles over Free Speech, Obscenity, Sexual Liberation, and Modern Art* (New York: Hill and Wang, 1996); Stanley Coben, *Rebellion against Victorianism: The Impetus for Cultural Change in 1920s America* (New York: Oxford University Press, 1991); Richard W. Fox and T. J. Jackson Lears, eds.,

The Culture of Consumption: Critical Essays in American History, 1880–1980 (New York: Pantheon, 1983).

2. Christopher Lasch, *The True and Only Heaven: Progress and Its Critics* (New York: Norton, 1991), 77, 78, 14.

3. Lester Frank Ward, *Pure Sociology: A Treatise on the Origin and Spontaneous Development of Society* (New York: Macmillan, 1903), 544. David W. Marcell, *Progress and Pragmatism: James, Dewey, Beard, and the American Idea of Progress* (Westport: Greenwood Press, 1974), 324.

4. Elsie Clews Parsons, "The Teleological Delusion," *Journal of Philosophy, Psychology, and Scientific Method* 14 (August 1917): 467; Mumford cited in Stuart I. Rochester, *American Liberal Disillusionment in the Wake of World War I* (University Park: Pennsylvania State University Press, 1977), title page.

5. Carl Edward Feigenbaum, "American Educational Historiography, 1900–1920: Review and Synthesis" (Ph.D diss., Cornell University, 1973), 289. For fuller treatment of later textbooks, see Milton Gaither, "Progress, Civilization, and American Educational Historiography, 1690–1960" (Ph.D. diss., Indiana University, 2000), 289–93.

6. George E. Arnstein, "Cubberley: The Wizard of Stanford," *History of Education Journal* 5 (1953–54): 73–81.

7. Ellwood Patterson Cubberley, *An Introduction to the Study of Education and to Teaching* (Boston: Houghton Mifflin, 1925), 20; data on book sales from Jesse Brundage Sears and Adin D. Henderson, *Cubberley of Stanford and His Contribution to American Education* (Stanford: Stanford University Press, 1957), 119–20.

8. Lawrence Cremin, "Recent Development of the History of Education as a Field of Study in the United States," *History of Education Journal* 7 (Fall 1955): 1–35; Sol Cohen, "The History of the History of American Education: The Uses of the Past," in his *Challenging Orthodoxies: Toward a New Cultural History of Education* (New York: Peter Lang, 1999), 9–19.

9. Bernard Bailyn, *Education in the Forming of American Society* (Chapel Hill: University of North Carolina Press, 1960), 9.

10. On the romantic historians, see David Levin, *History as Romantic Art: Bancroft, Prescott, Motley, and Parkman* (Stanford: Stanford University Press, 1959).

11. John Higham, *History: Professional Scholarship in America* (Baltimore: Johns Hopkins University Press, 1983), 94, 95.

12. Higham, *History*, 162. For the origins of the famous phrase "history is past politics," see Dorothy Ross, "On the Misunderstanding of Ranke and the Origin of the Historical Profession in America," in Georg G. Iggers and James M. Powell, eds., *Leopold Von Ranke and the Shaping of the Historical Discipline* (Syracuse: Syracuse University Press, 1990).

13. John Franklin Jameson, *The History of Historical Writing in America* (Boston: Houghton Mifflin, 1891), 142–43.

14. The most complete biography of Cubberley remains Sears and Henderson, *Cubberley of Stanford*, though it is in sore need of revision. On Paul Monroe, see Henry Suzzallo's introduction to I. L. Kandel, ed., *Twenty-five Years of American Education* (New York: Macmillan, 1924); and B. Edward McClellan's entry on him in *American National Biography*, vol. 15 (Oxford University Press: New York: 1999), 687.

15. On the influence of Monroe's *Cyclopedia*, see William W. Brickman and Francis Cordasco, "Paul Monroe's *Cyclopedia of Education*: With Notices of Educational Encyclopedias Past and Present," *History of Education Quarterly* 10 (Fall, 1970): 324–37. For analysis of his historical oeuvre, see Feignebaum, "American Educational Historiography," 208–219.

16. Albert Bushnell Hart, *National Ideals Historically Traced* (New York: Harper and Brothers, 1907), 70, 134, 223.

17. Cited in Sears and Henderson, *Cubberley of Stanford*, 57–58.

18. Ellwood Patterson Cubberley, *The History of Education* (Boston: Houghton Mifflin, 1948), x.

19. Dorothy Ross, *The Origins of American Social Science* (Cambridge: Cambridge University Press, 1991), 149; Morton White, *Social Thought in America: The Revolt against Formalism* (Boston: Beacon Press, 1957), 12. On the progressive historians, see Ernst A. Breisach, *American Progressive History: An Experiment in Modernization* (Chicago: University of Chicago Press, 1993).

20. Malcolm Cowley and Bernard Smith, eds., *Books That Changed Our Minds* (New York: Doubleday, Doran, 1939); Charles Beard, *An Economic Interpretation of the Constitution of the United States* (New York: Macmillan, 1913), 325, 324.

21. Vernon Louis Parrington, *Main Currents in American Thought: An Interpretation of American Literature from the Beginning to 1920* (New York: Harcourt, Brace, 1927–30), x, xi, xii; Robert Allen Skotheim, *American Intellectual Histories and Historians* (Princeton: Princeton University Press, 1966), 135. On Parrington and Beard, see Richard Hofstadter, *The Progressive Historians: Turner, Beard, Parrington* (Chicago: University of Chicago Press, 1979).

22. Ellwood Patterson Cubberley, *Public Education in the United States* (Boston: Houghton Mifflin, 1934), 164, 165.

23. Ross, *Origins*, 254; Cubberley, *Public Education*, viii.

24. Higham, *History*, 172.

25. Higham, *History*, 179.

26. Ellwood Patterson Cubberley, *Changing Conceptions of Education* (Boston: Houghton Mifflin, 1909), 62, 56–57; John Patrick Diggins, "Three Faces of Fascism: the American Right, Left, and Center," in *Mussolini and Fascism: The View from America* (Princeton: Princeton University Press, 1972), 204, 223.

27. Cubberley, *Public Education*, 486. On Cubberley's racism, see George E. Arstein, "Cubberley: The Wizard of Stanford," *History of Education Journal* 5 (Spring 1954): 73–81; and Feigenbaum, "Review and Synthesis," 145–50.

28. Bernard Bailyn, *Education in the Forming of American Society: Needs and Opportunities for Study* (Chapel Hill: University of North Carolina Press, 1960), 9; for Cubberley's citation of Eggleston, see Cubberley, *Public Education*, 38; and Cubberley, *Syllabus of Lectures on the History of Education with Selected Bibliographies and Selected Readings* (New York: Macmillan, 1904), 354.

29. Stuart McAninch, "Ellwood Cubberley as Architect of School Bureaucracy," paper presented at History of Education Society conference (Chicago, October, 1998); Robert Wiebe, *The Search For Order: 1877–1920* (New York: Hill and Wang, 1967), 166; William H. Whyte, *The Organization Man* (New York:

Simon and Schuster, 1956); Sloan Wilson, *The Man in the Gray Flannel Suit* (New York: Simon and Schuster, 1955).

30. Ernst A. Breisach, *American Progressive History: An Experiment in Modernization* (Chicago: University of Chicago Press, 1993); Edgar W. Knight, *Education in the United States* (Boston: Ginn, 1929).

31. Stuart G. Noble, *A History of American Education* (New York: Farrar and Rinehart, 1938), ix.

32. Stephen G. Rich, "Wanted: A Better History of Education," *Educational Administration and Supervision* 11 (April 1925): 239; Edgar B. Wesley, book review, *History of Education Journal* 4 (Summer 1953): 159–60. The growing appeal of cultural history among historians of this time is traced in Robert F. Berkhofer, Jr., "Clio and the Culture Concept: Some Impressions of a Changing Relationship in American Historiography," in Louis Schneider and Charles M. Bonjean, eds., *The Idea of Culture in the Social Sciences* (Cambridge: University Press, 1973).

33. For examples of anthropological appropriation by the schoolmen, see Allen Oscar Hansen, "Integrative Anthropological Method in History of Culture and Education," *Educational Forum* 1 (March 1937): 361–78; and for the discipline of geography, see Arthur Henry Moelhman, "Toward a New History of Education," *School and Society* 63 (January 26, 1946): 57–60. For an example of early quantitative educational history, see Jesse Brundage Sears, *Philanthropy in the History of American Higher Education* (Washington, D.C.: Government Printing Office, 1922). Examples of comparative educational history include Paul Monroe, *China: A Nation in Evolution* (New York: Macmillan, 1928) and *A Survey of the Educational System of the Philippine Islands* (Manila: Bureau of Printing, 1925); as well as I. L. Kandel, *Comparative Education: Studies of the Educational Systems of Six Modern Nations* (London: J. M. Dent, 1918); *Essays in Comparative Education* (New York: Teachers College, 1930); and *The New Era in Education: A Comparative Study* (Boston: Houghton Mifflin, 1955).

34. William W. Brickman, "Revisionism and the Study of the History of Education," *History of Education Quarterly* 4 (December 1964): 216–19.

35. Samuel Eliot Morison, *The Puritan Pronaos: Studies in the Intellectual life of New England in the Seventeenth Century* (New York: New York University Press, 1936); Monica Kiefer, *American Children through their Books, 1700–1835* (Philadelphia: University of Pennsylvania Press, 1948), 227.

36. Committee on the Role of Education in American History, *Education and American History* (New York: Fund for the Advancement of Education, 1965), 4. On the collaborations between progressive historians and educators, see Peter Novick, *That Noble Dream: The "Objectivity" Question and the American Historical Profession* (Cambridge: Cambridge University Press, 1988), 185–93; and Lawrence J. Dennis, *George S. Counts and Charles A. Beard: Collaborators for Change* (Albany: State University of New York Press, 1989). Beard's textbooks are discussed in Peter A. Soderbergh, "Charles A. Beard and the Public Schools, 1909–1939," *History of Education Quarterly* 5 (December 1965): 241–52. Curti and Beard's role at *The Social Frontier* is discussed in C. A. Bowers, "The *Social Frontier* Journal: A Historical Sketch," *History of Education Quarterly* 4 (September 1964): 169–71.

37. August Meier and Elliott M. Rudwick, *Black History and the Historical Profession, 1915–80* (Urbana: University of Illinois Press, 1986), 104–5; Christopher Berkeley, "Merle Curti," in *Encyclopedia of Historians and Historical Writing* (London: Fitzroy Dearborn, 1999), 1: 279. Curti was mentor to the first African American woman to receive a Ph.D. in educational history, Marion M. Thompson Wright, who completed her dissertation under him in 1940. On Curti, see Berkeley, "Merle Curti"; and Robert Allen Skotheim, *American Intellectual Histories and Historians* (Princeton: Princeton University Press, 1966), 135, 171–72.

38. Merle Curti, *Growth of American Thought* (New York: Harper, 1943), 222, 350, 351.

39. Social Science Research Council Committee on Historiography, *Theory and Practice in Historical Study: A Report of the Committee on Historiography* (New York: Social Science Research Council, 1946); Margaret Wooster Curti, *Child Psychology* (New York: Longmans, Green, 1930). On Margaret Wooster Curti, see *American National Biography*, vol. 5 (Oxford University Press: New York: 1999), 878–81.

40. Merle Curti, *The Making of An American Community: A Case Study of Democracy in a Frontier County* (Stanford: Stanford University Press, 1959).

CHAPTER FIVE

The opening quote is from James Truslow Adams, *The Epic of America* (Boston: Little, Brown, 1932), 366.

1. Christopher J. Lucas, *American Higher Education: A History* (New York: St. Martins, 1994), 204; Barbara Miller Solomon, *In the Company of Educated Women: A History of Women and Higher Education in America* (New Haven: Yale University Press, 1985), 63. On secularization, see George M. Marsden, *The Soul of the American University: From Protestant Establishment to Established Nonbelief* (New York: Oxford University Press, 1994); on bureaucratization, see Roger L. Geiger, *To Advance Knowledge: The Growth of American Research Universities, 1900–1940* (New York: Oxford University Press, 1986); and on popularization, see David O. Levine, *The American College and the Culture of Aspiration, 1915–1940* (Ithaca: Cornell University Press, 1986). On fears of declension and perversion among the first generation of academic women, see Lynn D. Gordon, *Gender and Higher Education in the Progressive Era, 1890–1920* (New Haven: Yale University Press, 1990).

2. Lucas, *American Higher Education*, 207–8; Willard B. Gatewood, *Aristocrats of Color: The Black Elite, 1880–1920* (Bloomington: Indiana University Press, 1990), 265–68. See also James D. Anderson, *The Education of Blacks in the South, 1860–1935* (Chapel Hill: University of North Carolina Press, 1988), 238–78.

3. Regarding racial terminology, I have endeavored to follow two general principles: where possible I have used the term preferred by the author or work under consideration, and elsewhere I have employed the terms *black* and *African American* interchangeably in the interest of prose style.

4. August Meier and Elliott M. Rudwick, *Black History and the Historical Profession, 1915–80* (Urbana: University of Illinois Press, 1986), 3. Ronald E. Butchart, "'Outthinking and Outflanking the Owners of the World': A Historiography of the African American Struggle for Education," *History of Education Quarterly* 28 (1988), 334. On Woodson, see Jacqueline Anne Goggin, *Carter G. Woodson: A Life in Black History* (Baton Rouge: Louisiana State University Press, 1993).

5. Carter Goodwin Woodson, *The Education of the Negro Prior to 1861: A History of the Education of the Colored People of the United States from the Beginning of Slavery to the Civil War* (New York: George Putnam, 1915).

6. Woodson, *Education of the Negro*, 2.

7. Woodson, *Education of the Negro*, 122, 152. On racial uplift, see Kevin Kelly Gaines, *Uplifting the Race: Black Leadership, Politics, and Culture in the Twentieth Century* (Chapel Hill: University of North Carolina Press, 1996).

8. Woodson, *Education of the Negro*, 144.

9. Woodson, *Education of the Negro*, 199–200.

10. On Du Bois, see David Levering Lewis, *W. E. B. Du Bois: Biography of a Race, 1868–1919* (New York: Henry Holt, 1993).

11. W. E. B. Du Bois, "The Conservation of Races," in *The American Negro Academy Occasional Papers* (Washington, D. C.: American Negro Academy, 1897), 7; W. E. B. Du Bois, "The Study of Negro Problems," in Herbert Aptheker, ed. *Writings in Periodicals Edited by Others*, vol. 1 (Millwood, N.Y.: Kraus-Thompson Organization, 1982), 46.

12. W. E. B. Du Bois, *The Negro Common School*, Atlanta University Publications, no. 6 (Atlanta: Atlanta University Press, 1901).

13. W. E. B. Du Bois, *The Philadelphia Negro* (Philadelphia: University of Pennsylvania Press, 1996), 97.

14. W. E. B. Du Bois, *The College-Bred Negro*, Atlanta University Publications, no. 15 (Atlanta: Atlanta University Press, 1910), 34, 114.

15. Du Bois, "Negro Common School," 37.

16. Lewis, *W. E. B. Du Bois*, 408.

17. W. E. B. Du Bois, *Black Reconstruction: An Essay toward a History of the Part Which Black Folk Played in the Attempt to Reconstruct Democracy in America, 1860–1880* (New York: Atheneum, 1969), 39, 38, 187, 190.

18. Du Bois, *Black Reconstruction*, 638, 653.

19. Du Bois, *Black Reconstruction*, 653, 665, 667.

20. On early African American social science, see John H. Bracey, August Meier, and Elliott M. Rudwick, eds., *The Black Sociologists: The First Half Century* (Belmont, Calif.: Wadsworth, 1971).

21. Horace Mann Bond, *The Education of The Negro in the American Social Order* (New York: Prentice Hall, 1934). On Bond, see Wayne J. Urban, *Black Scholar: Horace Mann Bond, 1904–1972* (Athens: University of Georgia Press, 1992); and Roger M. Williams, *The Bonds: an American Family* (New York: Atheneum, 1971).

22. Bond, *Education of the Negro*, 5, 13.

23. For a striking example of Bond's ability to use the rise-of-civilization thesis as an aid to his own integrationist objectives, see his "The Role of History in

Understanding the Struggle for Equalizing Educational Opportunity," *History of Education Journal* 1 (Spring 1950): 101–7. This text provides yet more evidence of the pervasiveness of broad culturalist definitions in the profession prior to 1960.

24. Bond, *Education of the Negro*, chaps. 6 and 7.

25. Horace Mann Bond, "Dr. Woodson Goes Wool-Gathering," *Journal of Negro Education* 2 (1933): 210.

26. Bond, *Education of the Negro*, 491, 465; Jonathan Kozol, *Savage Inequalities: Children in America's Schools* (New York: Crown, 1991).

27. Louis R. Harlan, *Separate and Unequal: Public School Campaigns and Racism in the Southern Seaboard States, 1901–1915* (Chapel Hill: University of North Carolina Press, 1958); James D. Anderson, *The Education of Blacks in the South, 1860–1935* (Chapel Hill: University of North Carolina Press, 1988); Vanessa Siddle Walker, *Their Highest Potential: An African American School Community in the Segregated South* (Chapel Hill: University of North Carolina Press, 1996).

28. Maxine Schwartz Seller, "An History of 'Women's Education in the United States': Thomas Woody's Classic—60 Years Later," *History of Education Quarterly* 29 (Spring 1989): 95.

29. Winifred Wandersee, *Women's Work and Family Values, 1920–1940* (Cambridge: Harvard University Press, 1981). On postsuffrage feminism's response to a diversity of opinions among women, see Nancy F. Cott, *The Grounding of Modern Feminism* (New Haven: Yale University Press, 1987); Margaret Mead, "The Higher Education Survey: A First Report of the Findings from the Questionnaire," *Journal of the American Association of University Women* 43 (Fall 1949): 10.

30. Willystine Goodsell, *History of the Family as a Social and Educational Institution* (New York: Macmillan, 1915), 5, 48. On Goodsell, see Robert Engel, "Willystine Goodsell: Feminist and Reconstructionist Educator," *Vitae Scholasticae* 3 (Fall 1984): 355–78.

31. Goodsell, *History of the Family*, 439, 441.

32. Willystine Goodsell, *The Education of Women: Its Social Background and Its Problems* (New York: Macmillan, 1923), 10, 12, 17, 28–29.

33. Willystine Goodsell, *Pioneers of Women's Education in the United States* (New York: McGraw-Hill, 1931), 7, 8.

34. Thomas Francis McHugh, "Thomas Woody: Teacher, Scholar, Humanist" (Ph. D. diss., University of Pennsylvania, 1973), 232–48; Thomas Woody, *A History of Women's Education in the United States*, vol. 1 (New York: Science Press, 1929), viii, 23, 124, 128, 301. Compare, for example, Alice Felt Tyler's account of women's education in *Freedom's Ferment: Phases of American Social History from the Colonial Period to the Outbreak of the Civil War* (Minneapolis: University of Minnesota Press, 1944), 250–54, or the Goodsellian work by Martha MacLear, "History of the Education of Girls in New York and in New England, 1800–1870," *Howard University Studies in History* 7 (December 1926): 5–123.

35. Woody, *Women's Education*, 2: 473.

36. Woody, *Women's Education*, 1: 58. Criticisms of aspects of Woody's work can be found in Seller, "An History of 'Women's Education in the United States'"; and Kim Tolley, "Science for Ladies, Classics for Gentlemen: A Comparative Analysis of Scientific Subjects in the Curricula of Boys' and Girls' Secondary Schools in the

United States, 1794–1850," *History of Education Quarterly* 36 (Summer 1996), esp. 136. Seller claims that current historians of women recognize, as Woody did not, "that schools can limit as well as liberate," but she can cite not a single historical work to demonstrate her point (104).

37. Viola Klein, *The Feminine Character: History of an Ideology* (New York: International Universities Press, 1946), 164.

38. Luella Cole, *A History of Education: Socrates to Montessori* (New York: Rinehart, 1950), vii, viii, ix.

39. Agnes E. Benedict, *Progress to Freedom: the Story of American Education* (New York: Putnam, 1942), 5–6, 291.

40. Ann Douglas, *The Feminization of American Culture* (New York: Knopf, 1978), 13; Benedict, *Progress to Freedom*, vii.

41. Eleanor Wolf Thompson, *Education for Ladies, 1830–1860: Ideas on Education in Magazines for Women* (New York: King's Crown Press, 1947); Vera M. Butler, "Education as Revealed by New England Newspapers Prior to 1850" (Ph.D. diss., Temple University, 1935); Monica Kiefer, *American Children through their Books: 1700–1835* (Philadelphia: University of Pennsylvania Press, 1948); Angie Burt Bowden, *Early Schools of Washington Territory* (Seattle: Lowman and Hanford, 1935); Marion M. Thompson Wright, *Education of Negroes in New Jersey* (New York: Teachers College, 1941); Lillian G. Dabney, *The History of Schools for Negroes in the District of Columbia, 1807–1947* (Washington, D.C.: Catholic University of America Press, 1949); Jeanne Noble, *The Negro Woman's College Education* (New York: Teachers College, 1956).

42. Ellen Condliffe Lagemann, "The Plural Worlds of Educational Research," *History of Education Quarterly* 29 (Summer 1989): 208, 212. Lagemann expands on these themes in *An Elusive Science: The Troubling History of Education Research* (Chicago: University of Chicago Press, 2000), 41–71. On Judd, see also Harold B. Dunkel, "Judd's Debt to Wundt," *School Review* 85 (August 1977): 535–51.

43. Charles Hubbard Judd, "Charles H. Judd," in Carl A. Murchison, ed., *History of Psychology in Autobiography*, vol. 2 (Worcester: Clark University Press, 1932), 214, 218, 223.

44. Charles H. Judd, "Standards in American Education," *School Review* 22 (September 1, 1914): 433–43; John Dale Russell and Charles H. Judd, *The American Educational System: An Introduction to Education* (Boston: Houghton Mifflin, 1940). On the junior high debates, see Edward Krug, *The Shaping of the American High School, 1880–1920*, vol. 1 (Madison: University of Wisconsin Press, 1969) 239–40, 327–35 and vol. 2 (Madison: University of Wisconsin Press, 1972), 47–53.

45. Charles H. Judd, "Prussia and Our Schools," *New Republic* 14 (April 20, 1918): 347–48.

46. Judd, "Prussia and Our Schools," 349.

47. Charles H. Judd, *Democracy and American Schools*, University of Chicago War Papers, no. 7 (Chicago: University of Chicago Press, 1918), 9; Charles H. Judd, *Evolution of a Democratic School System* (Boston: Houghton Mifflin, 1918), 2–3, 38, 45, 81; Charles H. Judd, *Introduction to the Scientific Study of Education* (Boston: Ginn, 1918).

48. Paul Monroe, "Further Considerations of Prussia and Our Schools," *School and Society* 7 (June 15, 1918): 691, 693, 694.

49. Charles H. Judd, "Shall We Continue to Imitate Prussia?" *School and Society* 7 (June 29, 1918): 752, 751, 753; Paul Monroe, "Shall We Continue to Advocate Reforms by False Arguments?" *School and Society* 8 (Sepember 7, 1918): 293.

50. James W. Fraser, *Between Church and State: Religion and Public Education in Multicultural America* (New York: St. Martin's, 1999), 127–53. For critiques of the historical arguments made by the Justices, see William E. Griffiths, *Religion, the Courts, and the Public Schools: A Century of Litigation* (Cincinnati: W. H. Anderson, 1966); and Edwin S. Corwin, "The Supreme Court as National School Board," *Thought* 23 (1948): 665–83. For defenses of the Court's argument, see Leo Pfeffer, "The Case for Separation," in John Cogley, ed., *Religion in America: Original Essays on Religion in a Free Society* (New York: Meridian Books, 1958), 52–94.

51. *Proceedings of the White House Conference on Children in a Democracy* (Washington, D.C.: U.S. Department of Labor, 1940), 31.

52. Sherman M. Smith, *The Relation of the State to Religious Education in Massachusetts* (Syracuse, N.Y.: Syracuse University Bookstore, 1926), iii. Lawrence Cremin's "Recent Development of the History of Education as a Field of Study in the United States," *History of Education Journal* 7 (Fall 1955): 1–35 is able to claim decline by exclusive attention to dissertations conducted at Teachers College. He has been followed in this regard by Ellen Condliffe Lagemann, *An Elusive Science: The Troubling History of Education Research* (Chicago: University of Chicago Press, 2000), 73–76.

53. Burton Confrey, *Secularism in American Education: Its History* (Ph.D. diss., Catholic University of America, 1931), 146, 150; Smith, *Relation of the State*, iv; Sadie Bell, *The Church, the State, and Education in Virginia: An Explanation of Present Day Attitudes toward Religion in Education from the Point of View of Their Historical Development* (Philadelphia: Science Press, 1930); see also Leo J. McCormick, *Church-State Relationships in Education in Maryland* (Washington, D.C.: Catholic University of America Press, 1942).

54. Cited in John F. Noll, *Our National Enemy Number One: Education without Religion* (Huntington, Ind.: Our Sunday Visitor Press, 1942), 290, 291.

55. Noll, *Our National Enemy*, 290; John Courtney Murray, *We Hold These Truths: Catholic Reflections upon the American Proposition* (New York: Sheed and Ward, 1960), 152; Henry Van Dusen, *God in Education: A Tract for the Times* (New York: Charles Scribner's Sons, 1951), 115.

56. Will Herberg, "Religion, Democracy, and Public Education" in John Cogley, ed., *Religion in America: Original Essays on Religion in a Free Society* (New York: Meridian Books, 1958), 118, 120, 123, 124.

57. Conrad Henry Moehlman, *School and Church, the American Way: A Historical Approach to the Problem of Religious Instruction in Public Education* (New York: Harper, 1944), x, 51; R. Freeman Butts, *The American Tradition in Religion and Education* (Boston: Beacon, 1950), xiv, 108.

58. Vivian T. Thayer, *Religion in Public Education* (New York: Viking, 1947), 1, 29; Vivian T. Thayer, *The Attack upon the American Secular School* (Boston: Beacon, 1951), 15.

59. R. Freeman Butts, "Our Tradition of States' Rights and Education," *History of Education Journal* 1 (Spring 1955): 213.

60. Lewis Paul Todd and Merle Curti, *Rise of the American Nation* (New York: Harcourt, Brace, and World, 1961), 81. Todd and Curti, *Rise of the American Nation, John Carroll Edition* (New York: Harcourt, Brace, and World, 1961), 81. Compare also at 526 where the public school version praises Parker and Dewey for two paragraphs and the Catholic school version substitutes a statement concerning the development of the parochial school system. I am indebted for this example to Leo J. Alilunas, "The Image of Public Schools in Roman Catholic American History Textbooks," *History of Education Quaterly* 3 (September 1963): 159–65.

61. William Clayton Bower, *Church and State in Education* (Chicago: University of Chicago Press, 1944), 30.

CHAPTER SIX

The opening quote is from Margaret Mead, *And Keep Your Powder Dry: An Anthropologist Looks at America* (New York: William Morrow, 1965), xii.

1. Archibald Anderson, "Bases of Proposals Concerning the History of Education," *History of Education Journal* 7 (Winter 1956): 41; Bernard Bailyn, "Education as a Discipline: Some Historical Notes," in John Walton and James L. Kuethe, eds., *The Discipline of Education* (Madison: University of Wisconsin Press, 1963), 132.

2. Bernard Bailyn, *Education in the Forming of American Society* (Chapel Hill: University of North Carolina Press, 1960), 5–9.

3. Edward Eggleston, *The Transit of Civilization: From England to America in the Seventeenth Century* (Boston: Beacon, 1959).

4. Robert Allen Skotheim, *American Intellectual Histories and Historians* (Princeton: Princeton University Press, 1966), 65.

5. Quoted in William Randel, *Edward Eggleston: Author of the Hoosier School Master* (New York: King's Crown Press, 1946), 259; Charles Hirschfeld, "Edward Eggleston: Pioneer in Social History," in Eric F. Goldman, ed., *Historiography and Urbanization: Essays in American History in Honor of W. Stull Holt* (Baltimore: Johns Hopkins Press, 1941), 200. On Eggleston's turn from religious piety to agnosticism, see Ronald Lee Cansler, "Edward Eggleston's 'An Agnostic: A Novel of the Soul'" (Ph.D. diss., University of Missouri–Columbia, 1986).

6. Edward Eggleston, *History of the United States and Its People for the Use of Schools* (New York: D. Appleton, 1888), iv; Eggleston, "The New History," in *Annual Report of the American Historical Association for the Year 1900*, vol. 1 (Washington, D.C.: Government Printing Office, 1901), 47.

7. Barrett Wendell, Review of *The Transit of Civilization, American Historical Review* 6 (July 1901): 804; Skotheim, *Intellectual Histories*, 64; Edward Eggleston, in *Annual Report of the American Historical Association for the Year 1890* (Washington, D.C.: Government Printing Office, 1891), 7; Eggleston, *Household History of the United States and Its People for Young Americans* (New York: D. Appleton, 1889), iv.

8. Eggleston, *Transit of Civilization*, 209, 208–9, 228–29.

9. Eggleston, *Transit of Civilization*, 233; Bailyn, *Education*, 6.

10. Bailyn, *Education*, 6; Harry Hutton and Philip Kalisch, "Davidson's Influence on Educational Historiography," *History of Education Quarterly* 6 (Winter 1966): 79–87. On Davidson's life, see Susan Ruth Fagan, "Thomas Davidson: Dramatist of the Life of Learning" (Ed.D. diss., Rutgers University, 1980).

11. J. J. Chambliss, "Origins of History of Education in the United States: A Study of Its Nature and Purposes, 1842–1900," *Pedagogican Historica* 19 (June 1979): 131; Thomas Davidson, *A History of Education* (New York: Charles Scribner's Sons, 1900), 1–2.

12. Welland Hendrick, *Joysome History of Education* (New York: Point of View, 1912), 34.

13. Kenneth Sylvan Launfal Guthrie, *Values of History of Education* (New York: Platonist Press, n.d.), 10, 21, 23. Internal evidence suggests for this work a date after 1899 but before 1908.

14. Edward Bellamy, *Looking Backward* (New York: Houghton, Mifflin, 1888); George Orwell, *1984* (New York: New American Library, 1949).

15. "U.S. at War," *Time*, August 20, 1945, 19; Dwight McDonald, *Memoirs of a Revolutionist* (New York: Farrar, Strauss, and Cudahy, 1957), 5; Bruno Bettelheim, "Individual and Mass Behavior in Extreme Situations," *Journal of Abnormal and Social Psychology* 38 (October 1943): 417–52; On Bettelheim's influence, see Wilfred McClay, *The Masterless: Self and Society in Modern America* (Chapel Hill: University of North Carolina Press, 1994), 229–34.

16. William Graebner, *The Age of Doubt: American Thought and Culture in the 1940s* (Boston: Twayne, 1991), xi, 41; Richard Hofstadter, *The Progressive Historians: Turner, Beard, Parrington* (Chicago: University of Chicago Press, 1979), 357.

17. Sidney B. Fay, "The Idea of Progress," *American Historical Review* 52 (January 1947): 231. On these themes, see Graebner, *Age of Doubt;* and Frank A. Warren, *Noble Abstractions: American Liberal Intellectuals and World War II* (Columbus: Ohio State University Press, 1999).

18. William C. Martin, *A Prophet with Honor: The Billy Graham Story* (New York: Morrow, 1991); Alexander Bloom, *Prodigal Sons: The New York Intellectuals and Their World* (New York: Oxford University Press, 1986).

19. United States Bureau of the Census, *Historical Statistics of the United States, Colonial Times to 1970* (Washington, D.C.: Government Printing Office, 1975), 382–83. On the growth of the research university, see Roger Geiger, *Research and Relevant Knowledge: American Research Universities since World War II* (New York: Oxford University Press, 1993).

20. R. Freeman Butts, untitled article, *History of Education Journal* 1 (Autumn 1949): 2.

21. Butts, untitled article, 4.

22. On the debates between functionalists and liberals, see Lawrence Cremin, "Recent Development of the History of Education as a Field of Study in the United States," *History of Education Journal* 7 (Fall 1955): 1–35; and Sol Cohen, "The History of the History of American Education: The Uses of the Past," in his *Chal-*

lenging Orthodoxies: Toward a New Cultural History of Education (New York: Peter Lang, 1999), 9–19.

23. Flaud C. Wooten, book review, *History of Education Journal* 1 (Autumn 1949): 35, 36. The correct spellings are Kluckhohn and Herskovits.

24. Adam Kuper, *Culture: The Anthropologists' Accounts* (Cambridge: Harvard University Press, 1999), 61; George W. Stocking, *Race, Culture, and Evolution: Essays in the History of Anthropology* (New York: Free Press, 1968), 213.

25. Thomas Woody, "Fields That Are White," *History of Education Journal* 2 (Autumn 1950): 3, 9.

26. George E. Arnstein, "Cubberley: The Wizard of Stanford," *History of Education Journal* 5 (Spring 1954): 76; George A. Male, review in *History of Education Journal* 6 (Spring 1955): 229; Bernard Mehl, "New Writings and the Status of the History of Education," *History of Education Journal* 8 (Spring 1957): 110.

27. H. L. Mencken, *A Book of Prefaces* (New York: Knopf, 1917), 201–2; Charles Francis Adams, *Massachusetts, Its Historians and History* (Boston: Houghton Mifflin, 1893), 57.

28. Kenneth B. Murdock, *Increase Mather: The Foremost American Puritan* (Cambridge: Harvard University Press, 1925); Samuel Eliot Morison, *Builders of the Bay Colony* (Boston: Houghton Mifflin, 1930); Morison, *The Puritan Pronaos: Studies in the Intellectual Life of New England in the Seventeenth Century* (New York: New York University Press, 1936); H. L. Mencken, *A Mencken Chrestomathy* (New York: Knopf, 1949), 624.

29. Bernard Bailyn, "Morison: An Appreciation," in *Proceedings of the Massachusetts Historical Society* 89 (1977): 115, 112; Gregory M. Pfitzer, *Samuel Eliot Morison's Historical World: In Quest of a New Parkman* (Boston: Northeastern University Press, 1991), xix.

30. Morison, *Intellectual Life*, 59.

31. Morison, *Intellectual Life*, 58; Samuel Eliot Morison, *The Scholar in America: Past, Present, and Future* (New York: Oxford University Press, 1961), 15.

32. Perry Miller, "The Plight of the Lone Wolf," *American Scholar* 25 (Autumn 1956): 445–51; Robert M. Calhoon, "Perry Miller," in Clyde N. Wilson, ed., *Twentieth Century American Historians* (Detroit: Gale Research, 1983), 284. On Miller, see Robert Middlekauff, "Perry Miller," Marcus Cunliffe and Robin W. Winks, eds., *Pastmasters: Some Essays on American Historians* (New York: Harper and Row, 1969), 167–90; and Anre Delfs, "Anxieties of Influence: Perry Miller and Sacvan Bercovitch," *New England Quarterly* 70 (December 1997): 601–16.

33. Perry Miller, *Errand into the Wilderness* (Cambridge: Harvard University Press, 1956), ix, vii.

34. Miller, *Errand*, 185; Perry Miller, *Jonathan Edwards* (New York: Sloane Associates, 1949); Perry Miller, "The End of the World," *William and Mary Quarterly* 8 (April 1951): 171–91; Perry Miller, "The Puritan State and Puritan Society," in *Errand into the Wilderness*, 141–52.

35. Perry Miller, "Education under Cross-Fire," in his *The Responsibility of Mind in a Civilization of Machines* (Amherst: University of Massachusetts Press, 1979), 83.

36. Miller, "Education," 86, 90, 80.

37. Echoes of Ferdinand Tönnies are hard to miss. *Gemeinschaft und Gesellschaft* was translated in 1955 and first published in this country in 1957 as *Community and Society* (East Lansing: Michigan State University Press). For interpretations of Bailyn's project, see Gordon Wood, "The Creative Imagination of Bernard Bailyn"; and Jack N. Rakove, "'How Else Could It End?' Bernard Bailyn and the Problem of Authority in Early America," both in James A. Henretta et al., eds., *The Transformation of Early American History: Society, Authority, and Ideology* (New York: Knopf, 1991), 16–50 and 51–69, respectively. Biographical information can be found in the introductory essay to this volume by Michael Kammen and Stanley N. Katz, "Bernard Bailyn, Historian and Teacher," 3–15. Bailyn himself has been generous in clarifying his understanding of the nature of history and his own works. See Bernard Bailyn, *On the Teaching and Writing of History* (Hanover: University Press of New England, 1994); Bailyn, *History and the Creative Imagination* (St. Louis: Washington University Press, 1985); and Bailyn, "Context in History," *Quadrant* 40 (March 1996): 9–16.

38. Bernard Bailyn, *The New England Merchants in the Seventeenth Century* (Cambridge: Harvard University Press, 1955); Bernard Bailyn and Lotte Bailyn, *Massachusetts Shipping, 1697–1714: A Statistical Study* (Cambridge: Harvard University Press, 1959).

39. Bernard Bailyn with Jane N. Garrett, *Pamphlets of the American Revolution, 1750–1776* (Cambridge: Harvard University Press, 1965); Bailyn, *The Ideological Origins of the American Revolution* (Cambridge: Harvard University Press, 1967); Nathan Huggins, *Harlem Renaissance* (New York: Oxford University Press, 1971); Ann Douglas, *Terrible Honesty: Mongrel Manhattan in the 1920s* (New York: Farrar, Straus and Giroux, 1995).

40. Bailyn, *History and Creative Imagination*, 10, 11, 12, 13.

41. Whitfield J. Bell, Jr., *Early American Science: Needs and Opportunities for Study* (Williamsburg, Va.: Institute of Early American History, 1955), iv.

42. Committee on the Planning of Research, *Historical Scholarship in America: Needs and Opportunities* (New York: Long and Smith, 1932), 95, 113.

43. Fund for the Advancement of Education, *Decade of Experiment: The Fund for the Advancement of Education, 1951–61* (New York: Fund for the Advancement of Education, 1961), 15, 16, 19, 9. On the Fund for the Advancement of Education, see Dennis Cornelis Buss, "The Ford Foundation and Public Education: Emergent Patterns," in Robert F. Arnove, ed., *Philanthropy and Cultural Imperialism: The Foundations at Home and Abroad* (Bloomington: Indiana University Press, 1980), 331–62. On Hutchins's role, see Mary Ann Dzuback, *Robert M. Hutchins: Portrait of an Educator* (Chicago: University of Chicago Press, 1991), 234–40.

44. Paul Woodring, *New Directions in Teacher Education: An Interim Report of the Work of the Fund for the Advancement of Education* (New York: Fund for the Advancement of Education, 1957), 17–18, 107–9; Correspondence with Bernard Bailyn, February 7, 2000, in possession of author; Fund for the Advancement of Education, *Report for 1954–56* (New York: Fund for the Advancement of Education, 1956), 91, 129, 48.

45. Paul H. Buck et al., *The Role of Education in American History* (New York: Fund for the Advancement of Education, 1957); Committee on the Role of Education in American History, *Education in American History* (New York: Fund for the Advancement of Education, 1965), 3–4.

46. Fund for the Advancement of Education, *Report for 1957–1959*, 73, 97, 99, 101, 102, 108, 110. The fund also supported such important work as Richard Hofstadter, *Anti-Intellectualism in American Life* (New York: Knopf, 1963); Hofstadter and Wilson Smith, *American Higher Education: a Documentary History* (Chicago: University of Chicago Press, 1961); and Jonathan Messerli, *Horace Mann: A Biography* (New York: Knopf, 1972).

47. Arthur Bestor, *Educational Wastelands: The Retreat from Learning in Our Public Schools* (Urbana: University of Illinois Press, 1953), 137, 144; Bailyn, *Education in the Forming*, 5, 4; Bestor, *Educational Wastelands*, 144.

48. Bailyn, *Education*, 5; Bernard Bailyn, "Politics and Social Structure in Virginia," in James Morton Smith, ed., *Seventeenth Century America: Essays in Colonial History* (Chapel Hill: University of North Carolina Press, 1959), 91; Bailyn, *Education*, 14.

49. Bailyn, *Education*, 15, 22, 48.

50. Maxine Seller, "Boundaries, Bridges, and the History of Education," *History of Education Quarterly* 31 (Summer 1991): 197; Peter Novick, *That Noble Dream: The "Objectivity Question" and the American Historical Profession* (Cambridge: Cambridge University Press, 1988), 573 ff.

51. Jennings L. Wagoner, "Historical Revisionism, Educational Theory, and an American *Paideia*," *History of Education Quarterly* 18 (Summer 1978): 201.

52. For such criticisms, see, for example, Daniel Walker Howe, "The History of Education as Cultural History," *History of Education Quarterly* 22 (Summer 1982): 205–14; Thomas G. Dyer, "From Colony to Metropolis: Lawrence Cremin on the History of American Education," *Review of Higher Education* 13 (Winter 1990): 237–44; and the comments of Robert L. Church, Michael B. Katz, and Harold Silver in "The Metropolitan Experience in American Education," *History of Education Quarterly* 29 (Fall 1989): 419–46.

53. David Tyack and Larry Cuban, *Tinkering toward Utopia: A Century of Public School Reform* (Cambridge: Harvard University Press, 1995), 6. Tyack's longtime affiliation with the house that Cubberley built adds dramatic irony to his professional trajectory. Maris Vinovskis, *History and Educational Policymaking* (New Haven: Yale University Press, 1999), 256; Ellen Condliffe Lagemann, *An Elusive Science: The Troubling History of Educational Research* (Chicago: University of Chicago Press, 2000), x, 246.

54. Jürgen Herbst, *The Once and Future School: Three Hundred and Fifty Years of American Secondary Education* (New York: Routledge, 1996); David F. Labaree, *How to Succeed in School without Really Learning: The Credentials Race in American Education* (New Haven: Yale University Press, 1997); David L. Angus and Jeffrey E. Mirel, *The Failed Promise of the American High School, 1890–1995* (New York: Teachers College Press, 1999); Diane Ravitch, *Left Back: A Century of Failed School Reforms* (New York: Simon and Schuster, 2000).

Index

About the Author

Milton Gaither is an assistant professor of education at Messiah College, in Grantham, Pennsylvania. He received his Ph.D. in history of education from Indiana University, Bloomington. He lives in Mechanicsburg, Pennsylvania, with his wife, Elizabeth, and their children, Rachel, Aidan, and Susanna.